Grenada

WORLD BIBLIOGRAPHICAL SERIES

General Editors:
Robert G. Neville (Executive Editor)
John J. Horton
Robert A. Myers   Ian Wallace
Hans H. Wellisch   Ralph Lee Woodward, Jr.

John J. Horton is Deputy Librarian of the University of Bradford and currently Chairman of its Academic Board of Studies in Social Sciences. He has maintained a longstanding interest in the discipline of area studies and its associated bibliographical problems, with special reference to European Studies. In particular he has published in the field of Icelandic and of Yugoslav studies, including the two relevant volumes in the World Bibliographical Series.

Robert A. Myers is Associate Professor of Anthropology in the Division of Social Sciences and Director of Study Abroad Programs at Alfred University, Alfred, New York. He has studied post-colonial island nations of the Caribbean and has spent two years in Nigeria on a Fulbright Lectureship. His interests include international public health, historical anthropology and developing societies. In addition to *Amerindians of the Lesser Antilles: a bibliography* (1981), *A Resource Guide to Dominica, 1493–1986* (1987) and numerous articles, he has compiled the World Bibliographical Series volumes on *Dominica* (1987) and *Nigeria* (1989).

Ian Wallace is Professor of Modern Languages at Loughborough University of Technology. A graduate of Oxford in French and German, he also studied in Tübingen, Heidelberg and Lausanne before taking teaching posts at universities in the USA, Scotland and England. He specializes in East German affairs, especially literature and culture, on which he has published numerous articles and books. In 1979 he founded the journal *GDR Monitor*, which he continues to edit.

Hans H. Wellisch is Professor emeritus at the College of Library and Information Services, University of Maryland. He was President of the American Society of Indexers and was a member of the International Federation for Documentation. He is the author of numerous articles and several books on indexing and abstracting, and has published *The Conversion of Scripts* and *Indexing and Abstracting: an International Bibliography*. He also contributes frequently to *Journal of the American Society for Information Science, The Indexer* and other professional journals.

Ralph Lee Woodward, Jr. is Chairman of the Department of History at Tulane University, New Orleans, where he has been Professor of History since 1970. He is the author of *Central America, a Nation Divided*, 2nd ed. (1985), as well as several monographs and more than sixty scholarly articles on modern Latin America. He has also compiled volumes in the World Bibliographical Series on *Belize* (1980), *Nicaragua* (1983), and *El Salvador* (1988). Dr. Woodward edited the Central American section of the *Research Guide to Central America and the Caribbean* (1985) and is currently editor of the Central American history section of the *Handbook of Latin American Studies*.

VOLUME 119

Grenada

Kai Schoenhals

Compiler

CLIO PRESS

OXFORD, ENGLAND · SANTA BARBARA, CALIFORNIA
DENVER, COLORADO

British Library Cataloguing in Publication Data

Schoenhals, Kai
Grenada. – (World bibliographical series,119)
1. Grenada – Bibliographies
I. Title   II. Series
016.9729845

ISBN 1–85109–126–2

Clio Press Ltd.,
55 St. Thomas' Street,
Oxford OX1 1JG, England.

ABC-CLIO,
130 Cremona Drive,
Santa Barbara,
CA 93117, USA.

Designed by Bernard Crossland.
Typeset by Columns Design and Production Services, Reading, England.
Printed and bound in Great Britain by
Billing and Sons Ltd., Worcester.

THE WORLD BIBLIOGRAPHICAL SERIES

This series, which is principally designed for the English speaker, will eventually cover every country in the world, each in a separate volume comprising annotated entries on works dealing with its history, geography, economy and politics; and with its people, their culture, customs, religion and social organization. Attention will also be paid to current living conditions – housing, education, newspapers, clothing, etc.– that are all too often ignored in standard bibliographies; and to those particular aspects relevant to individual countries. Each volume seeks to achieve, by use of careful selectivity and critical assessment of the literature, an expression of the country and an appreciation of its nature and national aspirations, to guide the reader towards an understanding of its importance. The keynote of the series is to provide, in a uniform format, an interpretation of each country that will express its culture, its place in the world, and the qualities and background that make it unique. The views expressed in individual volumes, however, are not necessarily those of the publisher.

VOLUMES IN THE SERIES

For my friends
Helma and Helmut Schweigert
and for
Belkisita

Contents

Preface

During the four-and-a-half years of the Grenadian Revolution, a poster used to be displayed on Grenada which pictured Maurice Bishop, Fidel Castro and Daniel Ortega. The caption underneath their portrait read: 'Grenada, Cuba and Nicaragua: three giants rising in the Caribbean.' The description of a tiny island of 133 square miles as a 'giant' seemed like a vast exaggeration. So did, of course, President Ronald Reagan's claim that Grenada constituted a threat to the national security of the United States.

The inflated importance of the Grenadian Revolution is reflected in the avalanche of books and articles published about this event since 1979. While trying to give this revolution its proper due, this compiler made every effort to unearth materials on Grenada which preceded or followed the half decade of the People's Revolutionary Government's rule. Yet, hard as I tried to redress the balance, I found in the end that both my introduction and bibliography contained more information on life during Grenada's revolutionary government than any other phase of that nation's history.

Research for this volume was carried out at the libraries of Kenyon College, the Ohio State University, the University of Michigan, the Michigan State University, The University of Florida at Gainesville, The Florida International University at Miami, the University of the West Indies at Cave Hill, Barbados, Marryshow House at St. George's, Grenada, and the US Library of Congress at Washington, DC. My special thanks go to Peter Berg and Anne Tracy of the Special Collections Division of the Michigan State University Libraries and to Carol Singer of the Olin-Chalmers Library at Kenyon College. Thanks also to Mary Hopper who carried out the arduous task of composing the manuscript and the index.

The compiling of this bibliography was made possible through several small grants by CICALS (Consortium for Inter-Institutional Collaboration in African and Latin American Studies) at Michigan State University and PICAS (Program for Inter-Institutional Collaboration in Area Studies) at the University of Michigan. I am especially indebted to the Faculty Affairs Committee of Kenyon College which made it possible for me to take a full year's sabbatical and provided me with funds to do research on Barbados and Grenada during the spring of 1990.

Introduction

A traveller flying into Grenada will see the contours of the entire island spread out below. Upon landing, a visitor can drive around the island of 133 square miles and 110,000 people in one hour (if the roads were better, it could be done in half that time). Living on Grenada is like residing in a small village where everybody knows each other, with the inhabitants even having memorized the license plates and owners of the cars existing on the island.

To speak of Grenada as one island is technically incorrect since that nation consists of one major island, Grenada, and the much smaller islands of Carriacou and Petit Martinique that are part of the chain of islands spread out between Grenada and St. Vincent and known as the Grenadines. (With the exception of Carriacou and Petit Martinique, all of the Grenadines belong to St. Vincent.)

Those visitors to Grenada who have had the opportunity to see the other islands of the West Indies, will almost invariably list Grenada as their favourite destination. This enthusiasm for the 'spice island' is derived from Grenada's lovely mountains covered with tropical vegetation, the capital St. George's with its magnificent harbour (the crater of an extinct volcano) as well as its pastel-hued houses dating back to the seventeenth and eighteenth centuries, Grand Anse beach which is rated as the Caribbean's finest, and the friendly Grenadians themselves who make tourists welcome on their soil. Some travellers have even claimed that the Grenadian air is filled with the aroma of nutmeg, mace, allspice, saffron and cinnamon, all spices which are cultivated on Grenada and exported to the far corners of the globe.

In spite of its minuscule size (before St. Kitts-Nevis obtained its independence in 1983, Grenada had been the smallest nation of the western hemisphere), Grenada has played at times an extraordinary role in the history of the Windward Islands. While displaying unique characteristics, it has also shared considerably the common traditions of the Caribbean.

Like the rest of the islands which stretch like an arc between Trinidad and Cuba, Grenada was settled by waves of Amerindians from South America whose war-prone Carib group gave its name to the entire region. Also like most of its Caribbean sister nations, Grenada was drawn into the vortex of European colonial rivalry after Christopher Columbus discovered the island during his third voyage in 1498. Spanish, English and French raiders met with stiff resistance from the Caribs who were not subdued until 1654 when French forces drove them to the northernmost point of the island. Refusing to surrender, the remaining Carib families committed suicide by throwing themselves in the ocean, an event commemorated in Grenadian history as a supreme act of heroism. The spot where the Caribs hurled themselves from a cliff is called la Morne des Sauteurs (Leapers' Hill).

French control over Grenada was to last for over a century and exercise a permanent influence on the island. Roman Catholicism, first introduced to Grenada by the French, continues to be the primary religion there in spite of subsequent British attempts to convert the population to the Anglican faith. More than half of the geographical nomenclature of Grenada remains French to this day (e.g., Gouyave, Sauteurs, Lance-aux-Epines, Grand Anse, Grand Etang, Carenage and Perdmontemps). Many of Grenada's leading citizens (including the late Prime Minister Maurice Bishop) are descendants of French colonialists and their black slaves.

The French settlers on Grenada at first cultivated tobacco, indigo and cotton, but by 1700 they had introduced sugar cane to the island. The production of sugar required large amounts of cheap labour, a requirement met by the importation of black slaves who numbered 12,000 by 1753. Today the descendants of these black slaves make up the majority of Grenada's population and African traditions continue on Grenada, especially on the island of Carriacou whose isolation protected the African customs of the slaves from being obliterated by European influences. One persistent custom on Carriacou is the maroon – a voluntary effort of the entire populace for the gathering of a crop or the raising of an edifice. The famous Big Drum Dances which have fascinated anthropologists, serve Carriacouans as an important link to their African past. Some of Grenada's rural people still believe in *obeah* (magic and witchcraft), a phenomenon exploited by former Grenadian Prime Minister, Eric Gairy, whose main support came from this segment of the island's population.

During the French occupation, Grenadian society was divided into three classes with the white French plantation owners at the top. An intermediate class of free mulattoes (the off-spring of white Frenchmen and their black slaves) were permitted to hold property. At the bottom were the black slaves who could be sold and mortgaged and were subjected to great cruelty if they dared to escape.

When the British seized Grenada in 1763, and then again in 1783 after a renewed period of French domination (1779-83), all three of the above-mentioned classes were to suffer because the English tried to anglicize the island and increase the work load of the slaves in order to make Grenada into the second most productive British sugar colony after Jamaica. The British confiscated the lands and building of the Catholic Church and proclaimed that all baptisms, marriages and funerals must be held in the presence of an Anglican minister. Roman Catholics were barred from political activity. These British actions created the perfect soil for a revolutionary upheaval which occurred on 2 March, 1795, when a Grenadian mulatto land owner, Julien Fedon, began a revolt to oust the British from Grenada.

Fedon's rebellion, which began as an effort of white Frenchmen and mulattoes to restore French rule, was soon transformed into a social upheaval when 24,000 black slaves began to kill their masters and burn down sugar estates and rum factories. Fedon was able to gain control over most of the island and capture the British governor, Ninian Home, as well as forty-seven members of his entourage, but the British succeeded in holding on to St. George's with its strategic forts. Fedon gave the British the choice of surrendering the Grenadian capital or face the execution of Ninian Home as well as the rest of the English captives. When this ultimatum was rejected, Fedon executed the British governor and most of his other British prisoners. A tablet in the Anglican church at St. George's lists the names of Fedon's victims.

The British now rushed reinforcements to Grenada from all over the West Indies and England itself, but it took them fifteen months to crush the revolt. Fedon apparently drowned while trying to flee to Trinidad. Thirty-eight of his lieutenants were executed. Many of the French-speaking whites, mulattoes and black slaves were deported. The crushing of the Fedon rebellion in June 1796 signalled the termination of French power on Grenada.

While the British on Grenada were desperately trying to hang on to slavery during the 1790s, changes were transpiring in their home country which made slavery all but obsolete. The Industrial Revolution, which gained its first victory in England, dealt a death blow to the mercantile system by which sugar production in the British West Indies had been protected against foreign competition. The free trade scheme introduced by the Industrial Revolution, eliminated the protective mercantile shield and forced the sugar producers on the small British islands in the Caribbean to compete with such giant sugar exporters as Cuba and Brazil. Disaster now struck the British sugar plantations and by 1856, forty-seven sugar estates on Grenada had been abandoned. The rapid decline of the demand for British West Indian sugar, reduced the need for African slaves and by 1838, slavery had been abolished in the British colonies.

After their emancipation, the majority of ex-slaves continued to work on the remaining estates, but one-third of them desired to cut ties with their former landlords by buying, renting or simply seizing small plots of land (between one and two-and-a-half acres) on which they cultivated fruits and vegetables. Thus the post-emancipation period on Grenada saw the rise of a class of peasant small holders which still exists today. Its presence ensures the lack of severe undernourishment on the island. The exportation of Grenadian fruits and vegetables to Trinidad originated at that time and continues to the present day with many a fragile vessel sinking while 'trafficking' agricultural products between Grenada and its southern neighbour. The exodus of a substantial number of former slaves from their estates, compelled the Grenadian plantocracy to seek new sources of cheap labour which were found among the cargoes of captured Spanish and French slave ships as well as indentured labourers from Malta, Madeira and the Indian subcontinent.

With the decline of sugar production, new agricultural products rose to prominence on Grenada. The mountainous terrain of the island was very favourable to the cultivation of cocoa which by the 1880s had become the major agricultural export item on the British colony. Grenadian plantation owners who had been sent by the British to Asia in order to assist in the development of sugarcane in the East Indies returned to their homeland with nutmeg seeds which were first put into Grenadian soil in 1843. Within a decade, the island was covered with nutmeg trees and nutmeg had become Grenada's second most important export item. Today nutmeg and mace (the fibrous covering of the nut) are the chief export products of Grenada. The symbol of a nutmeg is depicted in the centre of the country's national flag.

By the end of the nineteenth century, the development of commerce in such urban centres as St. George's, Gouyave and Grenville had given rise to a new social stratum made up mostly of mulattoes with a smattering of blacks and whites. This incipient bourgeoisie, which consisted of civil servants, lawyers, physicians and teachers, resented the power monopoly exercised by the crown and the plantation owners and demanded a voice in the political affairs of Grenada. Theophilus Albert Marryshow (1887-1958) became the leading spokesperson for this rising middle class as well as Grenada's most prominent citizen during the first half of the twentieth century.

In 1915, T. A. Marryshow and the Grenadian lawyer, C. F. P. Renwick, established a newspaper entitled *The West Indian* which was edited by Marryshow for twenty years. In this journal, Marryshow advocated Grenadian participation in the legislative council whose representatives were chosen by the British Crown, greater independence from England and the formation of a West Indian federation. The newspaper's slogan was: 'The West Indies must be West Indian'. By 1925, Marryshow's agitation had resulted in a new constitution for Grenada which provided for five elected members of a sixteen member legislative council (the remaining eleven members were still appointed by the Crown). Marryshow became one of the elected members and remained on the legislative council as representative of St. George's for thirty-three years.

The 1920s and 1930s were decades of turmoil for Grenada as they were for the rest of the world. The economic boom triggered by the First World War, was followed by an economic slump which saw a precipitous fall in the demand for cocoa and nutmeg, Grenada's chief export items. Grenadian soldiers who had fought for the British Empire during the Great War, found, upon returning to their native land, that they were unable to find employment. The World Depression of 1929 exacerbated the economic plight even further. When the West India Royal Commission (Moyne Commission) inspected Grenada in 1939, it discovered undernourishment, poor health care, deficient housing and the low minimum daily wage of twenty-four US cents for men and twenty US cents for women.

The Second World War set off another period of boom in the Caribbean. At Trinidad, the expansion of oil production and the construction of US military bases created a job market for thousands of Grenadian immigrants who were unable to find work at home. Other Grenadians (like Eric Gairy and the father of Maurice Bishop) left for the Dutch ABC islands (Aruba, Bon Air and Curacao) where the oil refineries were working at full capacity. For those Grenadians, however, who worked on the estates of the plantocracy, life continued to be one of abject poverty. Even though trade unions had been legalized on Grenada in 1933, their appeal was confined to urban workers. The decades of neglect of Grenada's rural estate labourers came to an end in 1951 when the Grenadian countryside exploded into violence.

It was a black Grenadian named Eric Matthew Gairy, himself hailing from this poorest segment of the island's society, who took up the cause of Grenada's agricultural proletariat upon returning from Aruba where he had worked as a primary school teacher and trade union organizer. He was to be the dominant political figure on Grenada from 1951 until March 1979. In 1950 he founded the Grenadian Manual and Mental Workers Union (GMMWU) and in 1951 the Grenada's People Party (GPP), which was later renamed

Introduction

Grenada United Labour Party (GULP). Both of these organizations constitute Gairy's political power base to this day.

The GMMWU was the most radical trade union ever to be founded on Grenada, and the plantation owners refused to recognize it as the bargaining agent for its estate workers. In response, Gairy called a general strike which turned into a rural uprising with peasants razing plantation houses, damaging the cocoa and nutmeg crops and blocking roads. The economic life of Grenada became paralyzed. When Gairy and his impoverished disciples staged a large protest march on York House, the seat of Grenada's parliament and highest court, the British colonial authorities rushed in reinforcements from St. Lucia and Trinidad and deported Gairy to Carriacou, measures which only helped to inflame the situation. The British were forced to bring Gairy back to Grenada in order to pacify his followers.

When elections were held in October 1951, it became apparent that Gairy had become a hero to Grenada's masses. His party garnered seventy-one per cent of the vote and six of the seven council seats. Soon after his electoral victory, it became evident that Gairy had abandoned the interests of his followers and was, instead, trying to ingratiate himself with the British officialdom and the Grenadian establishment that despised him for his low social origins and his eccentric behaviour. Rather than bringing social progress to the rural poor, Gairy tried to make an impression with his knowledge of witchcraft and unidentified flying objects (UFOs). A devastating hurricane (Janet), which struck the island in 1955 and killed more than a hundred people, aggravated the plight of the poor.

The disillusionment with Gairy became evident in 1957 when the Grenadian electorate elevated Herbert Blaize and his Grenadian National Party (GNP) to power. Even though the GNP had promised to help all strata of Grenadian society, it soon became clear that it espoused only the interests of the privileged, of which Blaize himself was a part as a proprietor from Carriacou. Between 1957 and 1960 the income of the plantation owners rose by 170 per cent while the wages of agricultural labourers increased by only fifteen per cent. By 1960, 42.6 per cent of the island's labour force found itself without work.

It came as no surprise that the Grenadian people concluded that Gairy's GULP, with all of its shortcomings, was preferable to the GNP which was defeated in 1961. Gairy's new reign, which was marked by corruption and highhandedness, was cut short after only fifteen months when the British colonial authorities suspended Grenada's constitution, dissolved the GULP government and put the island under the control of the colonial administration until new elections scheduled for September 1962.

By advocating Grenada's union with Trinidad (a scheme subsequently rejected by Eric Williams' government at Port-of-Spain), the GNP was able to regain power in the autumn of 1962. It was to be its second and last chance to reduce Gairy's appeal by expanding its power base beyond the plantocracy and business élite. Blaize, however, soon illustrated (as he was to do after 1983) that he lacked the imagination and resourcefulness to initiate new paths for his party. While granting plantation owners government subsidies for fertilizers and insecticides and helping the merchants by lifting the taxes on their businesses, the GNP offered nothing to the urban and rural workers. For the first time since 1951, Gairy, during the period 1962-67, took up the cause of the agricultural proletariat. Agitation by the GMMWU ensured that the wages of rural workers were raised by twenty-two per cent.

In 1967, the Grenadian electorate, which was never again to put its faith in the GNP, restored Gairy to power from which he was not ousted until March 1979. The 1967 elections coincided with Great Britain's granting of 'associated statehood' to Grenada which meant total domestic independence for the island with Great Britain keeping sole control of defence and foreign affairs. It also meant, of course, that Gairy was now able to assume unrestrained control of Grenada which he carried out by a combination of vote rigging, patronage and the formation of a terrorist squad known as the 'Mongoose Gang'. The granting of complete independence on 7 February 1974, enhanced Gairy's power even further. As prime minister of Grenada, he was now able to speak to international bodies such as the United Nations about UFOs and the Bermuda triangle. His buffoonery made him the laughing stock of the Caribbean.

For the Grenadian people, however, the final phase of Gairy's rule (1967-79) was far from laughable since almost all aspects of Grenadian life underwent serious deterioration. This was particularly true of the field of education which suffered grievously under Gairy. Most of Grenada's eighty-two schools were in disrepair. Of the four hundred secondary school teachers, only seven per cent possessed professional training. Of the 900 primary school teachers, only thirty-six per cent could lay claim to a professional background. Only fifteen per cent of the island's primary pupils went on to secondary schools. Classrooms with up to eighty students were not uncommon. The school texts consisted of discarded textbooks from the United States and Canada. Since Gairy's government owed US $1.5 million to the University of the West Indies, this institution was reluctant to admit any more Grenadians to its campuses on Jamaica, Barbados and Trinidad. All these deficiencies did not bother Gairy in the least since an ignorant Grenadian populace made it easier for him to impose his bizarre rule on it.

The condition of Grenada's health system, too, was abominable. The General Hospital at St. George's was known as 'a branch of La Qua's', Grenada's major funeral home. The hospital lacked the most elementary medical equipment, medicines, beds, and even sheets and pillows. Women often had to deliver their children on the concrete floors of the hospital. Rural people never saw a dentist in their life since there were no dental clinics in the countryside. Any Grenadian who could afford it, went for medical treatment to Barbados or the United States. When in November 1970, nurses from the General Hospital at St. George's protested against the intolerable conditions at their place of work, they were sent by Gairy to remote parts of the island. When they resumed their demonstrations in December, they were met with clubs and tear gas and twenty-two of them were jailed and tried.

The nurses were ably defended by two young lawyers, Maurice Bishop and Kenrick Radix, who were typical of a whole new generation of Grenadians who had studied during the 1960s at various universities abroad only to return to the repressive and corrupt atmosphere of their home country. These young iconoclasts, who were influenced by the writings of Walter Rodney, Frantz Fanon, Kwame Nkrumah, Martin Luther King, Jr. and Malcolm X (whose mother was Grenadian), had been swept up by the Black Power Movement. Their special admiration, however, was reserved for Fidel Castro's revolution in Cuba which they hoped to duplicate on Grenada.

In contrast to their middle class parents who were steeped in British traditions, they felt little loyalty to English institutions such as the Westminster model of parliamentary democracy. They scorned the existing political parties on Grenada and, above all, the clownish Eric Gairy whom they hoped to topple by the founding of grass root movements. Two such organizations were formed in 1972: the urban-based Movement for the Assemblies of the People (MAP) led by Bishop and Radix and the rural-centered Joint Endeavour for Welfare, Education and Liberation (JEWEL) headed by the young economist Unison Whiteman. On 11 March 1973, these two organizations fused to constitute the New Jewel Movement (NJM) whose manifesto called for greater social justice, better health care and education, equality for women, better housing, and full employment (unemployment at this time hovered around fifty per cent).

Gairy soon realized that the New Jewel Movement with its populist appeal was an infinitely greater threat to his authoritarian rule than the élitist GNP. When the NJM accused Gairy of corruption and murder and called for his resignation within two weeks or face the possibility of a general strike, Gairy decided to terrorize the young rebels into submission. When six of the NJM's top leaders met at Grenville on Sunday 18 November 1973, to plan a general strike, they were thrown into jail with common criminals, but not before three of them (Maurice Bishop, Selwyn Strachan and Unison Whiteman) were mercilessly beaten with axe handles, clubs and pistol butts. Maurice Bishop, who suffered a broken jaw and damaged back, was never fully to recover from this beating, which resulted in an outpouring of sympathy from all strata of Grenadian society. In the wake of 'Bloody Sunday', a frightened Gairy released the six prisoners and promised many reforms which, however, he failed to carry out once the situation had calmed down.

By January 1974, renewed protests occurred against Gairy's rule. On 21 January 1974 ('Bloody Monday'), a peaceful demonstration, consisting mostly of women and children, was viciously attacked by the Mongoose Gang that drove the protesters into several buildings facing St. George's waterfront. When Maurice Bishop's father, Rupert, a prominent businessman, approached members of the Mongoose Gang to plead with them for the safe passage of the panicky women and children, they killed him. In 1979, the massive Fort George was re-named Fort Rupert in the martyr's memory.

During the national elections of 1976, the NJM, GNP and UPP (a conservative faction that had broken off the GNP), formed a common anti-Gairy front known as the People's Alliance. By blatant electoral fraud and repression, Gairy succeeded in holding on to power, even though the opposition gained 48.5 per cent of the vote and six of the fifteen legislative seats. Maurice Bishop became the main spokesperson for the parliamentary opposition.

Abroad, Gairy was held in greater disdain than ever. The Trinidadian prime minster, Eric Williams, gave orders that he must never be seen in public with Gairy. The Barbadian head of state, Errol Barrow, labeled Gairy a 'political bandit'. But Gairy obtained support from Augusto Pinochet whom he visited in Chile during 1976. The Chilean dictator dispatched arms and ammunition for Gairy's armed forces (known as the 'green beasts') and trained members of the Mongoose Gang in Chile.

After forging an electoral alliance in 1976 with the élite (an alliance Herbert Blaize did not want to be reminded of after 1983), the NJM concentrated upon gaining new converts among Grenada's urban workers, youth and women. It was even successful in penetrating Gairy's police and army. When the Grenadian prime minister left on 12 March 1979, for a visit to the United States, NJM agents among the police warned the NJM leadership that Gairy had allegedly given orders to liquidate them during his absence from the island. During the night of 13 March 1979, forty-six armed members of the NJM ambushed Gairy's army of 230 men at True Blue barracks and routed them completely. By 4:30 p.m. on 13 March 1979, Grenada, Carriacou and Petit Martinique were under the control of the New Jewel Movement. Only three persons had been killed during the action. Bishop's first radio message which promised that 'this revolution is for work, for food, for decent housing and health services and for a bright future for our children and great-grandchildren' met with overwhelming approval. Jubilant crowds danced in the streets singing: 'Freedom come, Gairy go, Gairy gone with UFO'.

From the very beginning of its rule, the PRG maintained close relations with Cuba whose Fidel Castro was deeply admired by Grenada's revolutionary leadership. Bishop's mother, Alimenta, has described the friendship between Castro and her son as 'almost a father-son relationship'. The fact that the Cuban leader had successfully defied the United States since 1959, lent encouragement to the members of the PRG that they, too, could successfully challenge the 'colossus of the north'. For Castro, the revolutionary takeover of Grenada and the subsequent Sandinista victory in Nicaragua meant an end to Cuba's isolation in the Caribbean basin.

In the face of stern warnings from the US ambassador to the Eastern Caribbean, Frank Ortiz, Cuba and Grenada established full diplomatic relations on 11 April 1979. Soon thereafter, Cuban arms shipments and military instructors built up the fledgling People's Revolutionary Army (PRA). Cuban aid, however, was by no means confined to military assistance. Twelve Cuban physicians provided free medical care on Grenada through the PRG's four-and-a-half years. (Before the revolution, there were only seven medical doctors in all of Grenada.) The Cuban dentists, who were sent to the rural parts of Grenada and Carriacou, were especially appreciated because most Grenadian peasants had never been to a dental clinic before.

The Cuban government provided its ally with factories producing asphalt and cement blocks. It also delivered a stone-crushing facility as well as fishing vessels. The most impressive Cuban undertaking was the construction of a new airfield which could handle jets. Bringing their own heavy equipment and trucks, 300 Cuban construction workers laboured around the clock to complete the Point Salines airport by the fifth anniversary of the Grenadian Revolution on 13 March 1984.

By 1982, the Soviet Union had replaced Cuba as the chief arms supplier of the PRA. Moscow also donated a crop dusting plane and offered university scholarships to hundreds of Grenadian students. The German Democratic Republic sent technicians to keep Grenada's antiquated printing presses functioning and planned the modernization of the island's telephone system. North Korea dispatched arms and ammunition and promised to construct a sports stadium. Aid for the PRG was by no means confined to the Communist world. Muamar Qaddafi, who opened a 'people's bureau' at St. George's, sent substantial financial contributions in order to prevent the Communist nations from gaining a monopoly of power on Grenada. Among Latin American nations, Venezuela spearheaded help for Grenada in the form of petroleum products, dental clinics and school equipment. In spite of strong pressure from Washington, the European Economic Community (EEC) dispatched aid to Grenada. The United States, however, assumed a hostile attitude towards the Grenadian Revolution as soon as it became clear that the Bishop régime would establish close ties to Castro's Cuba.

The Carter Administration refused to accept the credentials of Grenadian envoy, Dessima Williams, and ordered the new US ambassador to the Eastern Caribbean, Sally Shelton, who had an initial meeting with Maurice Bishop, not to meet with the Grenadian prime minister in the future. When Hurricane Allen devastated Grenada's crops, Washington not only refused to send help but attempted to pressure other countries from rendering assistance. It must be emphasized, however, that the Carter Administration, which was beset by such major diplomatic problems as the Iranian hostage crisis, always regarded the Grenadian situation as a problem of secondary importance. All of this was to change by 1981, when the newly inaugurated President Ronald Reagan elevated the Grenadian–United States relationship to one of primary significance. Claiming that Grenada's planned international airport was really a Cuban-Soviet air force base in the making which threatened vital United States shipping lanes in the Caribbean, President Reagan asserted, in the course of a series of speeches during early 1983, that Grenada's revolutionary government constituted a threat to the national security of the United States. The Reagan Administration held massive, annual military manoeuvres in the Caribbean which were clearly designed to intimidate the PRG.

During one of these manoeuvres (Ocean Venture '81), United States troops attacked an imaginary country called 'Amber and the Amberines – our enemy in the Eastern Caribbean' in order to 'free hostages' and form a government 'favourable to our way of life'. These military actions caused the PRG to build up an army and militia out of all proportion to the minuscule size of the country which, in turn, was interpreted by the Reagan Administration as a scheme to spread the 'Marxist virus' throughout the Eastern Caribbean by force of arms.

In spite of its frequent preoccupation with foreign affairs, the PRG was able to carry out a number of significant domestic reforms during its four-and-a-half-year reign. Nowhere was this more apparent than in the field of education.

The Grenadian Revolution's educational strategy consisted of five main pillars: continuous education, education for all, new content in curriculum, a work-study approach, and the integration of school and community. Under the rubric of continuous education comes the campaign against illiteracy which was waged in the Grenadian countryside by the Centres for Popular Education (CPE). Under the slogan of 'Each One, Teach One!' and 'If You Know, Teach! If You Don't, Learn!' thousands of volunteers of all ages fanned out to reach the illiterate part of Grenada's population which in 1979 constituted seven to ten per cent of the island's inhabitants. By 1983, illiteracy had dropped to less than three per cent.

In order to spread 'education for all', the PRG encouraged thousands of Grenadians to enroll in adult education courses which taught English, mathematics and basic sciences. Secondary education was rendered free of charge for all those students who had passed a rigorous examination. Forty per cent of all Grenadian students were attending secondary school by 1983 in comparison to eleven per cent in 1979.

The third pillar of the Grenadian revolution's educational strategy, new content in curriculum, was first introduced in 1980 in connection with the anti-illiteracy campaign. Under the guidance of the prominent Brazilian educator, Paulo Freire, a reader was developed which dealt with aspects of the Grenadian revolution and stressed the necessity of Caribbean unity. By 1982 Grenadian educators and artists had designed new texts for primary school pupils who, heretofore, had been taught from antiquated British and Canadian primers that had no relevance to Grenadian life. The new books, which were printed in Cuba, were called Marryshow Readers in honour of Grenada's famous journalist and politician. They depicted the lives of ordinary Grenadians and were set in the Grenadian countryside where most Grenadians live, pursuing agricultural tasks. Avoiding stereotypes, the readers showed a father holding an infant and feeding it with a bottle. When his wife and mother join him, he does not hand the child over to them.

By the fourth pillar of the Grenadian education policy, the work-study approach, the Bishop régime tried to prevent educated Grenadians from ending up behind some desk in a private or government office. Instead, the PRG hoped that the new educational system would produce the skills that could be absorbed by the country's economy. As Maurice Bishop put it: 'we must produce the agriculturists, the mechanics, the engineers, the hoteliers and the boat captains that we need to man our agriculture, our agro-industries, our fisheries and our tourism'.

The fifth pillar consisted of the attempt to integrate the schools and the communities which surrounded them. This effort was spearheaded by the Community Educational Councils (CECs) which were in charge of planning school curricula, maintaining school buildings and facilitating the transition from school to life in the everyday world. By virtue of the Community School Day Program (CSDP), ordinary people from all walks of life were invited to take over classes for one day a week in order to transmit their special skills to Grenada's pupils. These guest lecturers included basket-makers, farmers, storytellers, carpenters, seamstresses and calypsonians (calypso-musicians).

Second in importance only to the educational reforms were the agricultural programmes of the PRG which were designed to pull Grenadian agriculture out of the doldrums of the Gairy era. When the PRG seized power in March 1979, one-third of all land lay fallow and the average age of the Grenadian rural worker was sixty-two years. Even though unemployment in 1979 hovered around fifty per cent, young people were reluctant to take up agriculture because of the low pay and social status connected with it.

Thus the PRG's primary task was to make farming an attractive occupation for young Grenadians. It attempted to achieve this aim by the creation of a National Cooperative Development Agency (NACDA) which supplied land, loans and training in farming, bookkeeping and marketing to unemployed young people who were expected to form cooperatives. In order to create a secure market for farmers and at the same time, lower the prices of agricultural products for the general public by eliminating the middle man, the PRG created a Marketing and National Importing Board (MNIB) which made sure that the prices for cement, fertilizers, sugar, vegetables and milk on Grenada were lower than in the surrounding Caribbean nations.

Before the revolution there was the anomalous situation that Grenadian stores were filled with imported jams, jellies, fruit juices and cans of fish, even though Grenada produces an abundance of these items herself. In order to put an end to this situation, the PRG founded its own agricultural–industrial business (Spice Island Products) at True Blue which used Grenadian papayas, soursops, mangoes, tamarinds, guavas and bananas to produce jellies, juices and chutneys which were sold all over the Caribbean as well as Great Britain. The government also constructed a coffee processing plant, a spice factory and a national fishing industry.

The Mirabeau Farm School that had been closed by Gairy was reopened by the PRG which also founded three more agricultural training centres on Grenada as well as one on Carriacou. One of the most successful innovations of the Bishop régime was the creation of the Grenada National Institute of Handicraft (GNIH) which organized the manufacture of wood carvings, furniture, wall hangings and other handicraft products which were distributed through Grencraft both at home and abroad, providing supplementary employment for Grenada's rural population.

More than any other PRG project, however, it was the construction of the new international airport (started in January 1980) which aroused the enthusiasm of the Grenadian people who formed local airport development committees and purchased many airport bonds. Grenadian labourers worked side by side with their Cuban colleagues in order to complete this immense undertaking by 1984, a year which was designated as 'the year of the international airport'. The idea of such an airport had by no means originated with the PRG, but had first been broached by the British colonial authorities in 1954. It was again taken up by the Gairy régime which ordered feasibility studies. But it was only under Maurice Bishop that concrete steps were undertaken to realize this long-held dream. The new airport project became a truly international undertaking in regard to its financial undergirding as well as construction.

While Cuba provided the bulk of both the financial and material effort for this project (US $60 million), substantial financial assistance was also granted by the European Economic Community (EEC), Venezuela, Nigeria, Algeria, Syria, Iraq and Libya. A Finnish company named METEX obtained the job of installing lighting equipment on the runway as well as providing for the parking apron, car park and access road. A British corporation, Plessey Airport Ltd. was entrusted with the installation of air traffic control mechanisms and the electronic equipment of the terminal building which had been designed by Cuban architects. Even a North American firm called Layne Dredging became involved when thirty of its workers were sent to Grenada to drain Hardy Bay over which the 9000-foot runway of Point Salines Airport passes.

The claim of the Reagan Administration that the airport was designed as a Cuban-Soviet military base has been proved groundless. Among the tons of secret Grenadian documents captured by the United States during its armed intervention in October 1983, not a shred of evidence was found which might substantiate Washington's assertions. According to a statement issued by Plessey Airport Ltd., the Point Salines airport lacked eleven facilities (e.g. underground fuel tanks) essential to a military facility.

It was the determination of the PRG to complete the airport by March 1983, come what may, which helped to foment the grave economic and political crisis of 1983 that was to tear the Grenadian Revolution apart and destroy it by the end of that year.

Certainly, the PRG found itself in a financial crunch by the summer of 1983. Promised monetary assistance from a variety of sources was either being delayed or cancelled outright. For the first time since March 1979, there was an increase in unemployment. Wages in the armed forces (PRA) were so pitiful that many soldiers left for Trinidad and other foreign destinations at a time when the Reagan Administration's rhetorical attacks against revolutionary Grenada were increasing month after month. In friendly Cuba, telephone service to the Grenadian embassy and the Grenadian ambassador's private residence was cut because the PRG was no longer able to pay its bills.

The economic hardships, however, were only one facet of a general crisis which made itself felt during the summer and autumn of 1983. The tremendous enthusiasm which had greeted the NJM's seizure of power in 1979 had long evaporated. The Bishop régime's failure to hold the free elections it had promised, its jailing without trial of prominent members of the business community, its suppression of all opposition newspapers and its undeviating support of Soviet foreign policy (including the invasion of Afghanistan) had alienated the bourgeoisie and the Roman Catholic Church. As the memories of the repressive and corrupt Gairy era were fading and the social measures of the revolution (e.g. free milk for mothers, free medical and dental care) were increasingly taken for granted, the material expectations of the Grenadian population were exceeding the revolution's ability to fulfill them. This general malaise also had, of course, an impact upon the leadership as well as the rank and file of the New Jewel Movement.

There was one other factor which powerfully contributed to the crisis of 1983: many of the most loyal and capable cadres of the NJM had been sent to institutes of higher learning in Cuba, the Soviet Union and other socialist nations. They left a vacuum which could not be filled by the remaining party and government officials who were totally overburdened by the many tasks demanded of them, a situation that resulted in numerous physical and mental breakdowns during 1983.

When a series of meetings during the summer failed to resolve the crisis, an Extraordinary Meeting of the Central Committee of the NJM was convoked for September 14-16. This convention was considered to be of such importance that even the Grenadian ambassador to Cuba and the Grenadian deputy defence minister who was studying military science in the USSR, were ordered home.

For the first time since the founding of the NJM in 1973, the 'Comrade Leader' came under attack during this gathering. While there was praise for his regional and international work as well as his popularity with the Grenadian masses, Bishop was criticized for his disorganized manner of running the country and his lack of leadership during the ongoing crisis. It was suggested that Deputy Prime Minister Bernard Coard should be brought back to the Central Committee and Politburo (from which he had resigned in 1982) and that Bishop and Coard should share supreme power over Grenada. The majority of the Central Committee voted in favour of 'joint leadership' and made it clear that it expected Bishop to abide by this decision. While a minority (Minister of Agriculture, George Louison, and Minister of External Relations, Unison Whiteman) disagreed with the idea, they, nevertheless, joined in the criticism of Bishop's conduct of the government. It is well to remember this fact, because the pro-Bishop faction today claims that the crisis of 1983 was artificially created by Coard's disciples who were supporting their leader's alleged attempt to seize power.

The captured Grenadian documents show no evidence of any conspiracy on Coard's part. As a matter of fact, during a series of meetings which the Grenadian deputy prime minister held with his followers (17-22 September) while Bishop was attending the independence celebrations on St. Kitts-Nevis, Coard emphasized that he was most reluctant to re-enter the Politburo and the Central Committee and that he was happy just running the economy. He did, however, express resentment over the fact that in the past he had been called upon to act as a 'hatchet man' who had to carry out all of the unpopular decisions while 'the Comrade Leader, vacillating between the Marxist-Leninist and petit-bourgeois trends in the party, was making only the easy ones'.

During the Extraordinary Meeting of the Central Committee (14-16 September), there was much debate over the question of releasing the records of that gathering to the general public and the general membership of the NJM (about 300 persons). Everybody agreed that the Grenadian people should not be informed about the details of that meeting, but it was decided (over the objections of Maurice Bishop) to divulge the minutes to the rest of the NJM members and have an Extraordinary General Meeting of Full Members of the NJM debate the issues raised by the Central Committee's Extraordinary Meeting.

When the NJM's full membership congregated on 25 September,

both Bishop and Coard were missing. Bishop, who had promised that he would make up his mind about the 'joint leadership' ideas by the time of his return from St. Kitts (22 September), announced that he could not come to the meeting because he needed more time to think about sharing power. With the 'Comrade Leader' refusing to attend, Coard, too, decided not to appear. The leaderless conference then overwhelmingly voted to demand their presence, which compelled both of them to show up after all.

After a series of workshops and debates, the NJM's general membership voted unanimously for the joint leadership plan. Bishop then went along with the vote and exclaimed that he now fully accepted the idea of sharing power with Coard. The two then embraced each other before an enthusiastic audience which sang the 'International'. The conference concluded on a note of relief and euphoria which left everyone convinced that the grave political crisis had been resolved with everybody pulling together in order save the revolution and the nation.

This newly established harmony, however, began to unravel as soon as Maurice Bishop left on 28 September for state visits to Czechoslovakia and Hungary. Once he had put some distance between himself and his native land, new doubts began to assail Bishop concerning the feasibility of dividing the leadership of Grenada with the deputy prime minister. For four-and-a-half years, the 'Comrade Leader' had basked in the glory of being the sole, idolized chief of the Grenadian Revolution. To be called upon now to share power with Coard, who had done an excellent job of running the Grenadian economy but was widely disliked for his brusque manners, was too much for him to accept genuinely. His renewed doubts were reinforced by two of his ministers, Unison Whiteman and George Louison, who were accompanying him on his East European journey and were even more adamantly opposed to the idea of joint leadership. Louison addressed a group of Grenadians who were studying in Budapest and told them that Bishop was now rejecting sharing power with Coard. Word of Louison's Budapest talk and Bishop's renewed vacillation trickled back to Grenada where it set off an angry reaction with the NJM's Central Committee that felt that Bishop had broken his word and ignored the decision of the overwhelming majority of the party.

Bishop's reneging on his promise to abide by the joint leadership decision, set off a chain of events which was to result in his own death as well as the destruction of the Grenadian revolution. The prime minister got a taste of what was awaiting him when he returned to Grenada on 8 October only to discover that nobody had shown up to greet him at the airport except for Coard's supporter, Selwyn

Strachan, who received him in an icy manner. During the following days, he was not given any of the daily briefing to which he was accustomed.

Having lost control of the Politbureau, the Central Committee and the armed forces, the prime minister now tried to break out of his isolation by going directly to the masses whom he knew were still idolizing him. He told one of his two security guards to contact a number of prominent citizens in order to inform them that Bernard Coard and his Jamaican-born wife Phyllis (who was widely hated in Grenada), were getting ready to kill him. The security guard, however, turned himself in to the pro-Coard forces who reacted with fury to what they perceived as Bishop's attempt to stir up the masses against them.

At a hastily convened meeting of the Politburo and Central Committee on October 12, Bishop and his supporters George Louison and Fitzroy Bain were subjected to withering criticism. Louison was expelled from the Central Committee and subsequently incarcerated. Bain was threatened with jail. The prime minister himself was accused of 'cultism,' 'one manism' and 'spreading rumours as a pre-condition for murdering the Central Committee and chasing the party off the street'. At the end of the meeting, Politburo and Central Committee member, Liam James, announced that Bishop was to be prevented from having any contact with the outside world by being placed under house arrest and having his telephone cut.

It was after the 12 October meeting that news of the intra-party struggle began to penetrate Grenada as well as the outside world. The Cuban ambassador to Grenada, who like so many other people on the island, had been unaware of what was transpiring with the NJM, was now informed by both the Bishop and Coard factions of their fratricidal strife. He immediately informed Fidel Castro, who on 15 October, sent a message to the PRG expressing his hope 'that the difficulties could be overcome with the greatest wisdom, calmness, loyalty to principles and generosity'.

Fidel Castro's exhortations fell on deaf ears as the Bishop–Coard conflict intensified during the following days. Protests against Coard occurred in all major towns and Pearls Airport had to be closed temporarily when school children sat down on its runway in order to express their disapproval of Bishop's house arrest. When Minister of National Mobilization, Selwyn Strachan, announced in downtown St. George's that Maurice Bishop had been replaced as prime minister by Bernard Coard, he was chased away by an angry mob. There was no doubt on whose side the Grenadian people stood in this feud between Grenada's two top political leaders.

The pro-Bishop demonstrations culminated in a massive gathering on St. George's Central Market Square on 19 October, a day which is remembered by Grenadians as 'Bloody Wednesday'. All offices, schools, factories, stores and restaurants were closed on that day as over 10,000 persons assembled with signs such as 'Give us Maurice, or the masses will blast!' and 'C for Corruption, C for Coard!' The crowd was addressed by Minister of External Relations, Unison Whiteman, who called for a march on Maurice Bishop's residence in order to free him. About 3,000 people (the majority school children) followed Whiteman's appeal and walked up the steep streets that led to Bishop's house which was surrounded by a hundred PRA soldiers who fired above the approaching people's heads in order to force them back. The protesters, however, continued their march, pushed the soldiers aside and freed the exhausted Comrade Leader who had refused to eat anything during his confinement for fear that his captors were intending to poison him.

The feeble prime minister was lifted onto a lorry which moved downhill towards the Central Market Square where Bishop was expected to address the huge crowd which had been waiting for his liberation. But Bishop decided that his supporters must first seize the headquarters of the PRA, Ft. Rupert (formerly Ft. George), which contained a large arsenal. Once again, as at Bishop's residence, the PRA soldiers guarding the fort refused to shoot at their advancing fellow citizens who broke into the arsenal in order to arm themselves. Among the folk that stormed the arsenal were not only followers of Bishop, but known enemies of the Grenadian Revolution. An armed showdown between the Bishop and Coard factions had now become all but inevitable.

Pro-Coard PRA officers at Ft. Frederick (located across the bay from Ft. Rupert) were horrified when they observed that the pro-Bishop crowd had succeeded in capturing the nerve centre of Grenada's defence which contained enough ammunition, shells and mines to blow up most of St. George's. They ordered the dispatch of three Soviet-built personnel carriers whose task it was to re-capture Ft. Rupert. The soldiers manning these carriers apparently thought that their mere appearance would cow the crowd at Ft. Rupert into surrendering. They were sitting on top of their vehicles, exposed to potential enemy fire, instead of inside, where they would have enjoyed the protection of the armoured plating. It seems that elements in the fort (possibly provocateurs who were eager to see the Bishop and Coard factions kill each other) opened up with AK-47 fire, killing and wounding several PRA soldiers on top of their personnel carriers. The crews of the armoured vehicles thereupon poured shells and machine gun fire into the fort, killing many civilians and causing a panic with people jumping fifty to ninety feet to their deaths from the high ramparts. In order to prevent even more bloodshed, Maurice Bishop ordered the surrender of Ft. Rupert.

The entering pro-Coard soldiers ordered everybody to evacuate the fort, except for the Prime Minister and his prominent followers who were placed under arrest. At 1 p.m. an execution squad led by Captain Lester Redhead and First Lieutenant Iman Abdullah lined up Maurice Bishop, his pregnant friend, Minister of Education, Jacqueline Creft, Minister of External Relations, Unison Whiteman, Minister of Housing, Norris Bain and agricultural labour leader, Fitzroy Bain, against a wall of the fort's inner courtyard and killed them. The murder of Maurice Bishop and his closest adherents signified the self-immolation of the Grenadian Revolution.

Two hours after the massacre, the Commander of the People's Revolutionary Armed Forces, Hudson Austin, related over Radio Free Grenada the day's events from the vantage point of the Coard faction. He also issued a twenty-four hour curfew that would last until 24 October. Austin threatened that anybody violating this curfew would be shot immediately. Finally, Austin announced that Grenada was now under the rule of a Revolutionary Military Council, led by himself. The commanders of Maurice Bishop's execution squad were two of the sixteen members constituting the RMC.

The massacre at Ft. Rupert evoked a wave of outrage in the Caribbean which was shared by some of the staunchest supporters of the Grenadian Revolution. Former prime minister of Jamaica, Michael Manley, warned that 'history will pass a terrible judgement on those who are responsible for this murder', and Fidel Castro of Cuba declared that 'no doctrine, no principle or proclaimed revolutionary position and no internal division can justify atrocious acts such as the physical elimination of Bishop and the prominent group of honest and worthy leaders who died yesterday'.

Given its pariah status on both the local and international level, it seems unlikely that this military wing of the pro-Coard faction could have survived for very long. As a matter of fact, the RMC was well aware of its isolation and undertook desperate efforts to ingratiate itself with the United States. Hudson Austin contacted the American St. George's University School of Medicine and assured its vice chancellor that he was free to travel anywhere on the island during the curfew. The head of the RMC also made sure that the American medical students had enough food and water during the curfew and offered to assist in any evacuation of the students if they desired to leave Grenada (which most of them did not). When members of the US embassy at Barbados flew into Grenada during the curfew, one of the leaders of the RMC, Leon Cornwall, assured them that the

Revolutionary Military Council was a temporary organization that would only serve for two weeks, after which it was to be replaced by a civilian administration. Cornwall then asked the American diplomats to help him in forming this future civilian government.

The attempts by the RMC to reach a *modus vivendi* with Washington, received an icy response from the Reagan Administration, which could not pass up the opportunity to deal the *coup de grâce* to the Grenadian Revolution which it had tried to isolate for years. At 5:00 a.m. on 25 October 1983, 1,900 US troops and a token force of 300 soldiers from Barbados, Jamaica, Dominica, Antigua, St. Kitts-Nevis, St. Lucia and St. Vincent, invaded Grenada. Although the Cuban construction workers and military advisors, as well as some Grenadian units, put up a stiff resistance, the outcome of the invasion was never in doubt given the overwhelming superiority of the US invasionary forces. Within less than a week, the United States and its allies had secured total control over Grenada.

In spite of their previous tough rhetoric, not a single leader of the pro-Coard faction fought the invaders. All of them hid out at various private residences, where they were captured, interrogated and, subsequently, jailed. Despite the dire predictions by opponents of the US intervention on Grenada that the American forces would stay for many years and create permanent military bases there, the United States withdrew its troops as soon as possible. There is no doubt that the majority of the Grenadian people greeted the US forces as liberators who had freed them from the military dictatorship of Maurice Bishop's murderers.

The Reagan Administration underlined the importance that it assigned to Grenada by setting up a US Embassy at St. George's, which assisted in the economic and political rehabilitation of the country. During the first two years after the armed intervention, the US Agency for International Development (AID) spent US $37 million on construction projects in Grenada. The bulk of this assistance (US $21.1 million) went towards the completion of the new international airport at Point Salines which was formally opened by President Ronald Reagan on the first anniversary (25 October 1984) of the invasion of Grenada. AID money was also funnelled into the once deplorable road system of the country, which has improved considerably. United States monetary contributions helped with the repair of St. George's port facilities as well as the renovation of the Central Market Square. The Richmond Hill Mental Hospital, which was mistakenly bombed by US war planes during the invasion, was re-built with AID contributions. Since 1986, AID has assisted in the building of an industrial park, a new sewage system, and the repairs of many schools.

In the political realm, the United States pursued three main objectives. First of all, it was eager to have all organizations and institutions of the Grenadian Revolution thoroughly dismantled. Secondly, it hoped for a complete purge of the Grenadian civil service of former adherents of the revolution. Finally, every effort was to be made to prevent former prime minister Eric Gairy from staging a comeback. The last-mentioned task proved to be the most difficult one.

As soon as the United States had established control over Grenada, Gairy returned from his exile in California, proclaiming that God had chosen him once again to lead the Grenadian people. He called for the establishment of a permanent US military base on the island and pledged that upon becoming prime minister again, he would name the new airport after Ronald Reagan. To everyone's surprise, Gairy could still count on substantial support among the poorest segment of Grenada's peasants who recalled his campaign during the 1950s against the plantocracy. Along with its eccentric leader, reappeared the Grenada United Labour Party (GULP) which Gairy had used for three decades for his personal aggrandizement.

When the first post-invasion national elections were held on Grenada in December 1984, the spectre of a potential Gairy victory loomed large since the other political parties were fragmented and quarrelling among themselves. Under pressure from the United States, these parties finally agreed to a last minute political merger in the form of the New National Party (NNP) which was led by a conservative businessman from Carriacou, Herbert Blaize, who had been Grenada's prime minister twice during the past. Much to Washington's relief, the NNP emerged as the clear winner of the 1984 elections, although Gairy's GULP made a respectable showing by garnering thirty-seven per cent of the vote. Until his death in December 1989 at the age of seventy-one, Grenadian politics were dominated by Prime Minister Blaize who left behind a mixed record.

On the one hand, it no doubt helped Grenada to have at its helm a prime minister whose conservatism was much appreciated by the Reagan Administration. On the other hand, Blaize's subservience to Washington offended many Grenadians. Grenada was the only black country in the United Nations which supported the Reagan Administration's opposition to imposing sanctions on South Africa. Another example of Blaize's kowtowing to Washington was his speech during the opening of the new airport. Blaize thanked the United States profusely for constructing the airport without ever mentioning the Cubans who had finished three-quarters of the work before the armed intervention. Nor did he allude to Maurice Bishop, who had been the driving force behind the airport project until his execution.

What Grenada needed more than anything else in the wake of the traumatic October events, was an era of reconciliation. Blaize, however, followed the opposite course by his purge, persecution and harassment of former members of the New Jewel Movement. The former Chief of Staff of the PRA, Einstein Louison, had his Grenadian passport confiscated so that he was unable to visit his wife and child in Cuba. Maurice Bishop's former press secretary, Don Rojas, and former PRG Attorney-General, Richard Hart, were deported when they arrived at the new airport.

Pamphlets and books praising the Grenadian Revolution were not allowed into the country and the liberal regional newspaper, *Caribbean Contact*, which was published by the Caribbean Council of Churches on Barbados, could no longer be sold on Grenada. Hundreds of Grenadian students, who were returning from various socialist countries after completing their studies, were told that their degrees would not be recognized. This happened to the grandson of T. A. Marryshow, Dr. Terry Marryshow, who had terminated his medical studies in Cuba, only to be told in his homeland that he would be barred from practising medicine there unless he passed the medical examinations of Grenada. As a consequence, Terry Marryshow is today the leader of the leftist Maurice Bishop Patriotic Movement (MBPM) which tries to perpetuate the ideals of the slain leader of the Grenadian Revolution.

The worst treatment, however, was to be reserved for Bernard and Phyllis Coard and their closest associates. After intensive interrogations by the US armed forces, the leading members of the Coard faction, were incarcerated at Richmond Hill Prison. There they were placed under the jurisdiction of a brutal Barbadian prison commissioner, Lionel Maloney, whose treatment of prisoners ranged from physical beatings, denial of medical care, and solitary confinement, to the refusal to forward mail and to allow visits by family members and friends.

In April of 1986, a trial was launched against the Coards as well as sixteen other defendants who stood accused of the murder of Maurice Bishop and five of his top followers as well as twenty other Grenadians. On 4 December 1986, a guilty verdict was handed down against seventeen of the eighteen accused, fourteen of whom (including the Coards, Selwyn Strachan and Hudson Austin) were sentenced to die by hanging. At the time of this writing (June 1990), the condemned prisoners are still awaiting their execution on death row.

By the time of his death in December 1989, Blaize's popularity had reached a nadir. Besides his vindictiveness towards erstwhile supporters of the Grenadian Revolution, his autocratic ways of running the government and his poor management of the Grenadian economy had alienated almost everybody. The carefully crafted coalition party (NNP) of 1984 had long disintegrated with two of Blaize's most capable ministers (George Brizan and Francis Alexis) resigning from his cabinet and forming an opposition party known as the National Democratic Congress (NDC).

When general elections were called for on 13 March 1990, fears arose, as they had in 1984, that given the opposition's disunity, Eric Gairy would once again become Grenada's prime minister. As it turned out, Gairy's GULP captured less than twenty-nine per cent of the popular vote, the lowest percentage ever recorded for GULP since the elections of 1951. The NDC emerged as the victor of the elections and when a GULP representative defected to its ranks, the National Democratic Congress was able to form the new government with its leader, Nicholas Brathwaite, as Grenada's new prime minister. George Brizan and Francis Alexis became respectively Minister of Finance and Minister of Legal Affairs in the new cabinet.

Shortly after the elections, Governor-General Sir Paul Scoon outlined during his Speech to the Throne the aims of the new government, which he described as the containment of inflation by the tight control of expenditures, the expansion of trade and development of Grenada's agricultural industries. As further goals, Scoon cited the development of adult education, the expansion of teachers' training programmes, the modernization of laws concerning women, the re-introduction of local government and more Grenadian programmes on national television. Spokespersons for the NDC expressed their regret that Grenada under Blaize had not supported the boycott of South Africa. The new government also lifted the ban on leftist books and periodicals and announced the formation of an independent commission which would make unannounced visits to Richmond Hill Prison in order to ascertain the observance of human rights in that penal institution.

Grenada is a small country where everybody seems to know each other and where societal fissures have a particularly devastating effect. Over three decades of political turmoil and division have left a traumatic heritage which can only be overcome by a policy of tolerance and national reconciliation. It seems that with the advent of the centrist NDC government of Nicholas Brathwaite, Grenada has finally attained such a leadership which will heal the wounds of the past and advance Grenada into a better future.

The Country and its People

1 **A short history of Grenada.**
Grenada Independence Secretariat, History and Literary Division.
San Fernando, Trinidad: Unique Services, 1974. 58p.
A brief history of Grenada, which was issued on the occasion of the country's independence from Great Britain on 7 February 1974. The volume contains an explanation of the symbols and colour scheme of Grenada's flag as well as the text and music score of Grenada's national anthem.

2 **This – is Carriacou.**
Frances Kay Brinkley. St. George's: Carenage, 1971. 31p. map.
A humorous introduction to the history and customs of Carriacou written by an author who wrote a similar booklet on Grenada.

3 **This – is Grenada.**
Frances Kay Brinkley. St. George's: Carenage, 1966. 128p. map.
A delightful, unorthodox introduction to life on Grenada written with humour as well as great affection for the people of this island.

4 **Grenada: island of conflict from Amerindians to people's revolution, 1498–1979.**
George Brizan. London: Zed, 1984. 381p. map. bibliog. (Latin American Series).
A thorough, economically-orientated survey of the history of Grenada from 1495 to 1979 with a particularly detailed account of the development of trade unionism and the educational system. After the demise of the Bishop régime, the author founded his own political party and served as education minister in the Blaize government until his resignation in 1987.

The Country and its People

5 **Grenada: the hour will strike again.**
Jan Carew. Prague: International Organization of Journalists, 1985.
278p.
A history of Grenada by a Guyanese novelist who sympathized with the Grenadian
Revolution (1979-83) and blamed Bernard Coard and his cohorts for destroying it.

6 **Country profile: Grenada.**
Caricom Perspective, vol. 44/45 (June 1989), p. 28-31.
When the Tenth Conference of the CARICOM (Caribbean Community) Heads of
State met at St. George's, Grenada, during 1989, CARICOM's official journal
published a survey of the history, political system, economy and outstanding
personalities of Grenada.

7 **Carriacou culture.**
Christine David. Carriacou, Grenada: Hectograph, 1975. 44p. map.
A charming essay by a Carriacouan who obviously loves her island for its unspoiled
atmosphere and simplicity of life. The booklet provides much information on
Carriacou's culture, economy, tourist attractions, education, agriculture and African
heritage.

8 **Grenada.**
Joyce Eisenberg. New York; New Haven, Connecticut; Philadelphia:
Chelsea House, 1988. 83p. 2 maps. (Places and Peoples of the World).
This volume contains much up-to-date information on the government, education,
economy, culture and the media on Grenada. A useful glossary accompanies the book
which explains mostly Grenadian cooking and calypso terms.

9 **Grenada.**
Richard A. Haggerty, John F. Hornbeck. In: *Islands of the
Commonwealth Caribbean*. Edited by Sandra W. Meditz, Dennis M.
Hanratty. Washington: US Government Printing Office, 1989, p. 349-84.
map. bibliog.
A description of the geography, population, education, health and welfare, economy,
government and politics, foreign relations and national security problems of Grenada.
This volume on the anglophone Caribbean islands was prepared by the Federal
Research Division of the Library of Congress under the County Studies-Area
Handbook Program. The section on Grenada contains a much needed discussion of
developments on Grenada since the October events of 1983. A useful bibliography can
be found on pages 701-05.

10 **The impact of migration on the metropolitan and folk society of
Carriacou, Grenada.**
Donald R. Hill. New York: Anthropological Papers of the American
Museum of Natural History, vol. 54 part 2, 1977. 391p. bibliog.
A professor of anthropology at the State University of New York at Stony Brook
wrote this superb ethnographic study of Carriacou, one of the three islands constituting

2

the nation of Grenada. The paper deals with all aspects of Carriacouan life and explains in detail the famous Big Drum Dance and the 'maroons'.

11 Caribbean landmarks: historic events and sites.
Lennox Honychurch.   Walton-on-Thames, Surrey: Thomas Nelson, 1986. 94p.

A Dominican artist, journalist and historian wrote this beautifully illustrated guide to important Caribbean landmarks. The important Grenadian sites which are listed are: the spice plantations, Grand Etang crater lake, the historic centre of St. George's, Ft. George, Sauteurs, boatbuilding on Carriacou, spice factories at Gouyave and the Grenada Museum.

12 Carriacou: an old world in the new.
Robert C. Kingsbury. *Journal of Geography*, vol. 59, no. 9 (Dec. 1960), p. 399-409.

In this essay, a cartographer and professor of geography at Indiana University, Bloomington, Indiana, deals with the historical background, population, exports, fishing industry, cotton and corn agriculture, and water problems of Carriacou. The article is accompanied by several useful maps as well as artistic drawings of the island's capital of Hillsborough.

13 The Grenadines.
Bruce G. Lynn.   Hollywood, Florida: Dukane, 1968. 52p. map.

A description of the Grenadines based upon four sailing trips through the islands by a practising attorney from Columbus, Ohio. Grenada, Carriacou and Petit Martinique figure prominently in this book. The accompanying photographs are marvellous and well-chosen.

14 Plan and policy for a system of national parks and protected areas in Grenada and Carriacou-Government of Grenada.
Washington: General Secretariat, Organization of American States, 1988. 130p. 3 maps. bibliog.

This important document discusses the geomorphology, geological history, natural vegetation and wildlife on Grenada and the climate, geology, land-use history and natural vegetation of Carriacou. It also presents a development strategy for a national park system for these two islands.

15 Carriacou – a time capsule from paradise.
Wilfred A. Redhead.   *The Greeting Tourist Guide*, vol. 1, no. 2 (Oct. 1988), p. 9-11.

An enthusiastic article about the amazing blend of cultures which formed the population of Carriacou. The author spent many years on Carriacou as Grenada's District Officer. Beautiful photographs of Hillsborough and Tyrrel Bay as well as of the adjacent island of Petit Martinique.

The Country and its People

16 **A city on a hill.**
Wilfred A. Redhead.   Barbados, West Indies: Letchworth, 1985. 120p.
Charming reminiscences of his youth by a retired Grenadian civil servant. The author recalls the history of many prominent streets and houses of the Grenadian capital of St. George's such as the Carenage, the Esplanade, York House, Ft. George, Mt. Helicon, and the Botanic Gardens.

17 **Truth, fact and tradition in Carriacou.**
Wilfred A. Redhead.   *Caribbean Quarterly*, vol. 16, no. 3 (Sept. 1970), p. 61-63.
A Grenadian civil servant, assigned for several years to Carriacou, attacks M. G. Smith's book *Kinship and community in Carriacou* (q.v.). Redhead accuses Smith of describing Carriacou as much more primitive than it is. He labels ancestor worship on Carriacou as 'fiction'.

18 **Grenada: isle of spice.**
Norma Sinclair.   London: Macmillan, 1987. 128p.
A very useful book which delves into all aspects of Grenadian life and even contains a section on Grenadian cooking (crab and callaloo soup, stuffed jacks). Equal attention is paid to all sections of the main island, and the smaller islands of Carriacou and Petit Martinique are not neglected. Stunningly beautiful photographs accompany the text.

19 **Grenada, an island state, its history and its people.**
Beverley Steele.   *Caribbean Quarterly*, vol. 20, no. 1 (March 1974), p. 5-43.
A concise survey of Grenadian geography, history, economy and culture by a sociologist who serves as the resident tutor of the University of the West Indies' Extra-Mural Department at St. George's.

20 **Grenada revisited.**
Veronica Gould Stoddard.   *Américas*, vol. 37, no. 5 (Sept.-Oct. 1985), p. 8-15.
Without even once mentioning the severe crises which have shaken Grenada, the author draws a rapturous, idealized picture of the island nation.

Geography

General

21 **Commercial geography of the Grenadines.**
Robert C. Kingsbury.   Bloomington, Indiana: Indiana University, 1960.
38p. maps.

The first of a series of twelve reports on the commercial geography of the anglophone islands in the Lesser Antilles, published by the Department of Geography of Indiana University. Since Carriacou is the largest, most heavily populated and longest continually occupied island in the Grenadines, there is a great deal of information on the island in this volume (p. 22-27). Information on Petit Martinique may be found on page 27.

22 **A bibliography of the Caribbean area for geographers.**
Compiled by A. V. Norton.   Mona, Jamaica: University of the West
Indies, 1971. 3 vols. (Occasional Publications no. 7).

A bibliography pertaining to geography in the Caribbean which was published in 1971 by the Department of Geography of the UWI. The bibliographical materials on Grenada can be found on pages 20 and 152.

Maps and atlases

23 **Grenada isle of spice map.**
Government of the United Kingdom, Ordnance Survey.   St. George's:
Government of Grenada, 1985,

Besides the major map of the entire island, there are four inserts portraying the boundaries of the island's six parishes, Grenada's location within the Caribbean Basin, the capital of St. George's and the South-West Peninsula where most of the tourist hotels and restaurants are situated. The city map of St. George's contains an index to buildings such as the police stations, churches, post office, general hospital, botanical gardens, banks, national museum and public library. The map's scale is 1:50,000.

24 **The printed maps of Dominica and Grenada.**
R. V. Tooley. London: Map Collectors' Circle, 1970. 15p. 12 maps.

A listing of Grenadian maps published between 1717 and 1873 accompanied by reproductions of twelve Grenadian maps.

Tourism

25 **Grenada: spice of the Caribbean.**
Sam Alcorn. *Travel-Holiday*, vol. 164, no. 2 (Aug. 1985), p. 54-58, 74.

A discussion of the tourist attractions of Grenada by a financial reporter who praises the slow, laid-back pace of life on the island.

26 **Falling in love with Grenada.**
Joan Carter. *The Greeting Tourist Guide*, vol. 1, no. 1 (May 1988),
p. 12-14.

A first time visitor's positive reaction to Grenada reflected in an article written to attract other tourists to the island. The article is accompanied by a useful guide for visitors to Grenada.

27 **Grenada: the best of bed and board on a spice island.**
Thelma Dickman. *Américas*, vol. 35, no. 5 (Sept.-Oct. 1983), p. 46-49.

A eulogy of some of Grenada's exquisite small hotels and the delicious Grenadian dishes they serve.

28 **America's adopted island in the sun.**
William B. Flanagan. *Forbes*, vol. 138, no. 10 (3 Nov. 1986), p. 216-22.

According to this article, Grenada has experienced a true renaissance since the US intervention in October 1983. Useful appendix of major hotels and their rates.

29 **Tranquil tropics: discover the quiet islands of Curaçao and Grenada.**
Dari Giles. *Essence*, vol. 19, no. 5 (Sept. 1988), p. 23-28, 152.

Like so many travel writers, the author praises the non-commercial, unspoiled atmosphere of Grenada.

30 **Grenada: isle of spice.**
Grenada Tourism Department. Brussels: Transtec, 1985. 64p.

This tourist guide, which was financed by the European Economic Community, gives a brief overview of Grenada's different regions, customs, sports, hotels, restaurants, and products. The booklet which is filled with colourful photographs, is written in English, French, German and Spanish.

31 Frommer's a shopper's guide to the Caribbean.
Jeanne Harman, Harry Harman III.   New York: Prentice Hall, 1988. 528p.

Up-to-date information on where to find arts and crafts, fashions, jewelry, perfume and cosmetics as well as spirits on Grenada.

32 The isle of spice.
Richard M. Huber.   *The Greeting Tourist Guide*, vol. 2, no. 2 (Oct. 1989), p. 33-38.

Two lengthy tours of the island are suggested for tourists by the author concentrating respectively on the northern 'cone' and southern 'cone'. The northern tour includes such sights as Ft. George, the towns of Gouyave, Victoria, Sauteurs and Grenville, the Levera National Park, the River Antoine Rum Distillery and the Grand Etang Forest Center. The southern cone tour encompasses Fort Frederick, the botanical splendour of Bay Gardens, La Sagesse Protected Seascape, Marquis village, Royal Fort and the islands of La Baye Rock and Marquis.

33 War and remembrance: Grenada six years after the American military intervention.
Peter Oliver.   *Travel-Holiday*, vol. 172, no. 1 (July 1989), p. 84-91.

A well-written, sensitive article about the wonders and problems of Grenada which stands in stark contrast to so many superficial articles about Grenada in travel magazines. The author comments approvingly that even though the number of visitors to Grenada has doubled since 1983, tourist development is still minimal compared to that in the rest of the Caribbean.

34 Grenada revisited: better than ever.
Alan Ponsford.   *World Press Review*, vol. 34, no. 2 (Feb. 1987), p. 63.

Commenting that in Grenada you will find no Woolworth's, no McDonald's or Kentucky Fried Chicken, little crime and virtually no drugs, a British writer eulogizes the unspoiled atmosphere of Grenada.

35 Grenada revisited.
Allyson Reid-Dove.   *Black Enterprise*, vol. 19, no. 10 (May 1989), p. 113-14.

This article is filled with up-to-date information on hotels, art galleries, restaurants, tours and other information helpful to prospective tourists.

36 Grenadians' attitudes to tourism.
Rustum J. Sethna.   Port-of-Spain: Key Caribbean Publications, 1976. 48p. bibliog.

A study of the Caribbean Tourism Research Centre (CRTC) carried out by a professor of social psychology at the Ryerson Institute of Toronto, Canada. The survey indicates that Grenadians generally welcomed the expansion of tourism, but felt that its benefits were not evenly distributed among the country's population.

37 **United States Department of State February 1985 Grenada post report.**
Washington: US Government Printing Office, 1985. 16p. bibliog.
Information on all aspects of Grenadian life designed for the use of official US government employees and their families who are going to be stationed on the island. The information contained in this booklet would also be most useful for tourists or foreigners who are contemplating taking up residence on the island.

38 **Spice island cruise.**
Julius Wilensky. *Yachting*, vol. 156, no. 8 (Aug. 1984), p. 78-79, 110-14.
For anyone interested in visiting Grenada with a yacht, this is the article to read.

39 **Spice island regatta.**
Marcia Wiley. *Yachting*, vol. 156, no. 8 (Aug. 1984), p. 76-77, 105-06.
A report on Grenada's 23rd Easter regatta. The author states that in contrast to Grenada under the People's Revolutionary Government, boats can now land once again anywhere they want to.

Travel guides

40 **The Caribbean.**
Frank Bellamy. Chester, Connecticut: Globe Pequot Press, 1987. 358p. map. (Cadogan Guides).
The director of Transatlantic Wings, a company specializing in inexpensive travel to the Caribbean, supplies information on the history, entry regulations, climate, population, hotels, nightlife, shopping and sport of Grenada and Carriacou on pages 209-14.

41 **1990 Caribbean island handbook.**
Edited by Ben Box, Sarah Cameron. Bath, England: Trade and Travel, 1989. 507p. map.
Information on the history, government, flora and fauna, beaches and water sports as well as the festivals of Grenada can be found on pages 347-58 of this book.

42 **Best of the Caribbean 1983**
Sandra Hart. New York; Easton, Maryland; Champaign, Illinois: Fisher Travel Guides, 1983. 276p.
Good information on hotels, restaurants, nightlife, shopping and sports on Grenada can be found on pages 72-85.

43 **Undiscovered islands of the Caribbean.**
Burl Willes.   Santa Fe, New Mexico: John Muir, 1988. 208p.

Two of the 'undiscovered islands' discussed in this book are Carriacou (p. 137-43) and Petit Martinique (p. 144-45). Carriacou's five hotels and three restaurants are evaluated. The author lists his favourite spots in and around Carriacou which are the Carriacou Museum with its Amerindian and European artifacts, Tyrrel Bay, and Sandy Island.

44 **The inn way – the Caribbean.**
Margaret Zellers.   Stockbridge, Massachusetts: Berkshire Traveller Press, 1978. 192p.

This book contains a description on pages 83-91 of the lovely inns of Grenada.

Geology

45 **A geological model of the lesser Antilles subduction zone complex.**
Tony F. Clark. PhD dissertation, University of North Carolina at
Chapel Hill, 1974, 101p. (Available from University Microfilms, Ann
Arbor, Michigan, order no. 74-26860).

An examination of the subduction zone complex of the eastern margin of the
Caribbean which contains five major north–south trending geological structures (the
Barbados Ridge, Tobago trough, Lesser Antilles Island Arc, Grenada Basin, and the
Aves Swell) all located east of the Venezuelan Basin.

46 **Form-process relationships on island coasts.**
Manuel Luis Hernandez-Avila. PhD dissertation, Louisiana State
University and Agricultural and Mechanical College, Baton Rouge,
Louisiana, 1974. 134p. (Available from University Microfilms, Ann
Arbor, Michigan, order no. 75-01930).

In this dissertation, variations in geometric properties and spatial arrangement of
major coastal morphological landforms (beaches, cliffs, rocky shore and swamps) of
the islands of Barbados, Dominica, Grenada, St. Lucia, and St. Vincent are compared
to coastal process sectors.

Travellers' Accounts

47 Caribbean and El Dorado.
John Crocker.   Fontwell, Sussex: Centaur, 1968. 405p. map.
A British tourist guide from the 1960s which discusses the history, economy, sightseeing, hotels, restaurants as well as sports and recreation on pages 198-213. The reader is informed that 'perhaps more than any other island, violence played a large part in the history of Grenada'. Eric Gairy is described as 'a talented young Negro demagogue'.

48 Six months in the West Indies.
Henry Nelson Coleridge.   London: John Murray, 1832. 311p. map.
After describing Grenada as the most beautiful of all Caribbean islands the author labels the freed black slaves on Grenada as 'good humored, vivacious and impudent'.

49 Intimate glimpses of the West Indies.
Frank R. Coutant.   New York: Vantage, 1957. 119p.
A very positive description of Grenada in the wake of Hurricane Janet may be found on pages 49-55. The author's prediction that Grenada's main export crop would shift from nutmegs to bananas has not been realized.

50 The traveller's tree: a journey through the Caribbean islands.
Patrick L. Fermor.   London: John Murray, 1955. 403p. map.
Like so many travellers before him, the author is smitten by the overwhelming beauty of Grenada and its capital of St. George's which he compares to 'a beautiful eighteenth-century Devonshire town in mid-winter'. Most of the descriptions of Grenada in this book may be found on pages 181-93.

Travellers' Accounts

51 **Love in a nutshell.**
Anita Leslie.   New York: Greenberg, 1952. 208p. maps.
An Englishwoman's description of a sailing trip from England via the Canary Islands to the West Indies. Chapters 18 and 19 are devoted to her impressions of Grenada where she approved of the charming colonial architecture of St. George's but not of the Grenadian blacks who, according to her, had dropped from slavery into total indolence.

52 **Travel accounts and descriptions of Latin America and the Caribbean 1800-1920: a selected bibliography.**
Compiled by Thomas L. Welch, Myriam Figueras.   Washington: Columbus Memorial Library, Organization of American States, 1982. 293p.
This bibliography contains seven books on Grenada which are listed on page 116.

Flora and Fauna

General

53 Up hill and down dale in Grenada.
Raymund Devas.   London: Sands, 1926. 93p. map.
A marvellous description of the flora and fauna of Grenada as well as its waterfalls and mountains. Although published in 1926, this book could still be of great use to tourists eager to explore the natural wonders of Grenada and Carriacou.

54 A natural history of the island of Grenada, W.I.
J. R. Groome.   Arima, Trinidad: Caribbean Printers, 1970. 113p.
This excellent book by the president of the Grenada National Trust (1967-69) gives a complete description of the flora and fauna of Grenada and Carriacou.

55 Camps in the Caribbees.
Frederick A. Ober.   Boston, Massachusetts: Lee & Shepard, 1880. 336p.
A North American ornithologist, who visited the Lesser Antilles under the auspices of the Smithsonian Institution in 1876 describes the fauna of Grenada including the tatou (armadillo), manicou (opossum) and the agouti (a rodent native to the West Indies).

Plants

56 **The vegetation of the Grenadines, Windward Islands, British West Indies.**
Richard A. Hoard. Cambridge, Massachusetts: The Gray Herbarium
of Harvard University, 1952. 129p. maps. bibliog.
The definitive work on the flora of the inhabited Grenadine islands which belong to
Grenada (Carriacou and Petit Martinique) as well as the uninhabited islets which
belong to that nation (Kick 'em Jenny and the Isle of Ronde).

57 **The Double Chaconia – a rare beauty.**
Alister Hughes. *Caribbean Life and Times*, vol. 1, no. 5 (1980),
p. 86-87.
An interesting account of Grenada's plant propagation station at Mirabeau and its
successful director Neville Burris.

58 **Grenada's Bay Gardens.**
Arbon Jack Lowe, Richard J. Gardner. *Américas*, vol. 30, no. 8 (Aug.
1978), p. 35-37.
Magnificent photographs of a garden displaying all specimens of flowers which grow on
Grenada. This garden was planted by two Grenadian brothers, Keith and Lyle St.
Bernard.

Birds

59 **Birds of the West Indies.**
James Bond. Boston, Massachusetts: Houghton Mifflin, 1985. 5th ed.
256p. maps.
The best work on birds in the West Indies by the curator of birds at the Academy of
Natural Sciences of Philadelphia. Over 400 species of birds, many of them found in
Grenada, are listed.

60 **Birds of Grenada, St. Vincent and the Grenadines.**
Raymund P. Devas. St. George's: Carenage Press, 1943. 85p. map.
A description of the sea birds, water birds and land birds of Grenada, accompanied by
excellent drawings.

61 **Birds on Grenada.**
David Lack, Andrew Lack. *Ibis*, vol. 115, no. 1 (Jan. 1973), p. 53-59.
An annotated list of thirty different birds seen and heard by the authors on slow walks
on Grenada during the first week of August 1971. They were surprised to discover an
Apus Apus (common swift) which had never been seen before in the West Indies.

Reptiles

62 **Reptiles of the eastern Caribbean.**
Garth Underwood.   St. Augustine, Trinidad: Department of Extra-
Mural Studies, University of the West Indies, 1962. 192p. (Caribbean
Affairs [New Series] no. 1).

Pages 162-64 of this book by a professor of zoology at the faculty of agriculture, UWI.
at St. Augustine, Trinidad, list the names of lizards and snakes which can be found on
Grenada.

Prehistory and Archaeology

63 **Field comments on the skull excavated in 1967 at Caliviny [sic] Island, Grenada, West Indies.**
Adelaide K. Bullen.   In: *Proceedings of the Second International Congress for the Study of pre-Columbian Cultures in the Lesser Antilles.* St. Ann's Garrison, Barbados: Barbados Museum, 1967, p. 44-46.
A Grenadian archaeologist speculates on the origin and significance of a rare skull which she found on Calivigny Island off the coast of Grenada.

64 **Archeological chronology of Grenada.**
Ripley P. Bullen.   *American Antiquity*, vol. 31, no. 2 (Oct. 1965), p. 237-41.
Basing his conclusions upon his investigation of ceramic shards on Grenada, Bullen asserts that pre-Arawak agriculturists, the Arawaks and the Caribs (and perhaps even the preceramic Ciboney) all entered the West Indies by way of Grenada.

65 **Salvage archaeology at Caliviny [sic] Island, Grenada: a problem in typology.**
Ripley B. Bullen, Adelaide K. Bullen.   In: *Proceedings of the Second International Congress for the Study of pre-Columbian Cultures in the Lesser Antilles*. St. Ann's Garrison, Barbados: Barbados Museum, 1967, p. 31-43.
Two Grenadian archaeologists report on their findings of Carib pottery shards on Calivigny Island, Grenada, which are similar to shards found on the South American mainland.

16

66   **The archaeology of Grenada, West Indies.**
Ripley P. Bullen.   Gainesville, Florida: University of Florida, 1964.
67p. map. bibliog. (Contributions of the Florida State Museum, social
sciences, no. 11).

A report on the results of archaeological research on Grenada which yielded findings
of the materials used by pre-Arawak, Arawak and Carib inhabitants. An appendix of
fifteen pages contains photographs of various shards and petroglyphs found on the
island.

67   **A study of shells and shelled objects from six PreColumbian sites in the
Grenadines of St. Vincent and Grenada.**
Lesley A. Sutton.   In: *Proceedings of the Seventh International Congress
for the Study of pre-Columbian Cultures of the Lesser Antilles.* Caracas:
Universidad Central de Caracas, 1978, p. 195-210.

An interesting article on the findings of Arawak worked shells on the Isle de Ronde
and Carriacou.

68   **Liaison Arawak – Calivigny – Carib between Grenada and St. Vincent,
Lesser Antilles.**
Lesley Sutty.   In: *Proceedings of the Ninth International Congress for
the Study of Pre-Columbian Cultures of the Lesser Antilles.* Santo
Domingo, 1981, p. 145-53.

The author concludes that 'most probably the Calivigny was an interphase, but of a
single tradition and a fairly small group living in a restricted area, mainly the
Grenadines between AD 700 and 1200'.

History

General

69 **From the beginning: a history of Grenada.**
D. Sinclair DaBreo. St. George's: Printers, 1973. 185p.
A Grenadian broadcasting journalist relates the history of his country from the arrival of the Indians to independence from Great Britain in 1974. The book is the result of fifteen years of research at the West India Committee, the Commonwealth Institute, and the Institute of Race Relations in London.

70 **The history of the island of Grenada 1650-1950.**
Raymund P. Devas. St. George's, 1964. 209p. map.
Although purporting to be a history of Grenada until 1950, this classic history of Grenada basically ends with Julien Fedon's rebellion (1795-1796). The author was a Catholic priest who resided on Grenada for many decades.

71 **From Camahogne to Free Grenada.**
Edward Frederick. St. George's: N.P., 1980. 130p. map. bibliog.
A brief history of Grenada which begins with the Caribs and ends with the overthrow of Eric Gairy by the New Jewel Movement under Maurice Bishop.

72 **Karibische Klein- und Mikrostaaten.** (Caribbean small and micro-states.)
Hans-Dieter Haas, Udo Bader, Jörg Grumptmann. Tübingen, West Germany: Attempto, 1985. 200p. map. bibliog.
The authors of this volume, in which Grenada figures prominently, come to the conclusion that the Caribbean mini-states have not been able to achieve a socio-cultural and economic integration after the formal end of colonialism in that region.

73   **Grenada – isle of spice.**
Flora L. Phelps.   *Américas*, vol. 27, no. 6-7 (June-July 1975), p. 30-24.
When Grenada became the twenty-fifth member state of the Organization of American States, this historical sketch of the island appeared in *Américas*, a journal of the OAS.

74   **Grenada – past and present.**
Norma Sinclair.   *The Greeting Tourist Guide*, vol. 1, no. 1 (May 1988), p. 6-11.
An informative survey of the history of Grenada from the days of the Ciboneys to the re-establishment of a multi-party system on Grenada in 1984. The author's description of the Grenadian Revolution, however, is neither useful nor balanced.

French colonial rule, 1654-1763

75   **L'histoire de l'isle de Grenade en Amerique.** (The history of the island of Grenada in the Americas.).
Edited by Jacques Petitjean Roget.   Montreal: Les Presses de l'Université de Montréal, 1975. 186p.
Although the title of the book by an anonymous author suggests a broad history of Grenada, this volume is limited to the history of the island between 1649 and 1659, i.e., the period during which Richelieu's 'Compagnie de Saint-Christophe' collapsed. The volume constitutes the first thorough account of the French occupation of Grenada.

French–British struggle over Grenada, 1763-83

76   **The mystery of Grenada's back-to-front forts.**
Alister Hughes.   *The Greeting Tourist Guide*, vol. 1, no. 1 (May 1988), p. 32-37.
This article describes the different roles played by the many powerful forts of St. George's (Ft. George, Ft. Frederick, Ft. Matthew, etc.) in the colonial wars between Great Britain and France as well as the War of American Independence.

British colonial rule, 1783-1974

77 **John Candler's visit to Grenada.**
John Candler. *Caribbean Studies*, vol. 4, no. 4 (Jan. 1965), p. 56-61.
A British merchant and member of the Society of Friends, John Candler (1787-1869), made four journeys to the West Indies on behalf of the anti-slavery cause. During his sojourn on Grenada, he noticed the collapse of the sugar industry.

78 **Fedon's rebellion 1795-96: causes and consequences.**
Edward L. Cox. *Journal of Negro History*, vol. 67, no. 1 (Spring 1982), p. 7-10.
The article emphasizes that Fedon's rebellion on Grenada must not be viewed as a localized act of rebellion, but must be seen within the wider context of world-wide revolutions inspired by the American and French Revolutions. The author believes that Fedon deserves his place along with Toussaint L'Ouverture, Nat Turner, Denmark Vessey, and a host of other blacks who sought to improve the condition of their brethren by violent means.

79 **Free coloreds in the slave societies of St. Kitts and Grenada, 1763-1833.**
Edward L. Cox. Knoxville, Tennessee: University of Tennessee, 1984. 197p.
A comparison between the free coloureds on St. Kitts and Grenada with a particularly useful chapter on Fedon's rebellion on Grenada.

80 **The shadow of freedom: freedmen in the slave societies of Grenada and St. Kitts, 1763-1833.**
Edward L. Cox. PhD dissertation, Johns Hopkins University, Baltimore, Maryland, 1977. 399p. (Available from University Microfilms, Ann Arbor, Michigan, order no. 77-19584).
The author concludes that freed slaves on Grenada found the road to economic salvation less hard than their counterparts on St. Kitts because on Grenada abundant land was available for the growing of cash crops.

81 **Crown colony politics in Grenada 1917-1951.**
Patrick Emmanuel. Cave Hill, Barbados: Institute of Social and Economic Research (Eastern Caribbean), University of the West Indies, 1978. 198p. bibliog.
The best study of political institutions and developments in the context of colonial society in Grenada in the first half of the present century. Special attention is paid to the political thought and activities of Theophilus Albert Marryshow.

82 **The decline of friendly societies in Grenada: some economic aspects.**
L. P. Fletcher. *Caribbean Studies*, vol. 12, no. 2 (July 1972), p. 99-111.
The inappropriate response by these friendly societies to inflationary conditions and rising real wages is blamed for their decline in Grenada.

83   **British West Indian culture.**
Anne Rainey Langley. *National Geographic Magazine*, vol. 79, no. 1
(January 1941), p. 1-46.
A visit to Grenada when it was still a British colony and contained only 89,000
inhabitants. The article gives an extensive account of nutmeg production on Grenada.

84   **Marryshow of Grenada: an introduction.**
Jill Sheppard.   Barbados, West Indies: Letchworth, 1987. 56p.
A brief but excellent account of the life and career of Theophilus Albert Marryshow
(1887-1958), an admired Grenadian journalist and politician who fought for racial
equality and the unity of the anglophone Caribbean in a West Indian Federation.

85   **The African custom of tooth mutilation in America.**
T. D. Stewart, John R. Groome.   *American Journal of Physical
Anthropology*, vol. 28, no. 1 (Jan. 1968), p. 31-42.
A discussion of the African custom of tooth mutilation as exemplified by the discovery
on Grenada of the skeleton of a male black with a West African type of dental
mutilation. The authors assert that intricate dental mutilation decreased the value of a
slave. Since slave ships first landed at Barbados before they reached Grenada, the
white plantation owners there had their first pick and sent the less physically attractive
slaves (including those with dental mutilations) to Grenada.

86   **A narrative of the revolt and insurrection in the island of Grenada.**
Gordon Turnbull.   London: A. Paris, Rolls' Buildings, 1796. 2nd ed.
183p.
A British officer who participated in the suppression of the Grenadian slave revolt led
by Julien Fedon in 1795, denies the allegations made by British lawyer, William Wise,
that the military disobeyed orders from the colonial authorities at St. George's which
delayed the seizure of Fedon and his forces at their mountain retreat of Belvidere.

87   **A review of the events, which have happened in Grenada, from the
commencement of the insurrection to the 1st of May by a sincere
wellwisher to the colony.**
William Wise.   St. George's, 1795. 107p.
An account of the initially successful, but ultimately doomed slave insurrection on
Grenada in 1795 which was led by Julien Fedon and backed by the French. The
author, an English lawyer, labels Fedon and his followers 'inhuman wretches' and
'monsters in human shape' who deserve 'to be extirpated from the earth'. Wise draws
an unflattering account of the British military units and their officers who were sent out
to capture Fedon and free his English hostages. The troops are portrayed as having
been drunk for days, with their officers disobeying instructions from the colonial
authorities at St. George's.

The Gairy era, 1950-79

88 **Political parties in the Commonwealth Caribbean.**
B. H. Barlow. *North South Nord Sud*, vol. 8, no. 16 (1983), p. 43-64.
A political scientist from the University of Regina, Canada, blames the New Jewel Movement's coup on 13 March 1979, upon Eric Gairy's perversion of the Westminster model of parliamentary democracy on Grenada.

89 **Colonial Office report on Grenada for the years 1950 and 1951.**
British Colonial Office.   London: HMSO, 1953. 38p. map. bibliog.
Part I of the report reviews the years 1950 and 1951. Part II deals with the population, occupations, wages and labour organisation, public finance and taxation, currency and banking, commerce, production, social services legislation, justice, police, prisons, public utilities and public works as well as communications. Part III takes up geography and climate, history, administration, weights and measures, newspapers and periodicals and a reading list.

90 **Colonial Office report on Grenada for the years 1952 and 1953.**
British Colonial Office.   London: HMSO, 1955. 40p. map. bibliog.
The report announces good cocoa sales, but a decline in the sales of nutmeg and mace for 1952-53.

91 **Colonial Office report Grenada report for the year 1954.**
British Colonial Office.   London: HMSO, 1957. 42p. map. bibliog.
According to this report, the biggest piece of news was Hurricane Hazel which wrought $80,000 worth of damage on Carriacou on 25 October 1954.

92 **Grenada report for the years 1955 and 1956.**
British Colonial Office.   London: HMSO, 1958. 47p. map. bibliog.
The years 1955 and 1956 were overshadowed by Hurricane Janet which killed 120 persons and rendered thousands homeless.

93 **Grenada report for the years 1957 and 1958.**
British Colonial Office.   London: HMSO, 1961. 47p. map. bibliog.
The report relates efforts which were undertaken during 1957 and 1958 to raise overall production to at least the pre-Hurricane Janet level with particular emphasis on the export crops, cocoa, nutmegs, bananas and cotton.

94 **Grenada report for the years 1961 and 1962.**
British Colonial Office.   London: HMSO, 1964. 46p. map. bibliog.
The report deals with the dissolution of the Legislative and Executive Councils of Grenada by the British government. General elections held during September 1962 resulted in a majority for the Grenada National Party (GNP) over Eric Gairy's Grenada United Labour Party (GULP).

95 **Grenada report for the years 1963 and 1964.**
British Colonial Office. London: HMSO, 1966. 56p. map. bibliog.
The report relates a plan by the GNP government to enter into a unitary state with Trinidad and Tobago.

96 **Grenada report for the years 1965 and 1966.**
British Colonial Office. London: HMSO, 1968. 57p. map. bibliog.
The report describes a visit by Queen Elizabeth and the Duke of Edinburgh, 'an occasion which was marked by intensely loyal demonstrations by the entire community'.

97 **The prostitution of a democracy.**
D. Sinclair DaBreo. Bridgetown: Edgar Chris, 1977. 62p.
The author, a former supporter of Eric Gairy, lambasts Gairy's reign of terror by his Mongoose Gang during the 1970s. DaBreo relates the details of Rupert Bishop's murder by the Mongoose Gang on Monday, 21 January 1974 and also describes his own personal encounters with Gairy's secret police.

98 **Varieties of megalomania.**
Eric Gairy. *Harper's*, vol. 271, no. 1624 (Sept. 1985), p. 24-28.
In an interview with a North American journalist, former Grenadian Prime Minister Eric Gairy displays megalomaniac tendencies.

99 **How the Gairy regime was overthrown.**
Ernest Harsch. *Intercontinental Press*, vol. 17, no. 44 (3 Dec. 1979), p. 1184-87.
Basically a summary of the decades of Eric Gairy's rule over Grenada which ended with the 13 March 1979 revolution.

100 **Black comedy in Grenada.**
Max Hastings. *Spectator*, vol. 251, no. 8103 (29 Oct. 1983), p. 10-11.
A British reporter lambasts the British government for ever turning Grenada over to Eric Gairy ('the poor man's Papa Doc') and for knighting him in 1977.

101 **The rise and fall of Gairy.**
Alister Hughes. *Caribbean Life and Times*, vol. 1, no. 1 (Aug. 1979), p. 15-19.
The prominent Grenadian journalist describes the drama of Eric Gairy's rise and fall as a three act play: 'Act One: the fight against the plantocracy. Act Two: the fight against the British. Act Three: the fight against the people' which ended in the revolution of 13 March 1979.

102 **Independence for Grenada – myth or reality?**
St. Augustine, Trinidad: Institute of International Relations, 1974. 159p. bibliog.
Proceedings of a conference on the implications of independence for Grenada sponsored by the Institute of International Relations of the University of the West

Indies, St. Augustine, Trinidad, 11-13 January 1974. Among prominent contributors were Beverley A. Steele, Selwyn Ryan, Archie Singham, Anthony Maingot and Richard Jacobs.

103 **Roots of revolution: Gairy and Gairyism in Grenada.**
Gordon K. Lewis.   San German, Puerto Rico: Universidad Interamericana de Puerto Rico, 1986. 18p.(CISCLA Documento de Trabajo, no. 24).
A distinguished Caribbeanist at the University of Puerto Rico, Rio Piedras, points out that without Eric Gairy's bizarre and repressive rule, there would have been no NJM takeover in 1979.

104 **Granada: la nueva joya del Caribe.** (Grenada: the new jewel of the Caribbean.).
Jorge Luna.   Havana: Editorial de Ciencias Sociales, 1982. 234p. maps.
The author, a Peruvian correspondent for the Cuban news agency Prensa Latina, reveals many details of the New Jewel Movement's fight against Eric Gairy as well as its seizure of power on 13 March 1979.

105 **Report of the Duffus Commission of inquiry into the breakdown of law and order, and police brutality in Grenada.**
Kingston: 1975. 235p.
The report of a Jamaican commission consisting of Herbert Duffus (chairman), H. Aubrey Fraser and Archbishop Samuel Carter that travelled to Grenada to investigate the human rights violations of the Gairy régime against the Grenadian people. The Commission looked particularly into the events surrounding Bloody Sunday (18 November 1973). The Duffus Report was highly critical of Gairy's Mongoose Gang and its chief, Inspector Innocent Belmar.

106 **Report on human rights developments in Grenada November 1982.**
St. George's: Grenada Committee on Human Rights, 1982. 69p.
A brochure published during the Bishop régime which dwells upon the human rights' violations of the previous Gairy period without mentioning the arrests carried out by the PRG.

107 **Contemporary political trends in the English-speaking Caribbean.**
Walter Rodney.   *Black Scholar*, vol. 7, no. 1 (Sept. 1975), p. 15-21.
A Guyanese teacher, writer and political activist, points to the striking continuities between pre-independence and post-independence West Indian society. Rodney uses as example Eric Gairy who ruled Grenada by thuggery both before and after independence.

108 **The hero and the crowd in a colonial polity.**
Archie Singham.   New Haven, Connecticut: Yale University, 1968.
389p. bibliog.
The definitive study of Grenadian politics during the 1951-62 period which is based on
hundreds of interviews and analysis of five elections.

109 **A summary of some important political events in Grenada from 1951 to
March 13, 1979.**
Lindel Smith.   *Bulletin of Eastern Caribbean Affairs*, vol. 5, no. 1
(March-April 1979), p. 11-18.
A summary of the events leading to Eric Gairy's rise to power, his twenty-eight-year
rule of Grenada and his overthrow on 13 March 1979.

110 **Grenada: maxi-crisis for a mini-state.**
Tony Thorndike.   *The World Today*, vol. 30, no. 100 (Oct. 1974),
p. 436-44.
An excellent summary of the political events leading up to Grenada's achievement of
full independence from Great Britain on 7 February 1974. Eric Gairy's twenty-eight
years' reign over Grenada prior to independence is examined with great fairness.

The Grenadian Revolution, 1979-83

111 **Grenada under the P.R.G.**
Michael Aberdeen.   Port-of-Spain, 1986. 67p. map.
A glowing account of the accomplishments of the Grenadian Revolution in the fields of
employment, health, education and housing by the international secretary of the
People's Popular Movement (PPM) of Trinidad and Tobago. The author worked in
Grenada for brief periods with both the PRG's Ministry of Education and the Ministry
of Housing.

112 **Reagan's fantasy islands.**
Donald Algeo.   *Progressive*, vol. 46, no. 9 (Sept. 1982), p. 42-3.
A professor of philosophy at Carnegie-Mellon Institute in Pittsburgh, Pennsylvania
found during a visit to revolutionary Grenada that 'there is no question that the vast
majority of the Grenadian people are better off, in terms of self-respect and the
prospect for materially rewarding lives, under the new regime than they were under
the old'.

113 **Grenada: the New Jewel revolution.**
Fitzroy Ambursley. In: *Crisis in the Caribbean.* Edited by Fitzroy
Ambursley, Robin Cohen. New York: Monthly Review Press, 1983,
p. 191-222.

A Trotskyite analysis of Grenada under Bishop which approves of the 'anti-imperialist
consciousness' of the population, but deplores 'the continuing hegemony of the
bourgeoisie in key areas of economic activity'.

114 **A united, conscious, organized, vigilant people can never be defeated.**
Maurice Bishop. St. George's: Government Printing Office, 1980.
16p.

Maurice Bishop's radio address on 19 June 1980, to the Grenadian people in which he
denounced the assassination attempt on himself and the entire PRG leadership at
Queen's Park at 3 o'clock of that same day. The Grenadian prime minister lamented
the death of two small Grenadian girls by the bomb and blamed the explosion on
foreign imperialists who, according to him, wanted to destabilize the country.

115 **Forward Ever! Against imperialism and towards genuine national**
independence and people's power.
Maurice Bishop. Havana: Political Publishers, 1980. 31p.

An address given at St. George's by the Grenadian prime minister in the presence of
Prime Minister Michael Manley of Jamaica and Daniel Ortega of Nicaragua on the
occasion of the first anniversary of the Grenadian Revolution. During his speech
Bishop remarked that 'if there had been no Cuban Revolution in 1959, there could
have been no Grenadian Revolution in 1979'.

116 **Grenada has chosen its road.**
Maurice Bishop. *World Marxist Review*, vol. 25, no. 4 (April 1982),
p. 63-67.

An interview of Maurice Bishop by Jeronimo Carrera, a member of the Central
Committee of the Communist Party of Venezuela. The Grenadian prime minister
explains at length why the NJM joined the Socialist International (SI).

117 **Grenada: revolution in the Caribbean.**
Maurice Bishop. *Political Affairs*, vol. 59, no. 3 (March 1980), p. 22,
36-40.

A national radio broadcast delivered by Maurice Bishop six months after his successful
overthrow of the Gairy régime.

118 **Marryshow day.**
Maurice Bishop. St. George's, 1982. 17p.

A speech delivered by Maurice Bishop on 7 November 1982 at York House at St.
George's in honour of T. A. Marryshow, a Grenadian journalist and politician, whom
the PRG, along with Fedon and Butler, elevated in the pantheon of Grenadian
national heroes. In his address, the Grenadian prime minister stressed the theme of
Caribbean unity which was a life-long dream of Marryshow who was an avid proponent
of a West Indian Federation.

119 **Maurice Bishop speaks: the Grenada Revolution 1979-83.**
Maurice Bishop. New York: Pathfinder, 1983. 341p.
Maurice Bishop's most important speeches (1979-1983) as well as an appendix which
contains three statements by the Cuban government concerning the Grenadian
Revolution's final crisis. In the introduction, the editor of the socialist newsmagazine
Intercontinental Press blames the destruction of the Grenadian Revolution solely upon
Bernard Coard's 'treachery and betrayal'.

120 **Maurice Bishop speaks to US workers.**
Maurice Bishop. New York: Pathfinder, 1983. 48p.
This little volume includes the speech which Maurice Bishop delivered on 5 June 1983,
to an audience of over 2,500 people at Hunter College in New York City during his last
visit to the United States.

121 **One Caribbean.**
Maurice Bishop. Stoneleigh, England: Britain–Grenada Friendship
Society, 1984. 29p.
Two speeches delivered by Prime Minister Maurice Bishop. The first speech was given
on 7 November 1982, at York House in memory of the Grenadian journalist and
politician, T. A. Marryshow (1887-1958), while the second speech occurred at the
Bloody Sunday Rally at Seamoon, St. Andrew's on 21 November 1982.

122 **Cacademo Grant: hero of the people's revolution.**
Shirley Romain Brathwaite. St. George's: Government Printery,
1983. 20p.
The life story of an agricultural worker, trade unionist and early supporter of the NJM,
who was declared a national hero by the PRG upon his death in 1982.

123 **A comment on some economic strategies of the People's Revolutionary
Government.**
Oris Bubb. *Bulletin of Eastern Caribbean Affairs*, vol. 7, no. 1
(March-April 1981), p. 36-40.
The state of agriculture, agricultural industries, tourism, fisheries and forestry two
years after the PRG's takeover in Grenada are discussed in this article.

124 **The Castroization of Grenada.**
Keith Charles. *National Review*, vol. 34, no. 18 (17 Sept. 1982),
p. 1144, 1148-50.
A Trinidadian lawyer draws a frightening picture of revolutionary Grenada, replete
with Cuban hit squads roaming the countryside and Grenadian youths shipped off for
combat in Angola and Nicaragua.

125 **Grenada: a workers' and farmers' government with a revolutionary proletarian leadership.**
Steve Clark. New York: Pathfinder, 1980. 36p.
Two leaders of the Socialist Workers Party of the United States render highly laudatory accounts of the Grenadian Revolution. This brochure also contains interviews with Maurice Bishop and Selwyn Strachan of the PRG, and Gilbert Pago, a revolutionist from Martinique.

126 **La revolucion Granadina 1979-1983**. (The Grenadian Revolution 1979-1983.)
Edited by Steve Clark. New York: Pathfinder, 1984. 86p.
The introduction takes up half of this book. The remainder consists of speeches by Fidel Castro and Maurice Bishop.

127 **Grenada replays the painful lesson of Suez.**
John Cole. *Listener*, vol. 110, no. 2833 (3 Nov. 1983), p. 5-6.
According to the author, both Suez and Grenada illustrate how little Great Britain's interests count when they run counter to the foreign policy of the United States.

128 **The Grenada Revolution.**
D. Sinclair DaBreo. Castries: MAPS Publication, 1979. 353p.
A St. Lucian, with definite sympathies for the New Jewel Movement, renders a description of the events which led to the Grenadian Revolution of 13 March 1979.

129 **Review of human rights in Latin America.**
Patricia M. Derian. *Department of State Bulletin*, vol. 80, no. 2043 (Oct. 1980), p. 51-55.
In an address to the Center for Inter-American Relations in New York on 24 April 1980, the Assistant Secretary for Human Rights and Humanitarian Affairs, Derian, criticizes the Bishop régime on Grenada for suspending the constitution, detaining opponents without legal representation, abridging freedom of assembly and private enterprise and abolishing the independent press.

130 **The Grenada documents: window on totalitarianism.**
Nicholas Dujmovic. Washington: Pergamon-Brassey's International Defense Publishers, 1988. 88p.
An instructor of US history and national security policy at the United States Coast Guard Academy, New London, Connecticut, analyses the captured Grenadian Documents and concludes that Grenada under the PRG was well on its way to becoming a totalitarian state.

131 **American intervention in Grenada: the implications of Project 'Urgent Fury'.**
Edited by Peter M. Dunn, Bruce W. Watson.   Boulder, Colorado; London: Westview, 1985. 185p.
A collection of essays of varying quality, dealing with the circumstances and import of Operation 'Urgent Fury'.

132 **The Grenada affair.**
J. S. Dunn.   Canberra: Commonwealth Government Printer, 1983. 17p. map.
A survey of the land, people, history, constitution, government and economy of Grenada as well as the Bishop régime, its collapse and the subsequent US intervention. The study was prepared by the legislative research service of the Australian Parliamentary Library.

133 **Was Bishop a social democrat? The speeches of Maurice Bishop.**
Carl Henry Feuer.   *Caribbean Review*, vol. 12, no. 4 (Autumn 1983), p. 37-39.
After reviewing the content of Maurice Bishop's speeches, a political scientist comes to the conclusion that the Grenadian prime minister's primary concern was national sovereignty and the social and economic development of his country.

134 **The foreign policy of the Grenada Revolution.**
Henry S. Gill.   *Bulletin of Eastern Caribbean Affairs*, vol. 7, no. 1 (March-April 1981), p. 1-5.
A research fellow at the Institute of International Relations, University of the West Indies, St. Augustine, Trinidad, examines the foreign policy of the PRG and finds it much more radical than its attitudes towards domestic matters.

135 **The assassination of hope.**
Jean Girard.   *Caribbean Contact*, vol. 11, no. 11 (April 1984), p. 5, 7.
A member of the Maurice Bishop Memorial Committee in Guadeloupe recalls what he considers the PRG's accomplishments in education, women's rights and participatory democracy which served as an example to the rest of the Caribbean.

136 **Debate about democracy in Grenada.**
Lennox Grant.   *Caribbean Contact*, vol. 8, no. 3 (July 1980), p. 2.
A Trinidadian journalist attacks Merle Hodge's ringing defence of the PRG's failure to hold elections, which the author states the PRG solemnly promised to hold upon seizing power.

137 **The Caribbean's stolen jewel.**
Andy Green.   *Marxism Today*, vol. 27, no. 12 (Dec. 1983), p. 11-13.
After reviewing the origins and achievements of the Grenadian Revolution, Green predicts that the collapse of the PRG in October 1983 will result in large-scale purges and the re-emergence of the Mongoose Gang.

138 **Grenada is not alone.**

St. George's: Fedon, 1982. 147p.

Speeches delivered by ministers of the PRG at the First International Conference in Solidarity with Grenada held at St. George's during November 1981. These speeches contain information on the economy, education, agriculture, health care and foreign policy of the PRG.

139 **Grenada: report of a British labour-movement delegation December 1983.**

London: Spiders Web, 1983. 44p. map.

A British delegation which was favourably disposed towards the Grenadian Revolution bitterly assails the United States intervention and its aftermath, claiming that drug use, corruption and prostitution have been its results.

140 **Grenada: the peaceful revolution.**

EPICA Task Force. Washington: Ecumenical Program for Interamerican Communication & Action, 1982. 132p. maps. bibliog.

A lively, well-written and beautifully illustrated survey of modern Grenada with heavy emphasis on the Bishop Revolution. During the Bishop régime, this volume, was greatly valued by the People's Revolutionary Government which contemplated making it required reading in all Grenadian schools.

141 **A British socialist views the revolution.**

Brian Grogan. *Intercontinental Press*, vol. 20, no. 21 (7 June 1982), p. 492-93.

Pat Kane, a leading member of the British section of the Fourth International, who spent over half a year in revolutionary Grenada as an electrician and correspondent, relates his experiences in an interview.

142 **Grenada answers charges at CARICOM summit.**

Ernest Harsch. *Intercontinental Press*, vol. 20, no. 35 (29 Nov. 1982), p.839.

During a 16 November 1982 news conference, held shortly after the opening of the CARICOM conference at Ocho Rios, Jamaica, Prime Minister Maurice Bishop explains his government's attitude towards Westminster parliamentary democracy.

143 **1200 in New York cheer leader of Grenada revolution.**

Osborne Hart. *Intercontinental Press*, vol. 17, no. 39 (29 Oct. 1979), p. 1050-51.

Excerpts from a speech delivered by Maurice Bishop before an audience of 1200 people at New York City Community College on 13 October 1979.

144 **Between populism and Leninism: the Grenadian experience.**
Colin Henfrey. *Latin American Perspectives*, vol. 11, no. 3 (Summer 1984), p. 15-36.
A member of the Center for Latin American Studies and the Department of Sociology at Liverpool University, examines the reasons for the collapse of the Grenadian Revolution.

145 **Das Volk Grenadas festigt Weg der Volksrevolution.** (The people of Grenada strengthen the road of the people's revolution.)
Matthias Herold. *Neues Deutschland*, vol. 37, no. 211 (May 1982), p. 6.
A correspondent for East Germany's party newspaper reports on a visit to Grenada during which Maurice Bishop told him that he was eager to see the Caribbean transformed into a 'sea of peace' instead of a staging area for naval manoeuvres by the United States and its NATO allies.

146 **Democracy in Grenada.**
Merle Hodge. *Caribbean Contact*, vol. 8, no. 1 (May 1980), p. 13.
A Trinidadian teacher and writer gives a ringing defence of the PRG's policy not to hold elections in Grenada.

147 **'Is freedom we making': the new democracy in Grenada.**
Merle Hodge, Chris Searle. St. George's: Government Information Service, 1980. 92p. map.
In this booklet, the PRG asserts that the improvement in health care, education, medical care and women's rights represent its 'new democracy' – not the Westminster parliamentary tradition.

148 **Maurice Bishop – premier in the spotlight.**
Alister Hughes, John Redman. *Caribbean Life and Times*, vol. 1, no. 2 (Dec. 1979), p. 11-15.
A summary of a two-hour interview with Maurice Bishop which sheds light upon the personalities and events that shaped the Grenadian leader's political development.

149 **Grenada's Revolution: the first two years.**
Maurice Jackson. *Political Affairs*, vol. 60, no. 6 (June 1981), p. 34-39.
A review of what the author considers the accomplishments of the Grenadian Revolution: improvements in agriculture, strides in education and increase in the status of women.

150 **Grenada: on the road to people's democracy.**
W. Richard Jacobs. *World Marxist Review*, vol. 23, no. 9 (Sept. 1980), p. 65-68.
The Grenadian ambassador to Cuba and the Soviet Union extols the accomplishments of the PRG during the first two years of its rule and compares them to the decades of corruption under Eric Gairy.

151 **The Grenada revolution at work.**
W. Richard Jacobs. New York: Pathfinder, 1981. 15p.
A Grenadian Rhodes scholar, who served as the PRG's ambassador to Cuba and the
Soviet Union, explains the development and the aims of the Grenadian Revolution of
1979.

152 **'We must be prepared to stand up and fight imperialism'.**
Liam James. *Militant*, vol. 44, no. 31 (29 Aug. 1980), p. 11-12.
A speech given by PRG member Liam James to the Caribbean solidarity rally held on
3 August 1980, at Oberlin College, Oberlin, Ohio.

153 **Interview with Carriacou leader.**
Pat Kane. *Intercontinental Press*, vol. 20, no. 9 (15 March, 1982),
p. 200-201.
An interview with the Deputy Secretary for Carriacou affairs, George Prime, who
discusses the changes brought about by the PRG on Carriacou.

154 **The revolution comes to Carriacou.**
Pat Kane. *Intercontinental Press*, vol. 20, no. 9 (5 March 1982),
p. 199-200.
Efforts by the PRG to bring the neglected and isolated island of Carriacou into the
mainstream of Grenadian life are recounted in this article.

155 **Prime Minister Maurice Bishop: before the storm.**
Kwando M. Kinshasa. *The Black Scholar*, vol. 15, no. 1 (Jan.-Feb.
1984), p. 41-59.
The last interview which Maurice Bishop held with a North American journalist in late
August 1983.

156 **Grenadian culture: the people wants to get up.**
Jo-Ann Kolmes. *NACLA Report on the Americas*, vol. 16, no. 5
(Sept.-Oct. 1982), p. 38-39.
An interesting account by a Canadian journalist of the PRG's efforts to make
Grenadians proud of their own culture as expressed in Creole and in calypso music.

157 **Grenada and the end of revolution.**
Charles Krauthammer. *New Republic*, vol. 190, no. 4 (30 Jan. 1984),
p. 16-20.
After perusing the captured Grenadian documents, a senior editor of the *New Republic*
concludes that the Grenadian Revolution was one big farce with the leaders of that
revolution mouthing Marxist jargon that they barely understood.

158 **Grenada documents: an overview and selection.**
Edited by Michael Ledeen, Herbert Romerstein. Washington: US
Government Printing Office, 1984. 882p.

A selection of the large number of documents which were seized by the United States
on Grenada in the wake of the armed intervention on 25 October 1983. These
documents were released jointly by the US Department of State and the US
Department of Defense during September 1984. The editing and selection of the
documents in this volume were carried out by Ledeen, a consultant to the Department
of State, and Romerstein, an official of the United States Information Agency. The
documents are divided by the editors into three major categories: life under the New
Jewel Movement, international activities, and the minutes of the Political Bureau and
the Central Committee.

159 **Marxist follies: backstage with the New Jewel Movement.**
Michael A. Ledeen. *Harper's*, vol. 268, no. 1605 (Feb. 1984),
p. 24-25.

One of the editors of the captured Grenadian documents quotes various parts of these
documents to ridicule the Grenadian Revolution.

160 **Reform and revolution in Grenada 1950 to 1981.**
David E. Lewis. Casa de las Américas, 1984. 254p. bibliog.

The most complete account of the development of the New Jewel Movement by the
son of the prominent Caribbeanist Gordon K. Lewis. The book received a prize from
the Casa de las Américas.

161 **Grenada: the jewel despoiled.**
Gordon K. Lewis. Baltimore, Maryland: Johns Hopkins University
Press, 1987. 231p.

A professor of political science at the University of Puerto Rico concludes that 'the
Grenada experiment was betrayed by the three forces of US imperialism, the ultra-
right wing of the West Indian bourgeoisie, and the ultra-left faction of the New Jewel
Movement'.

162 **Lessons from a revolution betrayed.**
Gordon K. Lewis. *Caribbean Contact*, vol. 11, no. 8 (Dec. 1983),
p. 6-7.

Professor Lewis suggests that there were three elements responsible for the collapse of
the Grenadian Revolution: '(1) the ultra-left faction of the People's Revolutionary
Government in Grenada itself; (2) the political leaderships of the Organisation of
Eastern Caribbean States (OECS) and of Jamaica and Barbados and (3) the American
Reagan administration'.

163 **The lessons of Grenada for the Caribbean Left.**
Gordon K. Lewis. *Caribbean Contact*, vol. 12, no. 2 (July 1984),
p. 7, 10.

A renowned Caribbeanist states that the supreme lesson of Grenada is that the
Caribbean Left movement must rediscover its conviction that socialism must go hand

in hand with democracy. The PRG régime was too much tempted to forget that lesson, so that it built up the paraphernalia of a left-wing authoritarian state in the name of Leninism.

164 **Education and the new Grenada.**
Charles Lynch. *Black Scholar*, vol. 12, no. 4 (July-Aug. 1981), p. 13-24.

After a visit to revolutionary Grenada in 1980, a professor at Empire State College, State University of New York, has become convinced that 'the programs and policies of the People's Revolutionary Government can wipe out illiteracy, strengthen Grenada's sovereignty, lessen poverty and joblessness, improve housing and health care, and allocate human, natural, and technical resources more effectively'.

165 **Grenada: from Bishop to the marines.**
Anthony P. Maingot. Miami, Florida: Latin American and Caribbean Center, Florida International University, 1983. 15p. (Occasional Papers Series Dialogues no. 18).

A professor of sociology at Florida International University examines the origins of the New Jewel Movement, its demise with the assassination of Maurice Bishop and the subsequent US intervention on Grenada. Maingot concludes that the nearly five-year reign of the PRG deviated drastically from the original aims of the NJM.

166 **Grenada: revolution in the Caribbean.**
Sam Manuel, Andrew Pulley. New York: Pathfinder, 1981. 35p.

An interview with two North American socialists who relate their positive impressions of revolutionary Grenada.

167 **In nobody's backyard: the Grenada Revolution in its own words.**
Edited by Tony Martin. Dover, Massachusetts: Majority, 1983. 264p.

A selection of articles from the Bishop régime's newspaper *Free West Indian*. The editor is a professor of black studies at Wellesley College, Massachusetts. The book contains the rarely printed manifesto of the New Jewel Movement from 1973.

168 **Grenada before and after.**
Michael Massing. *Atlantic Monthly*, vol. 253, no. 2 (Feb. 1984), p. 76-87.

Of the myriad articles written about the Grenadian Revolution, perhaps the most lucid and balanced one by a writer from New York who skilfully explores all of the many contradictions which surfaced during the four-and-a-half year reign of the PRG.

169 **Grenada, we will never know.**
Michael Massing. *Index on Censorship*, no. 13 (April 1984), p. 15-19.

The director of the Committee to Protect Journalists in New York explores the discrepancies between the official version of the conflict and the reports of correspondents on the spot.

170 **Maurice Bishop's 'line of march' speech September 13, 1982.**
Washington: United States Department of State, 1984. 12p. (Grenada Occasional Papers, no. 1).

The United States Department of State published this secret speech which Maurice Bishop delivered before a general meeting of the NJM in order to illustrate that the Grenadian prime minister was determined to create a Marxist-Leninist state on Grenada in spite of his willingness to cooperate with bourgeois elements for the time being.

171 **Revolution and intervention in Grenada: strategic and geopolitical implications.**
Alexander H. McIntire.   PhD dissertation, University of Miami, Coral Gables, Florida, 1984. 362p. (Available from University Microfilms, Ann Arbor, Michigan, order no. 84-16307).

An examination of the multifaceted changes brought about by the revolution on Grenada and the subsequent armed intervention.

172 **Grenada in historical and political perspective: an exclusive interview with Dessima Williams.**
Tesfatsion Medhanie.   *New World Review*, vol. 52, no. 3 (May-June 1983), p. 15-19.

In an interview with a *New World Review* assistant editor, Grenada's former ambassador to the Organization of American States places the Grenadian Revolution (1979-83) within the context of Grenadian and Caribbean history.

173 **The Grenada revolution: why it failed.**
Robert Millette, Mahin Gosine.   New York: Africana Research Publications, 1985. 164p. bibliog.

Two sociologists find little that was positive about the Grenadian Revolution and its leader Maurice Bishop.

174 **Big welcome for Grenada leader on US visit.**
Geoff Mirelowitz.   *Militant*, vol. 47, no. 22 (17 June 1983), p. 1, 8.

An enthusiastic account of Maurice Bishop's address at New York's Hunter College on 5 June 1983, which was attended by more than 2,500 people.

175 **Grenade – épices et poudre.** (Grenada – spice and powder.)
Frederic Morizot.   Paris: L'Harmattan, 1988. 382p.

A French agronomist who worked on an agricultural project in Grenada from 1980 until 1985, wrote this extensive history of the Grenadian Revolution of which he was a strong supporter.

176 **Detroit city council greets Bishop.**
Joanne Murphy. *Militant*, vol. 47, no. 22 (17 June 1983), p. 8.
A narration of Maurice Bishop's visit to Detroit, Michigan, on 2 June 1983, during which he met with congressmen John Conyers and George Crockett as well as mayor Coleman Young.

177 **An island betrayed.**
V. S. Naipul. *Harper's*, vol. 268, no. 1606 (March 1984), p. 61-72.
A skilfully written appraisal of the Grenadian Revolution by a distinguished Trinidadian writer who concludes that 'the revolution was a revolution of words'.

178 **The United States and the Grenada Revolution: who pushed first and why?**
Robert Pastor.   San German, Puerto Rico: Universidad Interamericana de Puerto Rico, 1986. 34p. (CISCLA Documento de Trabajo, no. 26).
Basing his essay on a perusal of the captured Grenadian documents as well as interviews with members of the PRG and the Carter and Reagan administration, the author concludes that the United States did not push the Bishop régime to the left – it was there already.

179 **Change in the Commonwealth Caribbean.**
Anthony Payne.   London: Royal Institute of International Affairs, 1981. 58p. map.
A lecturer in politics at Huddersfield Polytechnic, renders a positive appraisal of the PRG during the third year of the Grenadian Revolution.

180 **Grenada: revolution and invasion.**
Anthony Payne, Paul Sutton, Tony Thorndike.   New York: St. Martin's, 1983. 233p. bibliog. 2 maps.
Of all the books on Grenada which appeared shortly after the collapse of the Grenadian Revolution, this volume, written by three British scholars, is by far the best because of its sense of balance. There are excellent analyses of the Gairy years, US policy towards the Caribbean basin, the relationship between the PRG, the Commonwealth and CARICOM and, even, Grenada under Sir Paul Scoon and the interim government.

181 **Revolutionary politics in Grenada.**
Anthony Payne. *Round Table*, vol. 70, no. 280 (Oct. 1980), p. 381-88.
Eighteen months after the successful takeover of Grenada by the PRG, a British Caribbeanist draws a favourable picture of its policies which he claims 'constitute a fascinating test of the capacity of tiny Third World states to escape from their historical dependence upon the international capitalist economy'.

182 **The Grenadian experience: aberration or harbinger in the Eastern Caribbean?**
Phillip Pearson, Robertico Croes. San German, Puerto Rico: Universidad Interamericana de Puerto Rico, 1986. 36p. (CISCLA Documentos de Trabajo.)

This is the rapporteur's report for the conference on 'democracy, development and collective security in the Eastern Caribbean: the lessons of Grenada,' which met 17-19 October 1985, and was sponsored by the Caribbean Institute and Study Center for Latin America (CISCLA) of the Inter American University of Puerto Rico, San German, Puerto Rico and the Ford Foundation.

183 **Grenada: 'first free black country in world'.**
Andrew Pulley. *Militant*, vol. 44, no. 36 (3 Oct. 1980), p. 12-13.

A slightly abridged interview with Socialist Workers presidential candidate Andrew Pulley which was presented on 21 September 1980, on WHUR-FM in Washington, DC. Basing his remarks on his visit to Grenada, Pulley eulogizes the Bishop régime.

184 **A sad note for Grenada.**
Phil O'Keefe, John Soussan, Paul Susman. *Political Geography Quarterly*, vol. 3, no. 2 (April 1984), p. 152-60.

A one-sided and, at times, erroneous article on Grenada which is filled with uncritical praise for the Grenadian Revolution and bitter denunciations of the United States policy towards the Bishop régime.

185 **Grenada – no Bishop, no revo: US crushes Caribbean jewel.**
Ellen Ray, Bill Schaap. *Covert Action Information Bulletin*, vol. 5, no. 20 (Winter 1984), p. 3-20.

Writing for a magazine which is dedicated to the exposure of CIA activities around the world, the authors attempt to pin some of the blame for the destruction of the Grenadian Revolution on the Central Intelligence Agency. They assert that the St. George's Medical School was a haven for a number of CIA agents.

186 **What went wrong in Grenada?**
Andrew A. Reding. *Christian Century*, vol. 101, no. 12 (11 April 1984), p. 370-73.

The director of a charity organization who lived for several years in revolutionary Grenada, blames the destruction of the Grenadian Revolution upon the ideological rigidity of the Bishop régime.

187 **Bishop the victim of his own policies?**
David Renwick. *Caribbean and West Indies Chronicle*, vol. 100, no. 1578 (Feb./March 1984), p. 5-6.

While disapproving of the armed intervention on Grenada, the *Chronicle's* associate editor states that there should be no sympathy for Maurice Bishop who was 'hoist on his own petard' after abolishing all the political and social institutions that previously existed.

188 **Grenada revolution: a major setback for regional unity.**
David Renwick, David Jessop. *Caribbean and West Indies Chronicle*,
vol. 94, no. 1549 (April/May 1979).

The authors warn that 'to recognise Bishop would be to legitimise the very political technique that is anathema to CARICOM leaders reared in the civilised tradition of the Westminster electoral process'. The article is accompanied by interviews with Maurice Bishop and Eric Gairy.

189 **Revolution in der Karibik: Grenada.** (Revolution in the Caribbean:
Grenada.)
Hamburg, West Germany: Informationszentrum für Guyana und die
Karibik, 1982. 105p. map. bibliog.

Except for the short introduction, this book consists largely of articles from journals and newspapers favourably inclined towards the Grenadian Revolution.

190 **Grenadian friendship society leader speaks.**
Andy Rose. *Militant*, vol. 44, no. 37 (10 Oct. 1980), p. 17.

A report on a speech given by Don Bridgeman at the Socialist Workers campaign rally at Washington, DC on 14 September 1980, at which the treasurer of the US–Grenada Friendship Society praised the Grenadian Revolution for its accomplishments in the realm of health, education and women's rights.

191 **Blow by blow: a personal account of the ravaging of the revo.**
Akinyele Sadiq. *The Black Scholar*, vol. 15, no. 1 (Jan.-Feb. 1984),
p. 8-20.

Probably the most valuable and objective eye-witness account of the bloody events of 19 October 1983 and the subsequent ephemeral reign of the Revolutionary Military Council by a North American radio news reporter from San Francisco who worked for Radio Free Grenada.

192 **Grenada: the untold story.**
Gregory Sandford, Richard Vigilante.   Lanham, Massachusetts; New
York; London: Madison, 1984. 180p.

Written by a foreign service officer and a television producer who had access to classified US papers as well as the captured Grenadian documents, this volume claims that the NJM was determined to transform Grenada into a communist state even before seizing power on 13 March 1979.

193 **The New Jewel Movement: Grenada's Revolution, 1979-1983.**
Gregory Sandford.   Washington: Department of State Publication,
Foreign Service Institute, 1985. 205p.

A thoroughly researched history of the Grenadian Revolution (1979-83) by a foreign service officer who served as US vice consul in Barbados in 1980 and who travelled to Grenada after the collapse of revolution in order to interview hundreds of Grenadian eye-witnesses.

194   **The ideology of Grenada's Revolution: dead end or model?**
Harald M. Sandstrom.   In: *The Caribbean after Grenada.* Edited by
Scott B. MacDonald, Harald M. Sandstrom, Paul B. Goodwin, Jr. New
York: Praeger, 1988, p. 19-54. bibliog.
An associate professor of politics and government at the University of Hartford,
Connecticut, attributes the demise of the Grenadian Revolution to the clash between
the élitist leadership assumptions in Marxism-Leninism and the egalitarian thrust of
populism.

195   **A Caribbean Lilliput: scrutinizing the Grenada skirmish.**
Kai Schoenhals.   *Caribbean Review*, vol. 14, no. 2 (Spring 1985),
p. 34-35.
The author describes the Grenadian Revolution as 'the popular move of a small group
of radicalized middle-class intellectuals to put an end to a despised regime, and their
less successful attempt to construct a new society on their island, an attempt which was
doomed once it was headed for the maelstrom of super power rivalry which tore
Grenadian society from its natural moorings'.

196   **Revolution and intervention in Grenada.**
Kai Schoenhals, Richard A. Melanson.   Boulder, Colorado:
Westview, 1985. 204p.
Two essays on Grenada by an historian (Schoenhals) and a political scientist
(Melanson) at Kenyon College, Ohio. Schoenhals gives a detailed account of the birth
and death of the Grenadian Revolution. His essay is based upon interviews with
members of the PRG (Maurice Bishop, Jacqueline Creft, Hudson Austin, Selwyn
Strachan, etc.) as well as a close examination of the captured Grenadian documents.
Melanson, a student of US foreign policy since 1945, discusses the response of the
Carter and Reagan administrations to the Grenadian Revolution and the reactions of
members of the US Congress to the armed intervention on Grenada.

197   **Venezuela increases aid to Grenada.**
Kai Schoenhals.   *Caribbean Contact*, vol. 10, no. 11 (March 1983),
p.11.
Venezuelan aid to Bishop's Grenada consisted of such diverse items as playground
equipment, athletic supplies, 10,000 barrels of gas oil, 8,000 posters praising Grenada
as a tourist paradise, school desks and a dental clinic, according to this article.

198   **The Grenada papers.**
Edited by Paul Seabury, Walter A. McDougall.   San Francisco,
California: ICS, 1984. 346p. map.
A selection of the captured Grenadian documents is offered in this volume which is
unfortunately vitiated by the accompanying explanatory notes that contain errors and
distortions.

History. The Grenadian Revolution, 1979–83

199 **Carriacou and Petit Martinique: in the mainstream of the revolution.**
Edited by Chris Searle.   St. George's: Fedon, 1982. 128p. map.
One of a series of booklets published by the PRG's Ministry of Education. This volume contains interviews with Maurice Bishop and many of his supporters on Carriacou and Petit Martinique who praise the efforts of the PRG to bring the two islands into the main stream of Grenadian life.

200 **Grenada's revolution: an interview with Bernard Coard.**
Chris Searle.   *Race and Class*, vol. 21, no. 2 (Autumn 1979),
p. 171-87.
In an interview with British author Searle, the former Deputy Prime Minister and Minister of Finance, Trade and Industry and Planning in Grenada, places the Grenadian Revolution within a world-historical perspective.

201 **Grenada: 'let those who labour hold the reins'.**
Chris Searle.   London: Liberation, 1979. 22p.
An interview by the British educator and writer Chris Searle with Bernard Coard during which the Grenadian Deputy Prime Minister and Minister of Finance spelled out the aims of the Grenadian Revolution which had occurred four months before this interview.

202 **In nobody's backyard: Maurice Bishop's speeches, 1979-1983 – a memorial volume.**
Edited by Chris Searle.   London: Zed, 1984. 260p.
This volume for the most part contains Maurice Bishop's speeches that he gave during the last two years of his life. In a preface, the PRG's attorney-general, Richard Hart, renders a superb analysis of the demise of the Grenadian Revolution.

203 **Maurice Bishop on destabilisation: an interview.**
Chris Searle.   *Race and Class*, vol. 25, no. 3 (Winter 1984), p. 1-13.
The British educator Searle conducted this interview with the Grenadian prime minister during November 1982, but it was not proofread by Bishop until August 1983, nine weeks before his execution.

204 **The Soviet Union and Grenada under the New Jewel Movement.**
Peter Shearman.   *International Affairs*, vol. 61, no. 4 (Autumn 1985),
p. 661-73.
A superb article by a Lecturer in Government at the University of Essex, who concludes that 'Grenada's military build-up under the NJM was not designed for military intervention against neighbouring Caribbean states' but to defend Grenada against 'an attack by the United States'.

205 **Grenada's festival of the revolution – a grand showing of Caribbean flag.**
Rickey Singh.   *Caribbean Contact*, vol. 7, no. 2 (April 1980), p. 5-6.
A report on the activities accompanying the Grenadian Revolution's first anniversary celebration (13 March 1980) which was attended by Michael Manley of Jamaica and Daniel Ortega of Nicaragua.

206 Our stand on Grenada.

Rickey Singh. *Caribbean Contact*, vol. 9, no. 4 (Aug. 1981), p. 1.

The editor of *Caribbean Contact*, a staunch supporter of the Grenadian Revolution, nevertheless criticizes the PRG for not allowing free elections, closing opposition papers and holding 120 Grenadians in prison without trial.

207 The assassins.

Archie W. Singham. *Nation*, vol. 231, no. 2 (12 July 1980), p. 37-38.

A renowned scholar of the Caribbean, who teaches political science at Brooklyn College, castigates US policy toward revolutionary Grenada and recounts the attempt to kill the PRG leadership on 19 June 1982, which he witnessed in person.

208 Grenada: a reporter's notebook.

Baxter Smith. *Intercontinental Press*, vol. 20, no. 22 (14 June 1982), p. 517.

A report on the US government's deportation of a twenty-year-old Grenadian Suzanne Berkley from Puerto Rico, the state visit of Lieutenant-Colonel Desi Bouterse of Suriname to Grenada, and the installation of new printing equipment received as a gift from East Germany.

209 Mozambican president visits.

Baxter Smith. *Intercontinental Press*, vol. 20, no. 22 (14 June 1982), p. 516-17.

Remarks made by Mozambican President, Samora Machel, during a state visit to Grenada on the occasion of African Liberation Day (23 May 1982).

210 Rally hails progress on airport.

Baxter Smith. *Intercontinental Press*, vol. 20, no. 17 (10 May 1982), p. 399.

A report of the 19 April 1982 rally held at the Point Salines airport site during which Maurice Bishop hailed Cuban, Middle Eastern, West European and Venezuelan aid for the construction of the new airport.

211 Thousands celebrate May Day.

Baxter Smith. *Intercontinental Press*, vol. 20, no. 19 (24 May 1982), p. 442.

At the 1982 May Day rally, Prime Minister Maurice Bishop announces three pieces of legislation to benefit workers: a new Workman's Compensation Act, which will increase insurance coverage to workers injured on the job, a law augmenting the amount of coverage victims of bus accidents receive; and a Rent Restriction Act.

212 **St. Vincent, the Grenadines and Grenada: taking it as it comes.**
Ethel A. Starbird. *National Geographic Magazine*, vol. 156, no. 3
(Sept. 1979), p. 399-425.
The description of a visit to Grenada, Carriacou and Petit Martinique, six months after
the revolutionary coup of 13 March 1979, which included a visit to Richmond Hill
prison and an interview with then thirty-four-year-old Maurice Bishop.

213 **Grenada – the first year.**
Jeremy Taylor. *Caribbean Contact*, vol. 7, no. 11 (March 1980), p. 8.
Summarizing Grenada's first year under the PRG, the author concludes presciently:
'perhaps the major problem facing the PRG after its first year is not the
implementation of its programmes, which undoubtedly command wide support. It is
the credibility gap which does exist between its stated ideological commitments – on
neutrality, on free elections – and a significant degree of public scepticism, in and out
of Grenada. The failure to close that gap could put much at risk'.

214 **No peace for Grenada?**
Jeremy Taylor. *Caribbean and West Indies Chronicle*, vol. 100,
no. 1578 (Feb./March 1984), p. 7-8.
Putting the Grenada crisis of October 1983 in historical perspective, the author asserts
it was only an episode in the history of an island which has been marked by greater
violence than any other anglophone island nation in the Caribbean.

215 **Terrorists sentenced in bomb plot.**
Intercontinental Press, vol. 20, no. 35 (29 Nov. 1982), p. 836.
The two-week trial in St. George's, Grenada, which culminated in the 1 November
1982 death sentence of four defendants who were accused of the 19 June 1980 Queen's
Park bombing, an attack resulting in the death of three young girls.

216 **Grenada.**
Tony Thorndike. In: *Latin America and Caribbean contemporary
record, 1982-1983*. Edited by Jack W. Hopkins. New York; London:
Holmes & Meier, 1984, vol. 2, p. 690-97. bibliog.
A good overview of the political, social, foreign and economic affairs of Grenada
during 1982-83 by the head of the Department of International Relations and Politics
at the North Staffordshire Polytechnic, Stoke-on-Trent, England.

217 **Grenada: politics, economics and society.**
Tony Thorndike. Boulder, Colorado: Lynne Rienner, 1985. 199p.
bibliog. map. (Marxist Regimes Series).
Written by a prominent British Caribbeanist, this is one of the best histories of the
Grenadian Revolution

218 **How masses met invasion threat.**
Jim Upton. *Intercontinental Press*, vol. 21, no. 9 (16 May 1983),
p. 272.

A report about Maurice Bishop's call (23 March 1983) for the mobilization of
Grenada's militia, mass organizations and trade unions in the wake of perceived
threats by the United States.

219 **Return to Grenada.**
Geoffrey Wagner. *National Review*, vol. 35, no. 25 (23 Dec. 1983),
p. 1613, 1631.

The author claims that the Cubans were building a submarine base on Grenada, were
designing ration cards for all Grenadians and were planning to slice off the whole Point
Salines peninsula in order to transform it into a military base.

220 **The New Jewel: revolution in Grenada.**
Annette Walker. *NACLA Report on the Americas*, vol. 15, no. 1
(Jan.-Feb. 1980), p. 40-43.

A positive appraisal of the accomplishments of the Grenadian Revolution by the
Caribbean editor of WBAI-FM Radio, New York.

221 **Sovereignty, democracy and socialism: reflections on the Grenada
experience.**
Laurence Whitehead. San German, Puerto Rico: Universidad
Interamericana de Puerto Rico, 1986. 14p. (CISCLA Documento de
Trabajo, no. 25).

A professor at Nuffield College, Oxford University and the University of California,
San Diego, concludes that the 'almost unbridgeable gap between aspirations and
objective possibilities was at the heart of the NJM's difficulties, and goes far to explain
the manner of its collapse'.

222 **Inside Grenada: one year later, a witness to the upheaval looks back.**
Jean Wiley. *Essence*, vol. 15, no. 6 (Oct. 1984), p. 94-99, 148-55.

A North American black writer from Oakland, California who spent a year on
Grenada as the first Caribbean correspondent for WHUR, the Howard University
radio station, gives a gripping account of the Grenadian Revolution and its collapse by
citing many of her diary entries.

223 **A revolution that could have worked.**
Stephen Zunes. *Progressive*, vol. 48, no. 1 (Jan. 1984), p. 21.

A political scientist at Beacon College, Massachusetts, writes that the revolution in
Grenada was 'influenced more by New Left politics and the black power movement
than by Soviet-style communism', a statement which is contradicted by the captured
Grenadian document collection.

The Bishop-Coard schism, 1983

224 **An ambiguous turning point: Grenada and its aftermath.**
Fred Halliday. *NACLA Report on the Americas*, vol. 18, no. 6 (Nov.-
Dec. 1984), p. 20-31.
A brilliant appraisal of the Grenadian Revolution and its collapse by a lecturer in
international relations at the London School of Economics who visited the eastern
Caribbean in 1983.

225 **Divided they fall.**
George Alagiah. *South*, no. 38 (Dec. 1983), p. 13-16.
This article fails to see major ideological differences between Maurice Bishop and
Bernard Coard and claims that Grenada's leaders did not dream that their own
tensions would set the fuse for the destruction of their revolution.

226 **Driving in the wedge.**
George Alagiah. *South*, no. 38 (Dec. 1983), p. 17.
The author claims that efforts to peacefully resolve the Grenadian crisis of October
1983 by CARICOM were thwarted by the Reagan Administration which desired an
invasion of Grenada.

227 **Grenada: whose freedom?**
Fitzroy Ambursley, James Dunkerley.   London: Latin American
Bureau, 1984. 128p. maps. bibliog.
A concise and useful history of Grenada (1950-83). The authors carefully steer a
neutral course when they discuss the struggle between the Bishop and Coard factions
which destroyed the Grenadian Revolution.

228 **The Grenada affair.**
Kai Bird, Max Holland.   *Nation*, vol. 242, no. 14 (12 April 1986),
p. 512.
Two *Nation* correspondents repeat the often-cited myth that Maurice Bishop's visit to
the US during June 1983 contributed to his death because it incensed the 'hard-liners'
under Bernard Coard. There is no proof whatsoever that Coard objected to this
journey.

229 **Grenada.**
Jacqueline A. Braveboy-Wagner.   In: *Latin America and Caribbean
contemporary record, 1981-1982*. Edited by Jack W. Hopkins. New
York; London: Holmes & Meier, 1983. vol. 1, p. 566-76. bibliog.
Excellent survey of the political, social, foreign and economic affairs of Grenada
during 1981-82 by a distinguished scholar of Caribbean and Third World affairs.

230 **Five comments on Rojas interview.**

Philippe Pierre Charles. *Intercontinental Press*, vol. 22, no. 6 (2 April 1984), p. 170-171.

The leader of the Socialist Revolution Group of Martinique and Guadeloupe hails Maurice Bishop's former press secretary as a true revolutionary and denounces the Coard faction.

231 **The second assassination of Maurice Bishop.**

Steve Clark. *New International*, no. 6 (1987), p. 11-96.

A leading North American Trotskyist accuses former Grenadian Deputy Prime Minister, Bernard Coard, not only of ordering Maurice Bishop's assassination on 19 October 1983, but, in addition, of attempting to murder Bishop's reputation by lies and distortions expressed during Coard's murder trial. Steve Clark expresses outrage that former US attorney-general, Ramsey Clark, compared Coard to Nelson Mandela. Although a partisan piece of writing, this article sheds much additional light on the final Bishop–Coard showdown during October 1983.

232 **US aims deathblow at revolution.**

Steve Clark. *Intercontinental Press*, vol. 21, no. 21 (7 Nov. 1983), p. 629-32.

Taking a strongly pro-Bishop stance, the editor of *Intercontinental Press* denounces Hudson Austin's RMC as well as US claims that Cuba and the USSR were behind the killing of Maurice Bishop.

233 **The Grenada documents.**

Edited by Brian Crozier. London: Sherwood, 1987. 182p.

A presentation of some of the captured Grenadian documents which the editor felt were of particular interest to European readers. The volume contains the moving letter addressed by trade union leader, Vincent Noel, to the NJM's Central Committee on 17 October 1983, two days before his death.

234 **Grenada.**

Selwyn R. Cudjoe. Ithaca, New York: Calaloux, 1984. 16p.

This brochure consists of two essays by a Trinidadian poet and writer. The first essay examines the US armed intervention on Grenada and reviews the history of US interference in the Caribbean Basin since 1833. The second essay tried to fathom the reasons for the bloody denouement of the Grenadian Revolution. While blaming both sides for the final crisis, the author appears to be more sympathetic to the Coards and their followers than to Maurice Bishop.

235 **Journalistic perspectives on the Grenadian crisis.**

Marlene Cuthbert. Kingston: Press Association of Jamaica, 1985. 46p.

An evaluation of the press coverage of the Grenadian crisis of October 1983 by newspapers in the Caribbean, the US, Canada and Europe. The author is a Senior Lecturer in the Faculty of Art University of the West Indies, Mona, Jamaica.

236 **Interviewing George Louison: a PRG minister talks about the killings.**
Bernard Diederich. *Caribbean Review*, vol. 12, no. 4 (Autumn 1983),
p. 10-12.
In an interview with a New Zealander, the former PRG Minister of Agriculture,
George Louison, blames Bernard Coard for the bloody outcome of the Grenadian
Revolution's crisis on 19 October 1983.

237 **The Grenada massacre.**
Edited by Stafford Earle. St. Ann, Jamaica: Earle, 1983. 76p.
This booklet, published in Jamaica shortly after the armed intervention of 25 October
1983, contains many interesting photographs and many errors. On page 26, a picture of
the late president of Mozambique, Samora Machel, and Maurice Bishop, is entitled
'Austin and Bishop'. The deadly quarrel between Bishop and Coard is said to have
originated over a gate at Coard's house which his neighbour Bishop disliked!

238 **Revolutionary suicide and Commonwealth disarray: Grenada, October
1983.**
Peter D. Fraser. *Round Table*, no. 289 (Jan. 1984), p. 24-30.
The author, a researcher specializing in the Caribbean at the Institutes of Education
and Commonwealth Studies in the University of London asserts that it was 'the
breakdown of consensus among the revolutionary leaders and the absence of
mechanisms to mediate such disputes that ultimately destroyed the revolution'.

239 **George Louison and Kenrick Radix discuss internal events leading to the
US invasion of Grenada.**
New York: Grenada, 1984. 44p.
Two former ministers of the PRG and founders of the Maurice Bishop Patriotic
Movement (MBPM) ascribe the destruction of the Grenadian Revolution to the
sinister machinations of Bernard Coard and his disciples.

240 **The importance of the Grenadian Revolution to the eastern Caribbean.**
Ralph E. Gonsalves. *Bulletin of Eastern Caribbean Affairs*, vol. 5,
no. 1 (March-April 1979), p. 1-5.
A positive evaluation of the New Jewel Movement's coup on Grenada which removed
the corrupt and repressive régime of Eric Gairy. The author predicts that the
Grenadian Revolution will be of great significance to the region as a whole.

241 **Grenada crisis: the turmoil before the purge.**
The Bajan and South Caribbean, no. 360 (Nov. 1983), p. 4-17.
A report on the crisis leading up to the bloody events of 19 October 1983 which
contains the explanatory statement read on Monday 17 October 1983, by the People's
Revolutionary Army commander, General Hudson Austin, over Radio Free Grenada.

242 **Grenada: facing up to reality.**
David Jessop. *Caribbean and West Indies Chronicle.* vol. 94, no. 1552 (Oct./Nov. 1979), p. 12, 31.

An interview with Maurice Bishop by the editor of *Caribbean and West Indies Chronicle*, during which the Grenadian Prime Minister voiced his desire to see the entire Caribbean basin shed its artificial divisions and become one united entity. Bishop also urged that both CARICOM and OECS become more responsive to the ordinary people of the Caribbean.

243 **Bernard Coard's 'Creeping coup'.**
Leonor Kuser. *Intercontinental Press*, vol. 22, no. 8 (30 April 1984), p. 253-56.

During an interview at St. Paul's, Grenada, on 6 December 1983, former PRG minister, Kenrick Radix, gives an account of the events leading up to the execution of Maurice Bishop on 19 October 1983 which, in part, conflicts with the captured Grenadian documents in the US National Archives at Washington, DC.

244 **The alienation of Leninist group therapy: extraordinary general meeting of full members of the NJM.**
Barry B. Levine. *Caribbean Review*, vol. 12, no. 4 (Autumn 1983), p. 14-15, 48-59.

The minutes of the NJM's full membership meeting on 25 September 1983 during which Maurice Bishop finally seemed to accept the idea of sharing the leadership with Deputy Prime Minister Bernard Coard. The minutes are introduced by the editor of *Caribbean Review*.

245 **Grenadian students in Cuba send letter to Rojas on coup.**
Terry A. Marryshow. *Militant*, vol. 48, no. 5, p. 9.

A letter written by the chairperson of the Grenada Students Movement at Havana, Cuba, Terry A. Marryshow (now the head of the Maurice Bishop Patriotic Movement on Grenada) to Maurice Bishop's former press secretary, Don Rojas, in which Marryshow relates that the 150 Grenadian students studying at Cuban universities have been split into pro-Bishop and pro-Coard factions.

246 **Grenada: revolution counter-revolution.**
Trevor Munroe. Kingston: Vanguard, 1983. 165p.

A series of speeches dealing with the Grenadian Revolution by the general secretary of the Workers Party of Jamaica. The author blames primarily Maurice Bishop for the fateful demise of the revolution. He also criticizes Fidel Castro for not rushing military aid to the Revolutionary Military Council after Bishop's murder.

247 **Caribbean countries alive with discussion on Grenada events.**
Mohammed Oliver. *Militant*, vol. 48, no. 9 (16 March 1984), p. 8.

An analysis of the deep fissures produced within the radical movements of the Caribbean by the Bishop–Coard schism on Grenada.

248 **Eyewitness report from Grenada.**
Mohammed Oliver. *Militant*, vol. 47, no. 47 (23 Dec. 1983), p. 1-2.
The author ruefully reports that many Grenadians have become disillusioned with socialism after the murder of Maurice Bishop and his followers on 19 October 1983.

249 **Interview with George Louison.**
Mohammed Oliver. *Intercontinental Press*, vol. 22, no. 7 (16 April 1984), p. 208-17.
In an interview in February 1984 at his home at Concord on the west coast of Grenada, the former PRG Minister of Agriculture gives his version of the final crisis of the Grenadian Revolution and discusses his imprisonment by the US occupation authorities.

250 **New Jewel leaders speak to the press.**
Don Rojas, Caldwell Taylor. *Intercontinental Press*, vol. 21, no. 22 (14 Nov. 1983), p. 654-55.
The former editor of the *Free West Indian* and press secretary of Maurice Bishop as well as the former Grenadian Ambassador to the United Nations denounce Bernard Coard and his faction as well as the US invasion of Grenada.

251 **One people, one destiny.**
Edited by Don Rojas. New York: Pathfinder, 1988. 110p. 2 maps.
Speeches and documents from the 1984-88 meetings of the Anti-Imperialist Organizations of the Caribbean and Central America, edited by Don Rojas, the secretary for propaganda and information of that organization. Rojas, who is a member of the Maurice Bishop Patriotic Movement (MBPM) and served as press secretary to the late Grenadian prime minister, has been barred from entering Grenada by the Blaize Government.

252 **Open letter from Don Rojas.**
Don Rojas. *Intercontinental Press*, vol. 23, no. 6 (1 April 1985), p. 178-81.
An attack by Maurice Bishop's former press secretary upon all students of the Grenadian Revolution (like this compiler) who have blamed both Bernard Coard and Maurice Bishop for destroying the revolution.

253 **Behind the revolution's overthrow.**
Steve Wattenmaker. *Intercontinental Press*, vol. 21, no. 25 (26 Dec. 1983), p. 756-63.
In an interview with Steven Wattenmaker, Maurice Bishop's former press secretary sheds much light on the final crisis of the Grenadian Revolution which he blames on the OREL (Organization for Education and Libration) faction of Bernard Coard.

254 **'We will go forward – on our feet, not on our knees'.**
Kenrick Radix. *Militant*, vol. 48, no. 16 (4 May 1984), p. 7-8, 12-14.
A speech delivered by the PRG's former minister of legal affairs to an audience in New York City on 26 February 1984, in which he denounced the Bernard Coard faction of the NJM as well as the US intervention.

255 **The road to Fort Rupert: the Grenadian Revolution's final crisis.**
Kai Schoenhals. San German, Puerto Rico: Universidad Interamericana de Puerto Rico, 1986, 13p. (CISCLA Documento de Trabajo, no. 28).
This monograph, published by the Caribbean Institute and Study Center for Latin America (CISCLA), advances the unorthodox claim that Maurice Bishop and Bernard Coard bear an equal share of guilt in the destruction of the Grenadian Revolution.

256 **Grenada morning: a memoir of the 'Revo'.**
Chris Searle. London: Karia, 1989. 191p. map.
Chris Searle, who played a prominent role in the educational reforms of the PRG, provides an interesting glimpse of the leaders of the Grenadian Revolution with whom he was well acquainted. Searle refuses to take sides in the bitter Bishop–Coard controversy and praises both of them for their accomplishments prior to the October 1983 crisis.

257 **Requiem for a revolution.**
Jeremy Taylor. *Caribbean and West Indies Chronicle*, vol. 100, no. 1577 (Dec./Jan. 1984), p. 4-6.
The editor of *Caribbean and West Indies Chronicle*, after analysing the 19 October 1983 massacre and subsequent US armed intervention, assesses the impact of the Grenadian events upon Caribbean politics. Taylor believes that the Caribbean Left has been routed and discredited and CARICOM bitterly divided.

258 **Leninism in Grenada.**
Jiri Valenta, Virginia Valenta. *Problems of Communism*, vol. 33, no. 4 (July-Aug. 1984), p. 1-23.
The coordinator of Soviet and East European Studies, Department of National Security Affairs, US Naval Postgraduate School, Monterey, California, and his wife assert that the Soviet Union was behind Bernard Coard's conspiracy to oust Maurice Bishop.

259 **What it was like in Grenada.**
Geoffrey Wagner. *National Review*, vol. 35, no. 23 (25 Nov. 1983), p. 1472-74.
A professor emeritus at City University of New York discovers (non-existant) North Korean and Syrian embassies on Grenada and makes the bizarre claim that Soviet Ambassador Genady Sazhenev was behind the attempted assassination of the Venezuelan *chargé d'affaires*, Romulo Huebner in May 1983.

Armed intervention, October 1983

260 Human rights implications for US action in Grenada.
Elliott Abrams. *Department of State Bulletin*, vol. 84, no. 2083 (Feb. 1984), p. 24-26.

In an address before the Los Angeles World Affairs Council on 22 November 1983, the then Assistant Secretary for Human Rights and Humanitarian Affairs states that the United States armed intervention was justified because it followed a plea by the Organization of East Caribbean States (OECS) and Sir Paul Scoon, the Governor General of Grenada.

261 Urgent Fury: the battle for Grenada.
Mark Adkin. Lexington, Massachusetts: Lexington Books, 1981. 373p. maps. bibliog.

A North American participant in the invasion of Grenada attempts to refute point by point the allegation that the United States bungled a number of operations on that island.

262 The lynching of Grenada.
Herbert Aptheker. *Political Affairs*, vol. 62, no. 12 (Dec. 1983), p. 33-38.

A prominent North American communist claims that 'Reagan's verbiage and action have thrown the United States back into the days of youthful and uninhibited imperialism – the bully days of Theodore Roosevelt'.

263 Grenada and East Caribbean security.
Stanley Arthur. London: The Institute for the Study of Conflict, 1985. 24p. map.

A ringing endorsement of President Reagan's armed intervention on Grenada by a British diplomatist who served as British High Commissioner to Barbados and the Eastern Caribbean.

264 The empire strikes back.
Richard J. Barnet. *Progressive*, vol. 48, no. 1 (Jan. 1984), p. 16-18.

A senior fellow at the Institute for Policy Studies in Washington, DC, believes that the rapid North American military victory on Grenada could be a Pyrrhic one, if it emboldens the United States to strike at Nicaragua or Cuba.

265 The danger of rescue operations.
Errol Barrow. *Caribbean Review*, vol. 12, no. 4 (Autumn 1983), p. 3-4.

A highly critical assessment of the US-led invasion of Grenada on 25 October 1983 by the late prime minister of Barbados who claims that the invasion resulted in 'inevitable damage to Caribbean sovereignty and self-respect, not to speak of the systematic dismantling of the Caribbean community'.

266 **Operation 'Urgent Fury'.**
Alexander Baryshev. *New Times* (Moscow), vol. 51 (Dec. 183),
p. 10-11.
A Soviet writer accuses the US military personnel on Grenada of robbing and
plundering as well as using chemical warfare. He also predicts that the United States
will construct a military base on Grenada.

267 **Who prepared the invasion and how.**
Alexander Baryshev. *New Times* (Moscow), vol. 45 (Nov. 1983),
p. 13-15.
The author asserts that the US military intervention on Grenada was no spur-of-the-
moment decision but a plan carefully prepared for many years by the CIA and the
Pentagon.

268 **Grenada invasion protested.**
Michael Baumann. *Intercontinental Press*, vol. 21, no. 21 (7 Nov.
1983), p. 636.
An account of a protest meeting of 30,000 people at Managua, Nicaragua, during
which Daniel Ortega and Grenadian Ambassador to the OAS, Dessima Williams,
addressed the crowd in order to condemn the US intervention in Grenada.

269 **False prophecy and the American invasion of Grenada.**
Wendell Bell. In: *The Caribbean after Grenada*. Edited by Scott B.
MacDonald, Harald M. Sandstrom, Paul B. Goodwin, Jr. New York:
Praeger, 1988, p. 69-85.
The author claims that all of the Reagan Administration's justifications for invading
Grenada (threatened safety of US medical students, new airport designed as a Cuban-
Soviet military base and alleged communist plans to use Grenada for launching
takeovers of other Caribbean islands) were all patently false.

270 **The invasion of Grenada: a note on false prophecy.**
Wendell Bell. *Yale Review*, vol. 75, no. 4 (Summer 1986), p. 564-86.
A professor of sociology at Yale University and past president of the Caribbean
Studies Association declares as fraudulent the three major justifications of the Reagan
Administration for invading Grenada.

271 **That lying pretext.**
Piotr Bogomolov. *New Times* (Moscow), vol. 46 (Nov. 1983), p. 8-10.
A Soviet reporter who had visited Grenada and interviewed the Cuban construction
workers there who were building the new airport, reports on the reaction to the US
military intervention on Grenada in the Cuban capital.

272 **Special operations and the Grenada campaign.**
Daniel P. Bolger. *Parameters*, vol. 18, no. 4 (Dec. 1988), p. 49-61.
This article claims that of thirteen special operations forces' (SOF) missions on
Grenada, ten proved to be successful, thereby accelerating the revitalization of special

warfare capabilities undertaken in the wake of the failed Iranian hostage rescue mission.

273 The Grenada memorandum.
William Boot.   *Columbia Journalism Review*, vol. 22, no. 5 (Jan./Feb. 1984), p. 17-18.

A humorous (and spurious) memorandum which was supposedly sent by a Pentagon colonel to the US secretary of defence, reporting on the great victory over the press corps during the Grenada invasion.

274 International lawlessness in Grenada.
Francis A. Boyle, Abram Chayes, Isaak Dore, Richard Falk, Martin Feinrider, C. Clyde Ferguson Jr., J. David Fine, Keith Nunes, Burns Weston.   *American Journal of International Law*, vol. 78, no. 1 (Jan. 1984), p. 172-75.

Nine prominent North American professors of law, including Richard Falk, Milbank Professor of International Law at Princeton University, wrote this denunciation of the Reagan Administration's military intervention on Grenada which they label 'a gross violation of the most fundamental principles of international law'.

275 Missing the point on Grenada.
William F. Buckley, Jr.   *National Review*, vol. 35, no. 23 (25 Nov. 1983), p. 1504-05.

A vigorous defence of the US intervention in Grenada (October 1983) by the editor of *National Review*.

276 The lessons of Grenada.
William F. Buckley, Jr.   *National Review*, vol. 37, no. 22 (15 Nov. 1985), p. 62.

The editor of *National Review* is convinced that the liberation of Grenada from communism in October 1983 was a world-historical event because it meant that for the first time since 1917, a communist nation had been wrested from Soviet control.

277 Revolution and rescue in Grenada: an account of the US-Caribbean invasion.
Reynold A. Burrowes.   New York; Westport, Connecticut; London: Greenwood, 1988. 180p. bibliog.

A commodity floor specialist on the US stock exchange argues convincingly that the United States should try to work out foreign policy problems within regional organizations such as CARICOM and Contadora (an association of Central American countries headed by Panama) before initiating unilateral interventions such as the invasion of Grenada on 25 October 1983.

278 **Call for 'immediate cessation of the armed intervention and the immediate withdrawal of the foreign troops from Grenada'.**
In: *American Foreign Policy Current Documents 1983.* Washington: Department of State, 1985, Document 664, p. 1418.
Resolution 38/7 adopted by the UN General Assembly on 2 November 1983, which 'deeply deplores the armed intervention in Grenada'.

279 **The American invasion of Grenada and the struggle in the Caribbean.**
Horace Campbell. *The Black Scholar*, vol. 15, no. 1 (Jan.-Feb. 1984), p. 2-7.
While comparing the Reagan Administration's intervention in Grenada during October 1983 to the aggressive actions of Hitler and Mussolini, the author, a professor of political science at the University of Dar es Salaam, Tanzania, criticizes the NJM for not taking the 'masses' into its confidence during the political crisis (September-October 1983) in Grenada.

280 **A report from the 'battlefield'.**
Greg Chamberlain. *Caribbean Contact*, vol. 11, no. 17 (Nov. 1983), p. 20.
A fascinating eye-witness account of the combat on Grenada by a correspondent who circumnavigated the US armed forces' ban on journalists by taking a fishing boat from Carriacou to Grenada. Chamberlain and Bernard Diederich freed the prisoners of the PRG, journalist Alister Hughes, politician Winston Whyte, lawyer Tillman Thomas, former attorney-general Lloyd Noel, and businessman Leslie Pierre from their cells on Richmond Hill.

281 **The 'lessons' of Grenada.**
Steve Clark. *Intercontinental Press*, vol. 21, no. 22 (14 Nov. 1983), p. 646.
The editor of *International Press* expresses the belief that the Reagan Administration ordered the invasion of Grenada in order to overcome the American people's 'Viet Nam syndrome'.

282 **The Grenada affair: what intervention means.**
Colin Clarke. *Geographical Magazine*, vol. 55, no. 12 (Dec. 1983), p. 610-11.
A university lecturer in geography and official fellow of Jesus College, Oxford, doubts that there were any justifications for the armed intervention on Grenada on 25 October 1983.

283 **Condemnation of 'armed intervention in Grenada'.**
In: *American Foreign Policy Current Documents 1983.* Washington: Department of State, 1985, Document 662, p. 1412-13.
This comprises the UN Security Council Draft Resolution of 27 October 1983, which condemned the US operation in Grenada as a 'flagrant violation of international law'. The resolution, which was passed ten to one (with three abstentions), was vetoed by the United States.

284 **Eyewitness reports on Grenada invasion.**
Steve Craine. *Militant*, vol. 47, no. 44 (2 December 1983), p. 3.
A US medical worker who had served in Grenada for a year and a half, ridicules the notion that US forces were sent to the island in order to save North American citizens who, according to him, were never in any danger until the US troops invaded.

285 **Grenada.**
Selwyn R. Cudjoe. *Freedomways*, vol. 23, no. 4 (1983), p. 270-77.
A withering criticism of the United States and Organization of East Caribbean States (OECS) as well as Jamaican and Barbadian armed intervention on Grenada in October 1983. The author is a Trinidadian writer who has taught at Harvard and Cornell Universities.

286 **The origins, development, and impact of US participation in the Grenada mission.**
Kenneth W. Dam. In: *American Foreign Policy Current Documents 1983*. Washington: Department of State, 1985, Document 666, p. 1420-25.
An address by the Deputy Secretary of State, Dam, before the Associated Press Managing Editors' Conference at Louisville, Kentucky, on 4 November 1983, during which he strongly defended the US intervention on Grenada.

287 **Grenada and black anticommunism.**
John F. Davis. *Village Voice*, vol. 28, no. 45 (8 Nov. 1983), p. 18.
A criticism of the Black Caucus' mild reprobation of the Reagan Administration's military intervention on Grenada. The author urges the Congressional Black Caucus to use 'this invasion as an opportunity to organize and educate people to some of the Third World realities'.

288 **Planning for future Grenadas.**
Lyle Dennison. *Quill*, vol. 72, no. 1 (Jan. 1984), p. 10-13.
After some bitter confrontations between the Pentagon and the media over the initial exclusion of the press from 'Operation Urgent Fury,' both the Pentagon and the media are ready for a future compromise solution, according to the author, a journalist for the *Baltimore-Sun* (Baltimore, Maryland: The Sun, 1837–. daily).

289 **The rape of Grenada and international law.**
Yuri Deporov. *New Times* (Moscow), vol. 49 (Dec. 1983), p. 10-12.
A Soviet author claims that the US military intervention on Grenada was a gross violation of the UN and OAS (Organization of American States) charters as well as the Helsinki Final Act.

290 **Attack on Grenada.**
Derek T. Dingle. *Black Enterprise*, vol. 14, no. 6 (Jan. 1984), p. 11-12.
The author mentions that the Congressional Black Caucus condemned the invasion of Grenada by President Ronald Reagan who, according to this article, did not even

consult with black congresspersons beforehand, even though they had made many trips to Grenada and were probably more familiar with that island nation than the rest of Congress.

291 **Bringing the war back home.**
Ron Dorfman. *Quill*, vol. 72, no. 1 (Jan. 1984), p. 14-16.
According to the editor of the *Quill*, it was not national security considerations, but the desire 'to make concrete its own version of reality' which made the Reagan Administration decide to keep the press out of Grenada.

292 **A political journal.**
Elizabeth Drew. *New Yorker*, vol. 59, no. 38 (7 Nov. 1983), p. 159-73.
A good account of the congressional reaction to the Reagan Administration's decision to invade Grenada.

293 **Ein Jahr unter US-Besatzung: Grenada und die Probleme der 'Wiederherstellung der Demokratie'.** (One year under US occupation: Grenada and the problems connected with the restoration of democracy.)
Hamburg, West Germany: Karibik Informationszentrum, 1986. 31p. 2 maps.
Highly critical accounts of life on Grenada after the armed intervention by the US and its OECS (Organization of East Caribbean States) partners by West Germans who sympathized with the Grenadian Revolution.

294 **Sovereignty and the small underdeveloped states: the case of Grenada.**
Anselm Francis. *Bulletin of Eastern-Caribbean Affairs*, vol. 10, no. 1 (March-April 1984), p. 1-5.
An analysis of the question of Grenada's sovereignty in terms of both its revolutionary programme up to October 1983 and the US-led invasion.

295 **Grenada and the Eastern Caribbean.**
Philadelphia: American Friends Service Committee, 1984. 33p.
A report of an AFSC delegation visit (27 December 1983-9 January 1984) to Grenada which assessed the need for humanitarian aid, investigated conditions and treatment of military and political detainees, examined the role of the United States in the October 1983 crisis and weighed the impact of the Grenadian crisis upon the rest of the Caribbean.

296 **Mission to conquer: the Greeks had a word for it.**
Altaf Gauhar. *South*, no. 38 (Dec. 1983), p. 8-9.
The Pakistani editor-in-chief of *South* compares the Reagan Administration's 'rescue mission' on Grenada with the bullying of her neighbours by Athens 2,500 years before.

297 **Grenada: after the show of US muscle flexing.**
Beijing Review, vol. 26, no. 46 (14 Nov. 1983), p. 12.
Calling the US intervention 'a brazen and bloody invasion of a sovereign state', this article asserts that 'the events in Grenada show that the Reagan Administration cannot tolerate a regime that is not to its liking, despite the lip service paid to peace'.

298 **Grenada and the noble lords: voices in an island storm.**
Encounter, vol. 62, no. 1 (Jan. 1984), p. 39-42.
Excerpts taken from Hansard Parliamentary records (vol. 444, no. 66) of the debate on Grenada in the House of Lords on 1 November 1983. The lords quoted (Sir Gladwyn Jebb, Max Beloff, Sir Alex Douglas Home, Hugh Thomas) all support the armed intervention on Grenada.

299 **Grenada: background and facts.**
Washington: United States Information Agency, 1983. 16p.
A United States government pamphlet which was published shortly after the intervention on Grenada. The brochure contains lots of pictures of captured Soviet arms as well as excerpts from the televised address of President Ronald Reagan on 27 October 1983.

300 **Grenada-Berichte, Analysen und Dokumentation.** (Grenada-reports, analyses and documentation.)
Hamburg, West Germany: Karibik Informationszentrum, Grenada-Nachrichten no. 6 (Dec. 1983), 64p. map.
Of special interest in this brochure are the eye witness reports by two West Germans (Thomas Poese and Ulli Theis) about the events of 19 October 1983, the subsequent rule of the Revolutionary Military Council, and the armed intervention by the US and OECS on 25 October.

301 **Grenada: diary of an invasion.**
Race and Class, vol. 25, no. 3 (Winter 1984), p. 15-26.
Four foreigners who had come to Grenada to aid the revolution give their eye-witness accounts of the armed intervention on 25 October 1983.

302 **The Grenadian runway, an illegitimate Soviet military interest.**
In: *American Foreign Policy Current Documents 1983*. Washington: Department of State, 1985, Document 654, p.1392.
The transcript of a White House press briefing on 24 March 1983, which revolved around the construction of the new airport on Grenada.

303 **Grenada: the world against the crime.**
Havana: Editorial de Ciencias Sociales, 1983. 325p.
Despite its strident language, this book provides an interesting insight into the Cuban government's appraisal of the Grenadian crisis of October 1983. The volume contains the pictures, names, ages and professions of the Cuban soldiers and construction workers who died on Grenada fighting the US forces.

304 **Grenada: US armed invasion is condemned.**
Beijing Review, vol. 26, no. 44 (31 Oct. 83), p. 9-10.
An article condemning the US intervention on Grenada which is called a violation of the United Nations Charter and a gross violation of basic international behaviour.

305 **Grenada war powers: full compliance reporting and implementation.**
Markup before the Committee on Foreign Affairs House of
Representatives Ninety-Eighth Congress First Session on H. J. Res. 402,
October 27, 1983.
Washington: US Government Printing Office, 1983. 40p.
The vehement debate about the legality of the War Powers Resolution and the US armed intervention on Grenada which preceded the adoption of J. H. Res. 402 which declared that 'the War Powers Resolution became operative on October 25, 1983 when United States Armed Forces were introduced in Grenada'.

306 **Outcries against invasion.**
Yussuf Hanniff.   *Caribbean Contact*, vol. 11, no. 17 (Nov. 1983), p. 5.
A description of the world-wide opposition to the armed intervention on Grenada as well as a presentation of the nations and organizations which supported it.

307 **Air war Grenada.**
Stephen Harding.   Missoula, Montana: Pictorial Histories, 1984. 56p.
2 maps. bibliog.
A day-by-day account of 'Operation Urgent Fury' and a detailed listing of all types of aircraft used during the armed intervention on Grenada. This account by a military historian is accompanied by many photographs as well as maps which indicate the military installations of the PRA.

308 **US invaders meet stiff resistance.**
Ernest Harsch.   *Intercontinental Press*, vol. 21, no. 22 (14 Nov. 1983), p. 648-50.
The author asserts that the US troops which invaded Grenada met with stiff resistance from Grenadian troops and not only Cuban forces as the US command claimed.

309 **US lies start to unravel.**
Ernest Harsch.   *Intercontinental Press*, vol. 21, no. 22 (14 Nov. 1983), p. 650-51.
Reagan's three main justifications for invading Grenada are all called specious in this article.

310 **The case of Grenada.**
J. Bryan Hehir.   *Commonweal*, vol. 110, no. 22 (16 Dec. 1983), p. 681, 698.
After reviewing both critical and approving commentators on the intervention on Grenada, the author expresses his own forebodings about the US intervention although he admits that the Reagan Administration has won the public relations battle.

311 **Washington diarist: Gauging Grenada.**
Hendrick Hertzberg. *New Republic*, vol. 189, no. 21 (21 Nov. 83),
p. 51.
While conceding that there was much greater justification for US intervention in
Grenada than there had been in Chile or the Dominican Republic, the author
nevertheless points out all of the pitfalls that this intervention entails for US foreign
policy.

312 **Fixing the backyard fence.**
Merle Hodge. *Caribbean and West Indies Chronicle*, vol. 100,
no. 1578 (Feb./March 1984) p. 6-7.
A bitter article by a Trinidadian writer, who soon after the 13 March 1979 revolution
went to Grenada to work in the Ministry of Education. She accuses the Caribbean
media of a simplistic coverage of the intervention of October 1983 and their failure to
mention the real accomplishments of the revolution.

313 **Invasion: Guyana's principled position on the invasion of the sovereign
state of Grenada.**
Ministry of Information. Georgetown: Ministry of Information,
Publications Unit, 1984. 47p.
Besides a short review of Guyanese-Grenadian relations, this pamphlet contains
speeches by President Forbes Burnham and Minister of Foreign Affairs Rashleigh
Jackson which denounce the US intervention in Grenada.

314 **Documents pertaining to the Grenadian Intervention.**
In: *Latin America and Caribbean contemporary record, 1983-1984.*
Edited by Jack W. Hopkins. New York; London: Holmes & Meier,
1985, vol 3, p. 927-1011.
An impressive collection of documents on the Grenadian intervention which includes
US Ambassador Kirkpatrick's statement to the Security Council, an address by
Kenneth W. Dam. Deputy Secretary of State, before the Associated Press Managing
Editors' Conference, Louisville, Kentucky, 4 November 1983, and the Declaration of
the Ministry of External Relations of Cuba dated 28 October 1983.

315 **Grenada: ''twas a famous victory'.**
Irving Howe. *Dissent*, vol. 31, no. 1 (Winter 1984), p. 7-8.
The editor of *Dissent* wrote this sarcastic and bitter commentary on the Reagan
Administration's proffered reasons for invading Grenada.

316 **US out of Grenada!**
Cindy Jaquith. *Intercontinental Press*, vol. 21, no. 21 (7 Nov. 1983),
p. 626-28.
A vitriolic denunciation of the Reagan Administration's intervention on Grenada.

317 **JCS replies to criticism of Grenada operation.**
United States Joint Chiefs of Staff. *Army*, vol. 34, no. 8 (Aug. 1984),
p. 28-37.
A point-by-point refutation by the United States Joint Chiefs of Staff (JCS) of a report
highly critical of the 1983 Grenada operation issued during spring 1983 by the
Congressional Military Reform Caucus.

318 **The United States action in Grenada: reflections on the lawfulness of**
invasion.
Christopher C. Joyner. *American Journal of International Law*,
vol. 78, no. 1 (Jan. 1984), p. 131-44.
An assistant professor of political science and member of the School of Public and
International Affairs at the George Washington University observes that the
Grenadian affair bodes ill for both international law and regional security. The author
describes the US armed intervention as 'a case of unilateral intervention by the United
States, expressly approved in advance by neighboring island states and undertaken
without due regard for the territorial sovereignty and political independence of
Grenada'.

319 **D-Day in Grenada: the 82nd Airborne Division in action.**
George Kimura, Patrick J. O'Kelley. New York: Time, 1985. 96p.
map.
The actions of the 82nd Airborne Division during the invasion of Grenada is described
in great detail and glowing colours.

320 **International reaction to Grenada mission.**
Jeane J. Kirkpatrick. In: *American Foreign Policy Current Documents*
1983. Washington: Department of State, 1985, Document 663,
p. 1413-17.
In the course of an interview on the NBC programme 'Meet the Nation', the US
representative at the United Nations, Jeane Kirkpatrick, states that the US
intervention on Grenada rests on strong legal, political and moral grounds.

321 **Statement to the UN General Assembly, November 2, 1983.**
Jeane J. Kirkpatrick. *Department of State Bulletin*, vol. 83, no. 2081
(Dec. 1983), p. 76-77.
In her defence of US intervention on Grenada, Ambassador Kirkpatrick states that 'we
believe that the use of force by the task force was lawful under international law and
the UN charter'.

322 **Statement to the UN Security Council, October 27, 1983.**
Jeane J. Kirkpatrick. *Department of State Bulletin*, vol. 83, no. 2081
(Dec. 1983), p. 74-76.
The United States ambassador to the United Nations gives a strong defence of her
country's armed intervention in Grenada on 25 October 1983.

323 **The UN and Grenada: a speech never delivered.**
Jeane J. Kirkpatrick. *Strategic Review*, vol. 12, no. 1 (Winter 1984),
p. 11-18.
A bitter speech written by the United States permanent representative to the United
Nations during the Reagan Administration. In her speech, Kirkpatrick staunchly
defends the legality of the US intervention on Grenada. She was prevented from
delivering her oration on 2 November 1983, by a cloture motion introduced by the
People's Democratic Republic of Yemen which was carried by sixty votes to fifty-four,
with twenty-four abstentions.

324 **End of a decade – end of an era.**
Allan Kirton. *Caribbean Contact*, vol. 11, no. 8 (Dec. 1983), p. 1.
The general secretary of the Caribbean Conference of Churches (CCC) denounces the
abrupt revocation by the Barbadian government of the editor of *Caribbean Contact*,
Rickey Singh's work permit, and the order for Singh to leave Barbados by 3 December
1983. Singh had aroused Barbadian Prime Minister Tom Adams' wrath by condemning
the US intervention in Grenada.

325 **Grenada syndrome.**
Michael T. Klare. *Nation*, vol. 237, no. 15 (12 Nov. 83), 453-54.
The *Nation*'s defence correspondent and a fellow of the Institute for Policy Studies in
Washington, DC expresses his belief that the US armed action on Grenada is the
logical outcome of the Reagan Administration's military doctrine.

326 **Resistance to more Grenadas.**
Michael T. Klare. *Nation*, vol. 237, no. 19 (10 Dec. 1983), p. 591-92.
The *Nation*'s defence correspondent does not feel that Reagan's invasion of Grenada
heralds further actions against other nations that the US government regards as hostile
to its interests.

327 **After Grenada.**
Charles Krauthammer. *New Republic*, vol. 189, no. 25 (19 Dec.
1983), p. 9-10.
According to the senior editor of the *New Republic*, Reagan's great victory on
Grenada was not the successful military action, but rather the great increase in his
popularity as a result of the invasion which totally routed the opposition to the US
intervention in Congress.

328 **In mohgro land.**
Charles Krauthammer. *New Republic*, vol. 189, no. 24 (12 Dec.
1983), p. 9-10.
According to the author, the US intervention on Grenada 'served both its own
geopolitical interests and the interests of democracy'.

329 Lamming's challenge to Barbadians.
George Lamming. *Caribbean Contact*, vol. 11, no. 8 (Dec. 1983),
p. 9, 12.

During an address to students of the University of the West Indies at Cave Hill,
Barbados, the renowned Barbadian novelist, George Lamming, denounced Barbadian
Prime Minister Tom Adams' action against *Caribbean Contact* editor, Rickey Singh,
who had dared to denounce the military action on Grenada. Lamming told the
students that they faced two choices: 'you may take the road through Garvey and
James to Fanon and Rodney and Bishop. Or you may choose the other tradition which
leads down the defecated tracks of the black plantation mongrel'.

330 Lessons of Grenada.
Department of State. Washington: United States Department of State,
1985. 23p. (Department of State Publication 8457).

A justification of Reagan's 'rescue mission' with photographs of United States medical
students waving flags and kissing American soil after being 'rescued'.

331 Documents on the invasion of Grenada.
Compiled by Sybil Farrell Lewis, Dale T. Mathews. Rio Piedras,
Puerto Rico: Institute of Caribbean Studies, University of Puerto Rico,
1984. 139p.

The documents include statements by leaders of the governments of Barbados, Cuba,
Dominica, Guyana, Jamaica, Trinidad and Tobago, the United States of America,
Canada, Great Britain, the Soviet Union and France. The appendices include extracts
from the Caribbean Community Treaty and the Organisation of Eastern Caribbean
States Treaty.

332 Critical questions on Grenada.
Sol M. Linowitz. *Manchester Guardian Weekly*, vol. 129, no. 19
(6 Nov. 1983), p. 10.

A former US representative to the Organization of American States (1966-69)
questions both the need and legality of the US intervention on Grenada in October
1983.

333 Grenada revisited: an interim report.
Audre Lorde. *The Black Scholar*, vol. 15, no. 1 (Jan.-Feb. 1984),
p. 21-29.

A bitter criticism of the US intervention in Grenada by a poet and prose writer of
Grenadian parentage who visited Grenada during December 1983.

334 International brigandage and terrorism – weapons of US imperialism.
S. Losev. *International Affairs* (Moscow), vol. 144, no. 1 (Jan. 1984),
p. 12-19.

A virulent Soviet attack on the US intervention in Grenada. The author asserts that
'the invasion of the tiny Caribbean island is a warning to all small nations: international
terrorism and brigandage have been made part of US policy'.

335 **Volk lehnt sich gegen die Unterdrückung auf.** (The people rebel against oppression.)
George Louison. *Neues Deutschland*, vol. 41, no. 41 (23 April 1986), p. 14.

In a speech before the 11th Party Congress of the Socialist Unity Party at East Berlin, the PRG's former Minister of Agriculture and present member of the executive committee of the Maurice Bishop Patriotic Movement, lambasts the Reagan Administration for having made use of Grenada's internal crisis in order to invade and occupy that island nation.

336 **Central America, the Caribbean, and US security.**
Wesley L. McDonald, Paul F. Gorman. In: *American Foreign Policy Current Documents 1984*. Washington: Department of State, 1986, Document 505, p. 1020-31.

In testimony by the Commander in Chief, US Atlantic Command (McDonald) and the Commander in Chief, US Southern Command (Gorman), before the Senate Armed Services Committee, 23 February 1984, Admiral McDonald admits that the US forces did not even know that there existed a medical school campus of 200 students on Grand Anse Beach, a seemingly spectacular intelligence failure given the fact that the US intervention supposedly took place to rescue the US medical students on Grenada.

337 **Uncle Sam is true to type.**
Lev Makarevich. *New Times* (Moscow), vol. 52 (Dec. 1983), p. 28-30.

A shrill and vitriolic denunciation of the US intervention on Grenada which is compared to Theodore Roosevelt's 'Big Stick' diplomacy.

338 **Grenada: revolutionary shockwave, crisis, and intervention.**
Leslie Manigat. In: *The Caribbean and world politics; cross currents and cleavages*. Edited by Jorge Heine, Leslie Manigat. New York; London: Holmes & Meier, 1988, p. 178-221.

According to the former president of Haiti and professor of international relations at the Universidad Simón Bolívar, Caracas, Venezuela, the Grenada events reasserted US hegemony over the Caribbean.

339 **Flimsy excuses and collective cowardice.**
Michael Manley. *South*, no. 38 (Dec. 1983), p. 19.

The prime minister of Jamaica states 'that the invasion of Grenada by US forces was a political action carried out for political reasons in defiance of all international principles and precedents because certain prime ministers saw an opportunity to destroy a political system they did not like and which was stupid enough to provide them with the opportunity and the pretext'.

340 **Grenada in the context of history: between neocolonialism and independence.**
Michael Manley. *Caribbean Review*, vol. 12, no. 4 (Autumn 1983), p. 6-9, 45-47.
The Jamaican prime minister places the Grenadian Revolution and its end result, as well as the outside intervention on 25 October 1983 into an historical context. By and large, he views the intervention as a negative event for the Caribbean.

341 **Who is next?**
Michael Manley. *Nation*, vol. 237, no. 15 (12 Nov. 1983), p. 454, 468.
The author writes 'that the invasion and conquest of Grenada by US force was carried out for political reasons in defiance of international law'.

342 **US explanations of its actions and objectives in Grenada.**
William J. Middendorf. In: *American Foreign Policy Current Documents 1983*. Washington: Department of State, 1985, Document 660, p. 1408-10.
A ringing defence of the US intervention in Grenada by the US representative at the Organization of American States, Middendorf, before a special meeting of the Permanent Council of the OAS on 26 October 1983.

343 **Grenada and the international double standard.**
John Norton Moore. *American Journal of International Law*, vol. 78, no. 1 (Jan. 1984), p. 145-68.
A member of the board of editors of the *American Journal of International Law* expresses his disapproval of the United Nations General Assembly's response to the OECS' Grenada mission and observes that it is part of a trend toward an international double standard which is undermining the foundation of the international legal order.

344 **Grenada: low-intensity conflict and the use of US military power.**
James Berry Motley. *World Affairs*, vol. 146, no. 3 (Winter 1983-84), p. 221-38.
A study which examines the Grenada military intervention within the framework of low-intensity conflict and concludes that in terms of probabilities 'the United States will within the foreseeable future, become involved in other 'quick strike' military interventions similar to Grenada'. The author, a retired US army colonel, served in the office of the Secretary of Defense, with the Joint Chiefs of Staff, and with the Department of the Army General Staff.

345 **The background to US military operations in Grenada.**
Langhorne A. Motley. In: *American Foreign Policy Current Documents 1984*. Washington: Department of State, 1986, Document 498, p. 1001-05.
The prepared statement on the intervention in Grenada by the Assistant Secretary of State for Inter-American Affairs before the House Armed Services Committee on 24 January 1984.

History. Armed intervention, October 1983

346 **Banned from Barbados.**
Fitzroy Nation. *Columbia Journalism Review*, vol. 22, no. 5 (Jan./Feb. 1984), p. 7-8.
The Caribbean editor of Inter-Press Service renders an informative biographical sketch of the former editor of *Caribbean Contact*, Rickey Singh, a Guyanese journalist who had his work permit revoked by order of Prime Minister Tom Adams for criticizing the US intervention on Grenada.

347 **An act of banditry against Grenada.**
Eduard Nitoburg. *International Affairs* (Moscow), vol. 2 (Feb. 1984), p. 63-70.
According to this propagandistic article, 'the American invaders of Grenada occupied other people's land and turned it into a torture chamber for an entire nation'.

348 **Grenada: history, revolution, US intervention.**
Edited by Eduard Nitoburg. Moscow: *Social Sciences Today* Editorial Board, USSR Academy of Sciences, 1984. 143p.
Contributions by a variety of Soviet scholars and journalists dealing with the Grenadian Revolution. The essays contain many contradictions, factual errors and unfounded assertions such as the claim that the CIA had penetrated the entourage of Bishop and Coard and was ultimately responsible for the violent outcome of the Grenadian Revolution.

349 **Washington's gamble.**
David North. *Maclean's*, vol. 96, no. 45 (7 Nov. 1989), p. 26-29.
The foreign editor of *Maclean's* gives a careful appraisal of the US invasion of Grenada.

350 **Blacks in forefront of Grenada protests.**
Mohammed Oliver. *Militant*, vol. 47, no. 43 (25 Nov. 1983), p. 13.
The author points out that there was particularly intense opposition to the US intervention on Grenada on the part of North American black political leaders who sympathized with their black Grenadian brothers and held Maurice Bishop in high esteem.

351 **Grenada: confusion reigns as workers organize.**
Mohammed Oliver. *Militant*, vol. 47, no. 48 (30 Dec. 1983), p. 4, 23.
The author draws a convincing picture of the confused post-invasion atmosphere on Grenada during December 1983. Oliver finds the greatest remaining support for Maurice Bishop's ideals among the rank-and-file membership of Grenada's trade unions.

352 Organization of Eastern Caribbean States request for US assistance in Grenada.
In: *American Foreign Policy Current Documents 1983*. Washington: Department of State, 1985, Document 656, p. 1397-98.
The letter dated 23 October 1983, from the chairperson of the Organization of Eastern Caribbean States (OECS), Eugenia Charles to the United States Ambassador in the Eastern Caribbean, Milan D. Bish, in which the Dominican prime minister formally requested US assistance for an armed intervention on Grenada.

353 Grenada: an eyewitness account of the US invasion and the Caribbean history that provoked it.
Hugh O'Shaughnessy. New York: Dodd, Mead, 1984. 261p. maps. bibliog.
An interesting description of the self-immolation of the Grenadian Revolution and the subsequent US intervention which is highly criticized by the author, who writes for the *Observer* and the *Financial Times*.

354 The invasion of Grenada: a pre- and post-mortem.
Robert A. Pastor. In: *The Caribbean after Grenada*. Edited by Scott B. MacDonald, Harald M. Sandstrom, Paul B. Goodwin, Jr. New York: Praeger, 1988, p.87-105.
A former national security advisor during the Carter Administration and current professor of political science at Emory University at Atlanta, Georgia, questions the legal basis for the US intervention in Grenada. He also asserts that the safety of US citizens was endangered more by the invasion than the Revolutionary Military Council.

355 The old jewel: Grenada's invaders and critics.
Edward Pearce. *Encounter*, vol. 62, no. 1 (Jan. 1984), p. 39-42.
A sarcastic attack by a leader, writer, and parliamentary sketch writer with the *Daily Telegraph* in London against British Conservatives who criticized Reagan's intervention on Grenada.

356 Gunship diplomacy.
Denzil Peiris. *South*, no. 38 (Dec. 1983), p. 11-13.
The author claims that the armed intervention on Grenada 'is the logical development of the way US administrations from Washington to Reagan, have identified the international environment necessary for US security and prosperity'.

357 As Panama outcome is praised, details emerge of bungling during the 1983 Grenada invasion.
James M. Perry. *Wall Street Journal* (15 Jan. 1990), p. A12.
This article by a *Wall Street Journal* staff reporter, describes the intervention on Grenada by the United States as a series of blunders, many of which have been covered up by the Pentagon which has not admitted the true extent of US casualties. The author also confirms the Cuban claim that Fidel Castro had ordered his forces on Grenada not to fire upon North American troops unless they were fired upon. This order, which was strictly obeyed, saved the lives of many US rangers who were

parachuting into the Point Salines airport area which was defended by the Cuban construction workers.

358 **An autopsy of an invasion.**
Michael Posner. *Maclean's*, vol. 96, no. 46 (14 Nov. 1983), p. 28-29.
The Washington bureau chief of *Maclean's* gives a well-balanced assessment of the US intervention on Grenada.

359 **Operation Fury: inside Grenada.**
Michael Posner. *Maclean's*, vol. 96, no. 45 (7 Nov. 1983), p. 30-31.
An interesting eye-witness report on the US invasion of Grenada by *Maclean's* Washington bureau chief who was able to circumvent the US blockade of journalists.

360 **'An anniversary of honor'.**
Ronald Reagan. In: *American Foreign Policy Current Documents 1984*. Washington: Department of State, 1986, Document 542, p. 1103-04.
Remarks made by President Ronald Reagan on 29 October 1984 at the White House during a ceremony celebrating the first anniversary of the US military action on Grenada.

361 **Announcement of the sending of US troops into Grenada.**
Ronald Reagan, Eugenia Charles. In: *American Foreign Policy Current Documents 1983*. Washington: Department of State, 1985, Document 657, p. 1398-1401.
Statements and remarks made by US President Ronald Reagan and the prime minister of Dominica and chairperson of the OECS, Eugenia Charles, at a press conference on 25 October 1983 which was held to announce the reasons for the armed intervention on Grenada by the United States and seven Caribbean nations.

362 **'[Grenada] was a Soviet-Cuban colony being readied . . to export terrorism and undermine democracy. We got there just in time.'**
Ronald Reagan. In: *American Foreign Policy Current Documents 1983*. Washington: Department of State, 1985, Document 661, p. 1410-12.
President Reagan's nationwide television and radio address from the Oval Office of the White House on 27 October 1983, during which he made his famous remark that 'Grenada, we were told, was a friendly island paradise for tourism. Well, it wasn't. It was a Soviet-Cuban colony being readied as a major military bastion to export terror and undermine democracy. We got there just in time'.

363 **President's report to Congress on deployment of US troops in Grenada.**
Ronald Reagan. In: *American Foreign Policy Current Documents*
1983. Washington: 1985, Document 659, p. 1407-08.

A letter sent by President Reagan on 25 October 1983 to the Speaker of the House of
Representatives, Thomas P. O'Neill, in which the US president vowed that 'our forces
will remain only so long as their presence is required'.

364 **'They are the moral equal of our founding fathers'.**
Ronald Reagan. In: *American Foreign Policy Current Documents*
1985. Washington: Department of State, 1986, Document 540,
p. 973-74.

During an address to the Conservative Political Action Conferences 12th annual dinner
on 1 March 1985, President Reagan stated that in Grenada 'we only did our duty, as a
responsible neighbor and a lover of peace, then we went in and returned the
government to the people and rescued our own students'.

365 **'This was a rescue mission'.**
Ronald Reagan. In: *American Foreign Policy Current Documents*
1983. Washington: Department of State, 1985, Document 665,
p. 1419-20.

During a press conference on 3 November 1983, President Reagan states that the fact
that 108 nations condemned the US intervention on Grenada 'did not upset my
breakfast at all.'

366 **Cowboys and West Indians.**
Daniel Asa Rose. *Esquire*, vol. 107, no. 2 (Feb. 1987), p. 20-22.

A rapturous account of the love which Grenadians allegedly hold for their North
American rescuers.

367 **'Grenada he come from'.**
Paul Rose. *Contemporary Review*, vol. 244, no. 1416 (Jan. 1984),
p. 30-33.

The author laments the utter feebleness of the Caribbean mini-states as exemplified by
their roles as pawns of the superpowers. Rose calls for another attempt to revive the
defunct West Indian Federation. Like so many Englishmen, he denounces the invasion
of Grenada by the United States and remarks that democracy cannot be created from
the barrel of a gun.

368 **Conflicts in goals of media and government have created confrontation.**
Martin Rubenstein. *Television/Radio Age*, vol. 31, no. 17 (19 March
1984), p. 85-86.

In a speech before the California State Broadcasters' Association in Palm Springs, the
president of the Mutual Broadcasting System discusses the restrictions against the press
corps imposed during the Grenadian operation by the Pentagon by orders of the
Reagan Administration.

369 **The lessons of Grenada and the ethics of military intervention.**
Richard L. Rubenstein. Washington: Washington Institute for Values in Public Policy, 1984. 18p. bibliog.
After heaping scorn on the critics of US armed intervention on Grenada and dismissing the World Court and the United Nations as unacceptable judges of US policy, the author, a professor of religion at Florida State University at Tallahassee, proclaims the intervention as morally right since it involved the security and defence of the United States of America.

370 **What was uncovered in Grenada: the weapons and documents.**
Nestor D. Sanchez. *Caribbean Review*, vol. 12, no. 4 (Autumn 1983), p. 20-33, 59.
After reviewing the captured Grenadian documents, the US Deputy Assistant Secretary of Defense for Inter-American Affairs, comes to the conclusion that the arms captured on Grenada far exceeded the arms requirements of the People's Revolutionary Army. Sanchez speculates that the arms build-up on Grenada was designed as a subversive projection of power against Grenada's non-socialist neighbours.

371 **Background to Grenada: when the social scientists invaded.**
Aaron Segal. *Caribbean Review*, vol. 12, no. 4 (Autumn 1983), p. 40-44.
A pessimistic appraisal of Grenada's past and future by a professor of political science at the University of Texas at El Paso, who concludes that 'the invasion of Grenada was decided in Washington, but the crisis which prompted the invasion is internal and will not go away'.

372 **The conquest of Grenada: sovereignty in the periphery.**
Mohamed Shahabuddeen. Georgetown: University of Guyana, 1986. 266p.
The prominent legal scholar and vice-president of Guyana assails the United States intervention on Grenada as a violation of international law.

373 **Revo out. US in.**
Tim Shorrock. *Multinational Monitor*, vol. 4, no. 12 (Dec. 1983), p. 18-21.
An examination of the aid projects which the US Agency for International Development (AID) provided to Grenada in the wake of the armed intervention.

374 **Events leading to presidential decision to commit US forces in Grenada.**
George P. Shultz. In: *American Foreign Policy Current Documents 1983*. Washington: Department of State, 1985, Document 658, p. 1401-07.
The transcript of a press conference held by Secretary of State George Shultz on 25 October 1983, during which he explained the events leading up to the armed intervention on Grenada by the United States and seven Caribbean nations.

375 **The ethics of power.**
George P. Shultz. *Department of State Bulletin*, vol. 85, no. 2095 (Feb. 1985) p. 1-3.
In an address at the convocation of Yeshiva University in New York on 9 December 1984, Secretary of State Shultz states that 'Grenada shows that a president who has the courage to lead will win public support if he acts wisely and effectively'.

376 **Invasion cannot be justified.**
Rickey Singh. *Caribbean Contact*, vol. 11, no. 17 (Nov. 1983), p. 4.
In this commentary, the editor of *Caribbean Contact* condemned the armed intervention on Grenada by the United States and some CARICOM governments in strongest terms. It was this article which provoked the Barbadian government to revoke his work permit.

377 **The situation in Grenada. Hearing before the Committee on Foreign Relations, United States Senate Ninety-Eighth Congress First Session, October 27, 1983.**
Washington: US Government Printing Office, 1983. 46p.
A number of senators subject Deputy Secretary of State Kenneth W. Dam to intense questioning in regard to the US military intervention on Grenada and the initial exclusion of the press from that operation.

378 **The Grenada complex in Central America: action and negotiation in US foreign policy.**
Wayne S. Smith. *Caribbean Review*, vol. 12, no. 4 (Autumn 1983), p. 34-36, 64-65.
A senior associate at the Carnegie Endowment for International Peace and former chief of the US Interests Section, Havana, Cuba, fears that the Reagan Administration's intervention in Grenada bodes ill for any diplomatic resolution of the crisis in Central America.

379 **US marines in Grenada 1983.**
Ronald H. Spector. Washington: History and Museum Division Headquarters, US Marine Corps, 1987. maps. 35p.
A lieutenant colonel in the US Marine Corps Reserve and professor of history on leave from the University of Alabama, has written this official account of the US Marine Corps' role in the invasion of Grenada during late October 1983.

380 **Reagan's island.**
William Steif. *Progressive*, vol. 48, no. 1 (Jan. 1984), p. 18-20.
A former national and foreign correspondent for the Scripps-Howard newspapers, reports on a visit to Grenada six days after the marines landed there. He discovered almost unanimous support for the United States armed intervention as well as continued admiration for the slain Maurice Bishop among the Grenadian populace.

381 **Death of a revolution: an analysis of the Grenada tragedy and the US invasion.**
Cathy Sunshine, Philip Wheaton.   Washington: EPICA, 1984. 63p.

A bitter attack upon the United States' intervention on Grenada by two authors connected with the Ecumenical Program for Interamerican Communication and Action (EPICA). The text is written in both English and Spanish.

382 **Transnational violence in the Caribbean.**
Frank Taylor.   *Bulletin of Eastern Caribbean Affairs*, vol. 10, no. 1 (March-April 1981), p. 6-8.

The author, a lecturer at the faculty of arts and general studies, UWI, Cave Hill, Barbados, states that the October invasion of Grenada is a manifestation of the increasing transnational violence which began with the Cuban airline tragedy of 1976.

383 **The Grenada war: anatomy of a low-intensity conflict.**
Vijay Tiwathia.   New Delhi: Lancer International, 1987. 250p. maps. bibliog.

A highly critical account of the US intervention on Grenada which the Indian author contends 'had the subtlety of a sledgehammer, and the discretion of a Caribbean hurricane'.

384 **Grenada was different than World War II.**
Frank Tremaine.   *Editor and Publisher*, vol. 117 (4 Feb. 1984), p. 29, 56.

The former senior vice president of UPI who directed United Press coverage of most of the Korean War and of the Second World War in the Pacific, compares the close cooperation between the military and the press during the Second World War and the Korean War with the exclusion of the media from the assault on Grenada on 25 October 1983.

385 **US invades Grenada: the Soviet coverage.**
Current Digest of the Soviet Press, vol. 25, no. 43 (23 Nov. 1983), p. 1-8.

A collection of articles which appeared in the Soviet press during October 1983 dealing with the final crisis of the Grenadian Revolution and the subsequent intervention by the United States and other Caribbean countries.

386 **US military actions in Grenada: implications for US policy in the Eastern Caribbean Hearings before the Subcommittees on International Security and Scientific Affairs and on Western Hemisphere Affairs of the Committee on Foreign Affairs, House of Representatives Ninety Eighth Congress First Session November 2, 3 and 16, 1983.**
Washington: US Government Printing Office, 1984. 244p.

Prominent scholars and diplomats such as Sally A. Shelton Colby, Robert A. Pastor, A. W. Singham, Jaime Suchliki, Abraham F. Lowenthal and Anthony P. Maingot analyse the Grenadian Revolution and express their views of the military intervention by the United States on Grenada.

387 **International law under time pressure: grading the Grenada take-home examination.**
Detlev F. Vagts. *American Journal of International Law*, vol. 78, no. 1 (Jan. 1984), p. 169-71.
A member of the board of editors of the *American Journal of International Law*, contemplating the United States military intervention on Grenada during October 1983, states that 'reflecting on the performance of the international legal guild, myself included, one is beset by an uneasy sense that we did not do the best possible job of representing international law under the circumstances'.

388 **'We got there just in time'.**
James M. Wall. *Christian Century*, vol. 100, no. 33 (9 Nov. 1983), p. 1003-04.
An editorial severely criticizing the US action on Grenada.

389 **World protests condemn invasion.**
Steve Wattenmaker. *Intercontinental Press*, vol. 21, no. 22 (14 Nov. 1983), p. 653-54.
A member of the editorial staff of *Intercontinental Press* describes the world-wide protests which greeted the military intervention on Grenada in October 1983.

390 **The moral difference between the United States and the Soviet Union.**
Caspar W. Weinberger. In: *American Foreign Policy Current Documents 1984*. Washington: Department of State, 1986, Document 160, p. 417-24.
Remarks made by US Secretary of Defence, Caspar W. Weinberger at the Oxford Union Debate on 27 February 1984. Weinberger strongly rejected any comparison between the Soviet invasion of Afghanistan and the US intervention on Grenada which he claimed as justified since, in his opinion, the lives of 1,000 US medical students were at stake.

391 **NY meeting for ex-dictator of Grenada turns into pro-revolution demonstration.**
Arnold Weissberg. *Militant*, vol. 44, no. 36 (3 Octo. 1980), p. 7.
An account of the first public appearance of Eric Gairy in the United States after his overthrow as prime minister of Grenada on 13 March 1979.

392 **US-UK relations and the Grenada invasion.**
Caspar W. Weinberger. In: *American Foreign Policy Current Documents 1983*. Washington: Department of State, 1985, Document 283, p. 614 15.
During an interview at a NATO defence ministers' meeting at Montebello, Canada, on 28 October 1983, US Secretary of Defense, Weinberger was asked why the United

History. Armed intervention, October 1983

States invaded Grenada when such a move was clearly opposed by British Prime Minister Margaret Thatcher. Weinberger replied that his country had to intervene in order to save its 1,000 citizens on the island as well as respond to the plea for help from Caribbean nations which are located near Grenada.

393 **The impact of Grenada in Central America.**
Howard J. Wiarda. In: *The Communist challenge in the Caribbean and Central America.* Howard J. Wiarda, Mark Falcoff, Ernest Evans, Jiri Valenta, Virginia Valenta. Washington: American Enterprise Institute for Public Policy Research, 1987. p. 198-217. bibliog.

The author, a resident scholar at the American Enterprise Institute, concludes that 'the Grenadian intervention had significant long-term implications for guerrilla and revolutionary forces in Central America and the Caribbean Basin'.

394 **A West Indian reflects on Grenada.**
Margaret D. Wilde. *Christian Century*, vol. 100, no. 33 (21-28 Dec. 1983), 1171-72.

The article is based upon an interview with the general secretary of the Caribbean Conference of Churches (CCC), Allan Kirton, who criticized the US intervention on Grenada and is quoted as saying: 'the main casualty will be the movement toward Caribbean unity. A virus of dissension and divisiveness has been let loose in the Caribbean community, and we do not know where it is going to end'.

395 **Die Intervention in Grenada: Kollektive Verteidigung oder hegemoniale Konterrevolution?** (The intervention in Grenada: collective defence or hegemonistic counter-revolution?)
Manfred Wöhlcke. In: *Entwicklungen im karibischen Raum 1960-1985.*
Edited by Wolfgand Binder. Erlangen, West Germany: Universitätsbund Erlangen-Nürnberg, 1985, p. 259-72.

An essay dealing with the motives of the Reagan Administration, the Seaga government on Jamaica, and the Adams government on Barbados for invading Grenada on 25 October 1983. The author asserts that none of the official reasons which were given for the intervention are even remotely accurate. According to Wöhlcke, the United States invaded Grenada for domestic reasons and to frighten the Sandinistas in Nicaragua, whereas Jamaica and Barbados participated in order to obtain more aid from Washington.

396 **Grenada's tragedy.**
B. F. Zharova. Moscow: Planeta, 1984. 46p.

A shrill denunciation of the US intervention in Grenada by a Soviet writer.

Post-revolutionary Grenada, 1983-90

397 The alliance crumbles: the 1987 political situation in Grenada after the resignations of three government ministers.
Eudine Barriteau. *Bulletin of Eastern Caribbean Affairs*, vol. 13, no. 4 (Sept.-Oct. 1987), p. 38-42.
A research fellow at the Institute of Social and Economic Research (Eastern Caribbean) at UWI, Cave Hill, Barbados, reviews the events leading up to the resignation of three Grenadian ministers (Francis Alexis, George Brizan and Tillman Thomas) from the governing New National Party (NNP).

398 Grenada: embassy blacklist.
Kai Bird, Max Holland. *Nation*, vol. 241, no. 5 (31 Aug. 1985), p. 137.
The authors claim that the US embassy on Grenada has compiled a blacklist of Grenadians who served in the government of Maurice Bishop. This list is allegedly used to keep even innocuous officials, such as Jane Belfon (director of tourism – 1979-83) from obtaining any kind of government job.

399 'The Americans' man'.
George Black. *NACLA Report on the Americas*, vol. 19, no. 2 (March-April 1985), p. 8-10.
From an interview with a North American writer, former Grenadian prime minister and leader of the Grenada United Labour Party (GULP), Eric Gairy emerges as bizarre as ever. Gairy labels his political rivals, George Brizan and Francis Alexis, as communists and proclaims that he has always desired an American military base on Grenadian soil.

400 Into the plain land of progress and stability.
Herbert Blaize. *CARICOM Perspective*, vol. 44/45 (June 1989), p. 26-27.
Grenadian Prime Minister Herbert Blaize renders a glowing account of his six years as Grenada's head of state. As his great accomplishments, he lists the abolition of the income tax, the introduction of a Value Added Tax (VAT), the improvements of the road system and telephone service, and the greater availability of electricity.

401 The Anglophone Eastern Caribbean and British dependencies.
Gary Brana-Shute, Rosemary Brana-Shute. In: *Latin America and Caribbean contemporary record, 1985-1986*. Edited by Abraham F. Lowenthal. New York; London: Holmes & Meier, 1988, vol. 5, p. 425-67. bibliog.
Perhaps signifying the lesser importance of Grenada in world affairs since the collapse of the Grenadian Revolution, Grenada no longer rates a separate chapter in this annual volume, but is included in the discussion about the Eastern Caribbean by a cultural anthropologist and an historian.

402 **The Anglophone Eastern Caribbean and British dependencies.**
Gary Brana-Shute, Rosemary Brana-Shute. In: *Latin America and Caribbean contemporary record, 1986-1987.* Edited by Abraham F. Lowenthal. New York; London: Holmes & Meier, 1989, vol. 6, p. 405-58. bibliog.

A report on developments in Grenada during 1986-87 which indicates that unemployment rates remained high, the expected new jobs from US and other foreign investments remained an illusion, and the Blaize government had lost much popularity.

403 **NNP likely to have majority in Grenada elections.**
Farley Brathwaite, Roberta Clarke, Eudine Barriteau. *Caribbean Contact,* vol. 12, no. 7 (Dec. 1984), p. 1, 11-12.

The results of a survey, funded by ISER (Institute for Social and Economic Research), University of the West Indies, Cave Hill, Barbados, which correctly indicated that the New National Party was most likely to win in the 3 December 1984 elections on Grenada.

404 **Libya, Grenada and Reagan.**
Ramsey Clark. *Nation,* vol. 242, no. 17 (3 March 1986), p. 604-05.

After castigating Reagan for the 14 April 1986 bombing of Tripoli, Libya, which he compares to Reagan's invasion of Grenada, the former attorney general of the United States questions the legality of the Maurice Bishop murder trial whose defendants include Bernard and Phyllis Coard.

405 **Marking time in Grenada.**
Charles E. Cobb, Jr. *National Geographic Magazine,* vol. 166, no. 5 (Nov. 1984), p. 688-710.

This article appeared a month before the first national elections on Grenada since the destruction of the PRG. It contains photographs of the leading political contenders: Herbert Blaize, George Brizan, Eric Gairy and George Louison. It also contains photographs of the bullet-riddled wall of Ft. George where Maurice Bishop as well as three of his ministers, were executed. The author draws an optimistic picture for Grenada for the time being, but points out the many dangers that lurk in the future.

406 **After the press bus left: Grenada four years after.**
Alexander Cockburn. *In These Times,* vol. 11, no. 39 (14-20 Oct. 1987), p. 17.

A bitter article by Cockburn who accuses the US press of totally ignoring Grenada which, according to him, has sunk into a morass of unemployment, drug abuse and prostitution. The author lambasts Prime Minister Herbert Blaize for restricting freedom of expression on Grenada by an Emergency Powers Act, giving the government sweeping powers of arrest, detention without trial, and curfew. He also criticizes Blaize for attempting to curtail calypsos by the creation of a board to censor 'politically sensitive songs'.

407 **America invades Grenada: the making of a counterrevolution.**
Alexander Cockburn, James Ridgeway. *Village Voice*, vol. 28, no. 45
(8 Nov. 1983), p. 1, 8-9, 49.
This article relates the pressure which the Reagan Administration put on the administrators of the St. George's Medical School on Grenada to appeal to Washington for a 'rescue' of the medical students, most of whom supposedly felt safe until the United States intervened.

408 **A comment on the political situation in Grenada.**
Michael Cummins. *Bulletin of Eastern Caribbean Affairs*, vol. 10,
no. 1 (March-April 1984), p. 45-49.
An ISER research assistant describes the economic and political life of Grenada under the Interim Advisory Council which was set up in the wake of the collapse of the PRG and the US-led invasion.

409 **Caribbean general elections – 1984: an overview.**
Neville Duncan. *Bulletin of Eastern Caribbean Affairs*, vol. 10, no. 6
(Jan.-Feb. 1985), p. 1-5.
An analysis of the 1984 general elections in six Caribbean countries, including Grenada, by the campus dean of the faculty of social sciences at the University of the West Indies at Cave Hill, Barbados.

410 **The frame-up of Cecil Prime: five years of crimes against a Grenadian patriot.**
Friends of Jamaica. New York: Grass Roots, 1989. 42p.
A brochure published by an organization which has taken up the cause of Bernard and Phyllis Coard as well as the other members of the Coard faction who have been condemned to death for allegedly ordering the execution of Maurice Bishop and many of his followers. This pamphlet asserts that the Deputy Chief of Operations of the PRA, Cecil Prime, who supposedly had absolutely nothing to do with the execution of Bishop, has been framed and condemned to death because he refused to testify against his former comrades during the Maurice Bishop murder trial. The brochure contains poems by Cecil Prime who is being held as prisoner at Richmond Hill, Grenada.

411 **Grenada: the revo in reverse.**
NACLA Report on the Americas. vol. 23, no. 5 (Feb. 1990), p. 27-32.
A devastating account of the dismantling of all of the programmes and institutions of the PRG in the wake of the armed intervention in Grenada 1983. The government of Prime Minister Blaize is accused of intolerance, corruption and subservience to the United States. The article contains a useful listing of US aid projects for Grenada.

412 **Grenada trial update.**
Caribbean Newsletter, vol. 9, no. 5-7 (Summer 1989), p. 1-4.
A valuable account of the 23 May-9 June 1989 session of the 'Grenada 17' appeal of their death sentence for the murder of Maurice Bishop and his followers.

413 **Bitter fruits of revolution's defeat.**
Ernest Harsch. *Intercontinental Press*, vol. 22, no. 17 (17 Sept. 1984),
p. 543-49.
A description of the dismantling of the institutions of the Grenadian Revolution.

414 **700 at rally to launch new party.**
Ernest Harsch. *Intercontinental Press*, vol. 22, no. 14 (23 July 1984),
p. 452-54.
The managing editor of *Intercontinental Press* describes the launching of the Maurice
Bishop Patriotic Movement (MBPM) on 27 May 1984.

415 **US forces impose reign of repression.**
Ernest Harsch. *Intercontinental Press*, vol. 21, no. 23 (28 Nov. 1983),
p. 674-76.
A member of the editorial staff of *Intercontinental Press* reports that the US authorities
on Grenada are not only purging Bernard Coard's followers from all positions of
influence, but also anybody who had supported the Grenadian Revolution.

416 **US show trial in Grenada.**
Ernest Harsch. *Intercontinental Press*, vol. 22, no. 5 (19 March 1984),
p. 130-31.
The assertion that the United States will make use of the trial against Bernard Coard
and seventeen of his colleagues to smear the Grenadian Revolution as a whole.

417 **'Withdraw foreign forces'.**
Ernest Harsch, Mac Warren. *Intercontinental Press*, vol. 22, no. 5
(6 Aug. 1984), p. 5-7.
An interview obtained by *Intercontinental Press* with George Louison on 2 July 1984 at
St. George's in which the PRG's former minister of agriculture explains the aims of the
Maurice Bishop Patriotic Movement of which he is one of the founders.

418 **A tale of two elections: Nicaragua, October 31-November 6, 1984**
–Grenada, November 26-December 6, 1984.
John Hearne. In: *A tale of five elections*. Lawrence Coote, John
Hearne, Lynden Facey. Kingston: Bustamante Institute of Public and
International Affairs, 1985, p. 16-44.
A commentator for Jamaica's *Daily Gleaner* is angered by the fact that Maurice Bishop
is still revered by a large part of Grenada's population. Calling the murdered prime
minister 'an under-educated, pathetic aspirant to international communist high rank,'
Hearne suggests that his epitaph should read: 'He died without cause. Without
dignity.' The author is, however, delighted by Herbert Blaize's electoral victory in
1984. He regards Blaize as the only politician in Grenada who can achieve a national
reconciliation.

419 **In Grenada, victors' justice.**
Progressive, vol. 53, no. 3 (March 1989), p. 15-16.
The author, a spectator at the appeals court sessions of 28 November – 9 December
1988, involving the Grenada 17 accused of murdering Maurice Bishop, asked his or her
name withheld to protect the identity of the sources who gave information for this
article which describes the allegedly brutal treatment of John 'Chalky' Ventour, Leon
Cornwall and Dave Bartholomew by their prison guards.

420 **Lessons of Grenada are focus of Trinidad event.**
Nels J'anthony.   *Militant*, vol. 51, no. 27 (17 July 1987), p. 5.
An account of a meeting entitled 'the Caribbean after October '83' which was held at
Port-of-Spain, Trinidad, on 25 June 1987. The meeting was addressed by Cheddi Jagan
of the People's Progressive Party of Guyana, Dennis Thomas of the Maurice Bishop
Patriotic Movement of Grenada, David Abdullah of the Oil Fields' Workers Union of
Trinidad and Lucien Perutin of the People's Union for the Liberation of Guadeloupe.

421 **Picking up the pieces.**
Keith Jeremiah.   *Caribbean Contact*, vol. 12, no. 2 (July 1984), p. 2.
A report on the founding of the Maurice Bishop Patriotic Movement by three former
ministers of the PRG (George Louison, Kenrick Radix and Lyden Ramdhanny) who
had sided with Bishop against the Coard faction.

422 **John Butler, 33, a US envoy to Grenada, killed.**
JET, vol. 76, no. 15 (17 July 1989), p. 5.
An account of the murder of John Angelo Butler, a political officer with the US
embassy at St. George's, Grenada. Butler, one of the few black American diplomats
assigned in the Caribbean, was shot to death while conferring with leading Grenadian
police officers.

423 **Now Gairy to the 'rescue'?**
Allan Kirton.   *Caribbean Contact*, vol. 12, no. 1 (Jan.-Feb. 1984),
p. 3.
The acting editor of *Caribbean Contact* finds it ironic that former Grenadian Prime
Minister Eric Gairy returned to his native country after five years of exile in California
on 21 January 1984, the tenth anniversary of the murder of Rupert Bishop by Gairy's
Mongoose Gang.

424 **Club-med quickie.**
Gary Krist.   *New Republic*, vol. 200, no. 17 (24 April 1989), p. 10-11.
A North American writer draws a disturbing picture of the changed atmosphere on
Grenada where, rather than being admired as an American, he was made to feel 'like a
narc [police spy] at a disco'.

425 **After the revolution: the future of democratic government in Grenada.**
John Gaffar LaGuerre. *Caribbean Affairs*, vol. 1, no. 3 (July-Sept. 1988), p. 115-36.
A senior lecturer and head of the department of government at the University of the West Indies at St. Augustine, Trinidad, concludes that the prospects for a stable two-party system on Grenada will depend on the extent to which the opposition forces to the New National Party can unite into a viable alternative.

426 **Manifesto of new Grenadian party.**
Intercontinental Press, vol. 22, no. 15 (6 Aug. 1984), p. 476-82.
The text of the manifesto of the MBPM which was founded by survivors of the pro-Bishop faction of the NJM.

427 **A coalition for Grenada.**
Devonson LaMothe. *Caribbean Contact*, vol. 17, no. 11 (April 1990), p. 2, 5.
LaMothe discusses the March 1990 national elections in Grenada as the result of which none of the three major parties (NDC, TNP and GULP) won the eight or more seats necessary to form a government of its own. Only through the defection of a GULP parliamentary representative to the National Democratic Congress (NDC) was that party able to form a government under Nicholas Braithwaite.

428 **Blaize ousted from NNP leadership.**
Devonson LaMothe. *Caribbean Contact*, vol. 16, no. 9 (Feb. 1989), p. 7.
An account of the NNP convention during January 1989 when Herbert Blaize was replaced by Keith Mitchell as the party's leader.

429 **Emergency Powers Act passed.**
Devonson LaMothe. *Caribbean Contact*, vol. 15, no. 3 (Aug. 1987), p. 5.
A report on Prime Minister Blaize's successful effort during 1987 to enact an Emergency Powers Act which was opposed by Francis Alexis, George Brizan and Tillman Thomas, all former members of the NNP.

430 **Gairy's 'house-cleaning' causes perplexity.**
Devonson LaMothe. *Caribbean Contact*, vol. 16, no. 1 (June 1989), p. 6.
An analysis of Eric Gairy's purge of Dr. Raphael Fletcher who had been regarded as Gairy's potential successor as the head of GULP.

431 **Grenada: distress and perturbation.**
Devonson LaMothe. *Caribbean Contact*, vol. 17, no. 3 (Aug. 1989), p. 5.
An investigation into the slaying of Grenada's Acting Police Commissioner, Cosmos Raymond, and the United States diplomat John Butler by one of Grenada's assistant

Police Commissioners, Grafton Bascombe. The article also delves in the mysterious circumstances of Bascombe's subsequent suicide or murder.

432 **Grenada prefers carnival.**
Devonson LaMothe. *Caribbean Contact*, vol. 17, no. 4 (Sept. 1989), p. 2.
With the political situation confused and floundering, the author predicts a steady increase in the level of intolerance and, possibly, political violence.

433 **Grenada faces bleak prospects.**
Devonson LaMothe. *Caribbean Contact*, vol. 15, no. 1 (June 1987), p. 6.
A grim picture of Grenada under Prime Minister Blaize, who, according to this article, has increased unemployment and failed to establish a sound economy.

434 **Grenada's political party no. 6.**
Devonson LaMothe. *Caribbean Contact*, vol 17, no. 5 (Oct. 1989), p. 26.
An account of the launching of yet another Grenadian political party called the People's Party for Growth and Accountability (PEGA) by a former Grenadian island scholar and staff member of the International Monetary Fund (IMF), Dr. Davison Budhoo. Dr. Budhoo advocates a central bank, a food security programme, an agricultural diversification programme, a new constitution with a bill of rights to include basic economic entitlements for all citizens, a fiscal readjustment programme and people's participation in governmental decision making.

435 **Grenada's rage of bannings.**
Devonson LaMothe. *Caribbean Contact*, vol. 16, no. 2 (July 1988), p. 6, 11.
A report on the convention of the MBPM at Gouyave, Grenada on 28 and 29 May 1988, during which a thirty-five year-old medical doctor, Terry Marryshow, was chosen as the new party leader. The Blaize government had barred Marryshow from practising medicine in Grenada because he had received his medical degree in Cuba.

436 **Grenadians await elections' date.**
Devonson LaMothe. *Caribbean Contact*, vol. 17, no. 9 (Feb. 1990), p. 7.
A report on the intense political activity on Grenada in anticipation of the general elections of 1990. It had been expected that the elections would be held in January 1990, but Grenadian Prime Minister Ben Jones announced that his government had no money (Grenada's national debt stood at East Caribbean $250 million) at that time.

History. Post-revolutionary Grenada, 1983-90

437 How free is Grenada?
Devonson LaMothe. *Caribbean Contact*, vol. 16, no. 12 (May 1989), p. 16.

An account of the Blaize government's consistent efforts to ban leftist books, newspapers and magazines from Grenada as well as its deportation of foreign visitors who wish to attend functions of the MBPM.

438 Mitchell-Blaize war still on.
Devonson LaMothe. *Caribbean Contact*, vol. 17, no. 2 (July 1989), p. 2.

A report on the bitter Mitchell–Blaize feud within the ruling New National Party which threatens the NNP's leading position during the upcoming national elections of 1989.

439 Severe spiritual crisis in Grenada.
Devonson LaMothe. *Caribbean Contact*, vol. 16, no. 6 (Nov. 1988), p. 2.

In Grenada, according to this article, the cult of Maurice Bishop has been replaced by the cult of money which has led to wide-spread corruption.

440 October remembered.
Devonson LaMothe. *Caribbean Contact*, vol. 17, no. 6 (Nov. 1989), p. 6.

LaMothe describes the efforts of the MBPM to make 19 October (the day Maurice Bishop was killed in 1983) a Grenadian national holiday, a suggestion opposed by the Blaize government which has designated 25 October (the day of the armed intervention by the United States on Grenada in 1983) as a national holiday called 'liberation day' or 'thanksgiving day'. The author also comments on the harassment meted out by the Grenadian immigration authorities to Kwame Toure (formerly Stokely Carmichael) who was the main speaker at the 19 October 1989 MBPM memorial rally for Maurice Bishop.

441 Uneasy atmosphere in Grenada.
Devonson LaMothe. *Caribbean Contact*, vol. 16, no. 3 (Aug. 1988), p. 2.

According to the author, an increase in armed robberies, the influx of cocaine, a steep rise in prices and three confirmed deaths from AIDS have all contributed to a feeling of malaise on Grenada.

442 Will Gairy win again?
Devonson LaMothe. *Caribbean Contact*, vol. 17, no. 10 (March 1990), p. 7.

The author laments the fact that the 1990 national elections on Grenada have not dealt with the important fiscal issues confronting the country. Instead, the election campaign revolved around political personalities and leadership questions. LaMothe, while expressing some fear that Eric Gairy's GULP might make a strong showing, predicts that the NDC (National Democratic Congress) of Nicholas Brathwaite has the best chance of winning the elections on 13 March 1990.

443 Elections for Grenada?

Hamlet Mark. *Caribbean Contact*, vol. 15, no. 7 (Dec. 1987), p. 12.

An analysis of three major Grenadian political parties: the New National Party (NNP), the National Democratic Congress (NDC), and the Grenada Unity Labor Party (GULP).

444 Grenada: period of uncertainty.

Hamlet Mark. *Caribbean Contact*, vol. 14, no. 12 (May 1987), p. 1, 12.

An account of the resignation during April 1987 of Legal Affairs Minister, Francis Alexis, and Education Minister, George Brizan, from the cabinet of Prime Minister Herbert Blaize, over Blaize's decision to fire 1,800 public service workers.

445 Grenada's police under strain.

Hamlet Mark. *Caribbean Contact*, vol. 15, no. 11 (April 1988), p. 13.

This outlines the wave of robberies and murders which shook Grenada in early 1988 and the police's lack of success in solving these crimes.

446 Grenada's time of trouble.

Hamlet Mark. *Caribbean Contact*, vol. 17, no. 3 (Aug. 1989), p. 1.

A report on the disintegration of the New National Party which might enable Sir Eric Gairy to emerge as victor during the next national elections in Grenada.

447 New party in Grenada.

Hamlet Mark. *Caribbean Contact*, vol. 15, no. 3 (Aug. 1987), p. 5.

Details about the founding of a new political party on Grenada during 1987 under former NNP minister, George Brizan.

448 NNP divided..

Hamlet Mark. *Caribbean Contact*, vol. 17, no. 1 (June 1989), p. 7.

A description of the deep schism within the New National Party between the factions led by Herbert Blaize and by Keith Mitchell.

449 Bad construction: a look at post-invasion Grenada.

Jill Nelson. *Guardian*, vol. 40, no. 31 (4 May 1988), p. 10-11.

This article, although basically nostalgic for the four and a half years of the Bishop revolution, contains an interesting interview with Colonel Glenn A. Mignon, the head of the Special Security Unit (SSU), a special Grenadian paramilitary unit set up by the United States after the intervention of 1983.

450 Hanging out in Grenada: loveboat diplomacy.

Peter Pringle. *New Republic*, vol. 189, no. 22 (28 Nov. 1983), p. 11-12.

A correspondent for the London *Observer* reports of the strange paradox that the Grenadians almost unanimously welcomed the arrival of the US troops, yet continue to admire the slain Maurice Bishop.

451 **Elections in Grenada.**
Ronald Reagan. In: *American Foreign Policy Current Documents 1984*. Washington: Department of State, 1986, Document 553, p. 1115-16.
In a statement issued on 4 December 1984, President Reagan hails the holding of democratic elections on Grenada on 3 December 1984, as 'an achievement of historic importance, the first occasion in which a nation has returned to democracy after being freed from Marxist-Leninist rule'.

452 **Group condemns confiscation of books by Grenada.**
Calvin Reid. *Publishers Weekly*, vol. 235, no. 14 (7 April 1989), p. 36.
An account of the censorship practised by the Blaize government on Grenada which has prohibited books by Nelson Mandela, Maurice Bishop and Malcolm X from entering the country.

453 **Grenada's hallucinations.**
Mike Richards. *Caribbean Contact*, vol. 14, no. 10 (March 1987), p. 5.
A depressing reportage from Grenada which by the beginning of 1987, according to the author, faced a continual decline of the economy, high unemployment, crime and social disorder and intense bickering between Prime Minister Herbert Blaize and two of his ministers George Brizan and Francis Alexis.

454 **Grenada needs honest, hardworking leadership to settle down.**
Peter Richards. *Barbados Advocate* (14 April 20), p. 10-11.
A report on the government of Grenadian Prime Minister Nicholas Brathwaite that was formed as a result of the 13 March 1990 elections, during which none of the competing parties received enough seats to form a government without having to enter into a coalition with rival parties. Brathwaite promised to relieve the unemployment problem on Grenada by creating 15,000 new jobs through the expansion of tourism and foreign trade.

455 **'Grenada's government today, is a government of the tiny rich minority, not of the working people'.**
Don Rojas. *People's Daily World* (12 March 1987), p. 12-13.
In an interview with the press organ of the Communist Party of the USA, Maurice Bishop's former press secretary and present representative of the Maurice Bishop Patriotic Movement at Havana, Don Rojas, denounces the government of Herbert Blaize as 'neo-colonialist' and asserts that 'the vast majority of Grenadians today are poorer both materially and spiritually' than they were under Bishop.

456 **The man in the gray fedora.**
George Russell. *Time*, vol. 124, no. 25 (17 Dec. 1984), p. 57.
A description of the resounding electoral victory of Herbert Blaize in 1984, which, according to the author, suggests that the Grenadian people desired a moderate leader after the radical reign of the PRG.

457 Good times in Grenada.

Dan Sewell. *Editor and Publisher*, vol. 117 (4 Feb. 1984), p. 8.

The Caribbean news editor of the Associated Press reports that a state of normality has returned to Grenada which also means that the press, by and large, is no longer interested in the island.

458 The side you haven't heard: Maurice Bishop murder trial – testimony by the defendants and analysis by the NJM and other Grenadians.

New York: Friends of Jamaica, 1987. 2 vols.

Volume 1 contains statements by former US Attorney General Ramsey Clark and former Attorney General of the PRG, Richard Hart , questioning the legality of the Maurice Bishop murder trial. It also includes Bernard Coard's testimony before the court. The testimonies of Lieutenant Colonel Ewart Layne and Phyllis Coard, as well as Phyllis Coard's prison diary are part of the second volume.

459 Disasters, drugs and Grenada's debacle.

Rickey Singh. *Caribbean Contact*, vol. 17, no. 5 (Oct. 1989), p. 4-5.

In his monthly column, Guyanese journalist Singh points out that Grenada is once again becoming politically destabilized with parliament prorogued and the pro-United States Caribbean Democratic Union (CDU) abandoning its erstwhile favourite, Prime Minister Herbert Blaize, and throwing its support behind Blaize's chief rival, Keith Mitchell.

460 Grenada and a letter to Kingston.

Rickey Singh. *Caribbean Contact*, vol. 17, no. 4 (Sept. 1989), p. 4.

An account of the parliamentary manoeuvres initiated by Prime Minister Herbert Blaize in order to stay in power until March 1990.

461 Unpredictable future for Grenada.

Rickey Singh. *Caribbean Contact*, vol. 17, no. 11 (April 1990), p. 4-5.

The author points to the fact that the 1990 national elections on Grenada reflected the political disillusionment of the Grenadian people (thirty-four per cent of the eligible voters boycotted the elections). He predicts 'a new and agonising phase of political instability and social tension'.

462 Paradise leased: the selling of Grenada.

Gar Smith. *San Francisco Bay Guardian*, vol. 20, no. 18 (19-26 Feb. 1986), p. 7-10.

The tale of the wholesale dismantling by the Blaize government of the social service features of the PRG and the alleged insensitivity of that government towards the poor, women and youth, all elements courted by the Bishop régime.

463 A doctor's dilemma.

William Steif. *Progressive*, vol. 53, no. 1 (Jan. 1989), p. 10.

A freelance writer based on the US Virgin Islands criticizes the Blaize government's decision to bar the leader of the MBPM from practising medicine on Grenada.

464 **Harassment of PRG associates continues.**
Cathy Sunshine, Norman Faria. *Caribbean Contact*, vol. 12, no. 7 (Dec. 1984), p. 13.
A report on the arrest by armed Immigration and Naturalization Service agents at Washington, DC of the PRG's ambassador to the Organization of American States, Dessima Williams, and the expulsion from Grenada of two Canadians who had maintained contacts with members of the Maurice Bishop Patriotic Movement.

465 **Rescue mission or occupation?**
Cathy Sunshine. *Guardian* (6 June 1984), p. 10-11.
During a visit to Grenada, six months after the United States intervention, a staff member of the Ecumenical Program for Interamerican Communication and Action (EPICA) witnesses the wholesale dismantling of the social welfare programmes of the Grenadian Revolution.

466 **Gairy to be kingmaker.**
Andy Taitt. *Caribbean Contact*, vol. 17, no. 9 (Feb. 1990), p. 11.
A survey of the political situation on Grenada which finds that there are basically only three parties which will contest the upcoming elections: the National Democratic Congress (NDC) led by Nicholas Brathwaite and Francis Alexis, the New National Party (NNP) headed by Keith Mitchell, and Sir Eric Gairy's Grenada United Labour Party (GULP). According to Taitt, both the NDC and NNP warn that a victory by Gairy's GULP would be a disaster for Grenada.

467 **Grenada.**
Tony Thorndike. In: *Latin America and Caribbean contemporary record, 1983-1984*. Edited by Jack W. Hopkins. New York; London: Holmes & Meier, 1985, vol. 3, p. 791-807. bibliog.
One of the finest brief accounts of the denouement of the Grenadian Revolution, the US intervention, and the restoration of the multi-party system on the island.

468 **Grenada.**
Tony Thorndike. In: *Latin America and Caribbean contemporary record, 1984-1985*. Edited by Jack W. Hopkins. New York; London: Holmes & Meier, 1986, vol. 4, p. 717-26. bibliog.
The collapse of the revolution, the interim administration, the December 1984 election, trade tourism and population are all covered in this excellent survey.

469 **Grenada: fünf Jahre danach.** (Grenada: five years after.)
Maritta Tkalec. *Berliner Zeitung* (25 October 1988), p. 2.
On the occasion of the fifth anniversary of the armed intervention on Grenada, a German reporter finds that all of the institutions of revolutionary Grenada have been thoroughly dismantled, drug addiction is rising, and the unemployment rate has risen to forty per cent.

470 **Trial of Grenada coup conspirators is major problem for country.**
Lloyd Noel. *Jet*, vol. 66, no. 8 (30 April 1984), p. 9.
Former Grenada attorney-general, Lloyd Noel, who himself had been jailed at
Grenada's Richmond Hill Prison, complains about the jailing without a trial of
Bernard Coard and his followers at that same prison.

471 **Are we losing Grenada again?**
Geoffrey Wagner. *National Review*, vol. 36, no. 24 (14 Dec. 1984),
p. 32-33.
One year after the collapse of the Grenadian Revolution, the author expresses his fear
that the delays in bringing Bernard Coard and his followers to justice as well as
the alleged failure to purge the bureaucracy of PRG members threaten the fragile
democracy on Grenada.

472 **Red calypso: the Grenadian Revolution and its aftermath.**
Geoffrey Wagner. Washington: Regnery Gateway, 1988. 261p.
A worthless diatribe filled with errors and distortions. The renowned Barbadian author
George Lamming is dismissed as 'an indifferent novelist who looks like a Bajan bear
after having lost a tussle with a lawn mower'. Reggae music is described as 'a sort of
musical itch'.

473 **Some fell slow and some fell fast.**
Geoffrey Wagner. *National Review*, vol. 39, no. 10 (5 June 1987),
p. 32-33.
The author welcomes the fact that almost four years after the murder of Maurice
Bishop, Bernard and Phyllis Coard and twelve of their followers have been sentenced
to hang, but he also expresses his fear that legal manoeuverings will prevent the
carrying out of this sentence for years to come.

474 **The death of Herbert Augustus Blaize.**
Caribbean Contact, vol. 17, no. 8 (Jan. 1990), p. 3.
A surprisingly laudatory editorial about the political career of Grenadian Prime
Minister Blaize in a monthly which seldom had anything good to report about Blaize's
five years as prime minister (1984-89) of post-PRG Grenada. The editorial was
occasioned by Blaize's death on 19 December 1989.

475 **A tragic island's revival.**
Dwight Whylie. *Maclean's*, vol. 97, no. 51 (17 Dec. 1984), p. 38.
A sympathetic portrayal of Prime Minister Herbert Blaize who is described as a 'self-
effacing, deeply religious man'.

476 **The Caribbean struggle against dependency: Grenada: showcase or
victim?**
Ake Widfeldt. Gothenburg, Sweden: PADRIGU, 1989. 94p, bibliog.
A Swedish graduate student, who interviewed many supporters as well as opponents of
the Grenadian Revolution, concludes that the NJM did not live up to its promise to
create a new society on Grenada. He also believes that Grenada, since October 1983,

History. Post-revolutionary Grenada, 1983-90

has hardly been transformed into the 'showcase of democracy' the Reagan Administration predicted it would become.

477 The man from GULP returns.
Fay Willey. *Newsweek*, vol. 103, no. 4 (30 Jan. 1984), p. 45.

A description of former Grenadian Prime Minister Eric Gairy's return to his native island which, according to the author, does not bode well for the future of democracy on Grenada.

478 Restoring the sovereignty of Grenada.
Dessima Williams. *The Black Scholar*, vol. 15, no. 3 (May-June 1984), p. 8-11.

The former ambassador of Grenada to the Organization of American States outlines the goals and objectives of the Grenada Foundation which she helped to found in order to preserve the memory of Maurice Bishop and his followers who were slain on 19 October 1983.

Population

479   An analysis of the 1750 Carriacou census.
Frances Kay Brinkley.   *Caribbean Quarterly*, vol. 24, no. 1-2 (March-June 1978), p. 44-60.

A description of the census which was carried out on the Grenadian island of Carriacou in 1750 by the French commandant of Carriacou, Lieutenant De la Bourgerie du Sablon, upon the orders of the French governor of Grenada, de Poincy. The island, then part of the French colonial empire contained 199 'souls'.

480   Grenada 1985-1987 population and vital statistics report.
Ministry of Finance.   St. George's: Statistical Department, Ministry of Finance, 1990. 58p.

Statistical data on the population, fertility, morbidity, mortality and marriages and divorces of the Grenadian people.

481   Population growth in Grenada in the twentieth century.
Jack Harewood.   *Social and Economic Studies*, vol. 15, no. 2 (June 1966), p. 61-84.

The director of the Government Statistical Service in Trinidad examines the contributions made by births, deaths and migration to the growth of population on Grenada in the period 1921-60. The author warns that if a population increase of the same order continues, Grenada, by the year 2060 would have a population density of 1,800 persons per square mile.

482   1980-1981 Population Census of the Commonwealth Caribbean, Grenada.
Kingston: Statistical Institute of Jamaica, 1985. 3 vols.

Topics which were covered by this 1980 census of Grenada include population, size and growth, demographic characteristics, economic activity, education, race and religion, marriage and union status, fertility, and housing and households.

Nationalities and Minorities

483 **Indians in the Caribbean.**
Edited by I. J. Bahadur Singh. New Delhi: Sterling, 1987. 428p.
bibliog.

A collection of essays dealing with the Indian Diaspora in the Caribbean. Noorkumar Mahabir of the Caribbean Institute of Indian Studies and Research at Trinidad deals with the Indian minority on Grenada (p. 370-404) which, according to him, numbers 9,700 persons.

484 **East Indian indenture and the work of the Presbyterian Church among the Indians in Grenada.**
Beverley Steele. *Caribbean Quarterly*, vol. 22, no. 1 (March 1976), p. 28-37.

A pioneering study of the influx of East Indians to Grenada after the middle of the nineteenth century. According to this article, schooling through the Presbyterian Church allowed East Indians to reach positions of distinction within a generation of arrival, but it also served as an agent of deculturation.

Overseas Populations

485 **'England I want to go': the impact of migration on a Caribbean community.**
Donald R. Hill.   PhD dissertation, Indiana University, Bloomington, Indiana, 1973. 960p. (Available from University Microfilms, Ann Arbor, Michigan, order no. 73-23013).

This dissertation contains three sections. Section one deals with the subsistence and money economy of Carriacou. Section two is concerned with the culture and social relations of the inhabitants of Carriacou, particularly the massive male emigration which has resulted in the ratio of two women for each man on that island. Section three deals with the folk religion of the islanders and the active part which ancestors play in the daily life of Carriacouans.

486 **Look into the eyes.**
Shiva Naipul.   *Spectator*, vol. 251, no. 8104 (5 Nov. 1983), p. 8-9.

A brilliant essay which examines the contemptuous attitude of Trinidadians towards immigrants from Grenada.

487 **Differential adaptation of Grenadian emigrant communities in London and New York.**
Peter M. Tobias.   *Social and Economic Studies*, vol. 25, no. 1 (March 1976), p. 77-79.

The author discovers great contrasts between the 'migrant social relations and island ties' of Grenadians in London and New York. Given the fact that Grenadians regard New York as a much more 'dangerous and predatory' place, the Grenadian immigrants in New York are much more willing to lend assistance to fellow Grenadians than is the case of Grenadians in London.

488 **'How you gonna keep 'em down in the tropics once they've dreamed New York?': some aspects of Grenadian migration.**
Peter M. Tobias.   PhD dissertation, Rice University, Houston, Texas, 1975. 240p. (Available from University Microfilms, Ann Arbor, Michigan, order no. 75-22073).

This dissertation deals with the phenomenon of migration from Grenada. The author claims that most Grenadians have little concrete information about the destination of their migratory desire and that whatever information they do obtain 'is created and transmitted during "liming" [loitering/hanging about] interactions which are the basic male activities in the Grenadian context'.

489 **Eastern Caribbean migrants in the USA: a demographic profile.**
Averille White.   *Bulletin of Eastern Caribbean Affairs*, vol. 13, no. 4 (Sept.-Oct. 1987), p. 8-28.

This article deals with the demographic characteristics of East Caribbean migrants in the United States of America, including Grenadian immigrants.

Languages and Dialects

490 **Learn the lingo.**
Alister Hughes. *The Greeting Tourist Guide*, vol. 2, no. 1 (March 1989), p. 16-20.
A fascinating, witty article about the special vocabulary used by Grenadians, which is derived from their African, British and French ancestors. A glossary accompanies the article which contains such expressions as 'to give bus iron' (to drive fast), 'to fire one' (to have a strong drink), and 'doctor shop' (pharmacy).

491 **Non-standard English of Grenada.**
Alister Hughes. *Caribbean Quarterly*, vol. 12, no. 4 (Dec. 1966), p. 47-57.
A renowned Grenadian journalist and editor analyses the influence of the Amerindians, French, Africans, Spanish, and East Indians upon the English spoken on Grenada.

492 **Bilingual aspects of language in a Creole community.**
Ronald Kephart. In: *Bilingualism: social issues and policy implications.* Edited by Andrew W. Miracle, Jr. Athens, Georgia: University of Georgia, 1983, p. 107-17.
The author calls for the formalization of bilingual education on Carriacou and urges that 'Carriacouans be taught to read and write in Creole before they tackle Export English'.

Languages and Dialects

493 **'It have more soft words': a study of Creole, English and reading in Carriacou, Grenada.**
Ronald F. Kephart.   PhD dissertation, University of Florida, Gainesville, Florida, 1985. 358p. (Available from University Microfilms, Ann Arbor, Michigan, order no. 86-06724).

A fascinating dissertation by a scholar of anthropological linguistics who spent many years on the Grenadian island of Carriacou studying the Creole English spoken there as well as assisting the local educational system.

494 **Verbal categories in Carriacou Creole English.**
Ronald Kephart.   *SECOL Review*, vol. 10, no. 2 (Summer 1986), p. 116-30.

A description of the verbal categories of Carriacou Creole English, the language spoken by most people in Carriacou, Grenada.

Religion

495 **Handbook of churches in the Caribbean.**
Compiled by Lisa Bessil-Watson. Bridgetown: Cedar, 1982. 134p.
This handbook contains a history of the churches of the Caribbean as well as statistical data and a list of theological colleges of the region. References to church life on Grenada can be located throughout this volume.

496 **Handbook of churches in the Caribbean.**
Edited by Joan A. Brathwaite. Bridgetown: Christian Action for Development in the Caribbean, 1973. 234p.
Information on the churches of Grenada can be found throughout this important handbook. For instance, the names, addresses and telephone numbers of the priests of the Roman Catholic Diocese of St. George's may be located on pages 218-19. Information on the Presbyterian Church of Grenada can be found on pages 65-66.

497 **The Rastafarians in the Eastern Caribbean.**
Horace Campbell. *Caribbean Quarterly*, vol. 26, no. 4 (Dec. 1980), p. 42-61.
An interesting report on the substantial support which the Rastafarians gave to the New Jewel Movement after having suffered persecution under Eric Gairy.

498 **From out of the rubble.**
Edward W. Desmond. *National Review*, vol. 36, no. 24 (14 Dec. 1984), p. 35, 52.
A freelance writer who had examined the captured Grenadian documents, discusses the various secret schemes by which the PRG attempted to reduce the influence of the Roman Catholic Church on Grenada which it regarded as a major threat to the establishment of socialism on the island.

499 **Conception Island or the troubled story of the Catholic church in Grenada, B.W.I.**
Raymund Devas. London: Sands & Sons, 1932. 430p. map. bibliog.
Based upon research in Grenada, the American Antiquarian Society at Worcester, Massachusetts, the New York Public Library and the British Museum, this extensive history of the Catholic Church in Grenada appeared on the occasion of the centenary of the Catholic emancipation in Grenada.

500 **'New Wave' missionaries invade Grenada.**
Devonson LaMothe. *Caribbean Contact*, vol. 15, no. 12 (May 1988), p. 7.
A criticism of the influx into Grenada of missionaries from the United States who belong to conservative Protestant organizations and, according to the author, behave in an aggressive and arrogant way instead of tailoring their activities to local circumstances.

501 **Wrestling with the Bible in the Caribbean basin.**
N. Samuel Murrell. *Caribbean Journal of Religious Studies*, vol. 8, no. 1 (April 1987), p. 12-23.
A visiting lecturer at the Caribbean School of Theology, Jamaica Theological Seminar at Kingston, Jamaica, states that 'it is clearly a case of psychological conditioning and Machiavellianism to allege that the US-backed administration or any of the past governments of Grenada originated with God, for the records show just the reverse'.

502 **A church in the sun.**
John A. Parker. London: Cargate, 1959. 109p. bibliog.
Although this book deals primarily with the development of the Methodist Church on Grenada, it contains an interesting account of the O'Hannonist schism within the Catholic Church of Grenada. O'Hannon, a Roman Catholic priest, championed the cause of black slaves and poor whites on the island, antagonizing both state and Church hierarchy until he made his submission to Rome in 1838.

503 **A very British island.**
Amit Roy. *New Society*, vol. 67, no. 1102 (5 Jan. 84), p. 5-6.
This article asserts that Christian values and the British heritage saved Grenadians from the Cuban Marxists in the past and will save them from the North American influence in the future.

504 **Black religions in the new world.**
George Eaton Simpson. New York: Columbia University Press, 1978. 415p. maps. bibliog.
The Catholic church and the Shango cult in Grenada are examined in this volume and the religious cults of Grenada are compared with those in Trinidad, Jamaica and St. Vincent. The author also explains the origins and significance of the Big Drum Dance on Carriacou.

505 **Dark Puritan: the life and work of Norman Paul.**
    M. G. Smith.   *Caribbean Quarterly*, vol. 5, no. 1 (June 1957),
    p. 34-47; vol. 5, no. 2 (Feb. 1958), p. 85-98; vol. 5, no. 4 (June 1959),
    p. 284-91.

A fascinating autobiographical sketch by a Grenadian revivalist preacher which illuminates the socio-economic conditions of Grenadian estate workers and their blend of African and European traditions.

506 **A note on truth, fact and tradition.**
    M. G. Smith.   *Caribbean Quarterly*, vol. 17, nos. 3 & 4 (Sept.-Dec.
    1974), p. 128-36.

An ethnographer and author of *Kinship and community in Carriacou* (q.v.) strongly rebuts the criticisms which the Grenadian civil servant Wilfred A. Redhead levied against his book. According to Smith, Redhead's denial of the existence of strong, non-Christian religious and folk traditions on Carriacou, reveals the typically superior attitudes which Grenadians of brown skin colour have displayed towards black Carriacouans.

507 **Rastafari in transition – cultural confrontation and political change in
    Ethiopia and the Caribbean (1966-86).**
    Ikael Tafari.   *Bulletin of Eastern Caribbean Affairs*, vol. 15, no. 1
    (March/April 1989), p. 1-13.

Part of this article deals with the relationship between the PRG and the Rastafarians on Grenada. The author asserts that the Rastafarians played an important role in the initial success of the 13 March Revolution which was led by Maurice Bishop who had defended Rastafarians in court during the oppressive Gairy era. As the Coard faction gained in influence, tensions arose between the PRG and the Rastafarians, some of whom were detained at Hopevale Plantation until the US intervention in 1983.

508 **In bloody terms: the betrayal of the church in Marxist Grenada.**
    Andrew J. Zwerneman.   South Bend, Indiana: Greenlawn, 1986.
    113p.

Although marred by a number of factual errors, this volume represents an important contribution to the study of the Grenadian Revolution by exploring the relationship between the predominant Roman Catholic Church and the Bishop régime.

Social Conditions

Social problems and social stratification

509 **The Grenadian peasantry and social revolution 1930-1951.**
George I. Brizan. Kingston: Institute of Social and Economic
Research of the University of the West Indies, 1979. 52p.
This brochure examines the economic conditions prevalent among the black peasant
underclass of Grenada during the 1930s and 1940s and explores its grievances which led
to the 1951 uprising under Eric Gairy.

510 **Bitter-sweet and spice.**
Frederick McDermott Coard. Ilfracombe, England: Arthur H.
Stockwell, 1970. 208p. map.
The fascinating autobiography of a Grenadian civil servant who sheds much light on
the class structure of his country.

511 **Youth in the English-speaking Caribbean: the high cost of dependent
development.**
Meryl James-Bryan. *Cepal Review*, no. 29 (Aug. 1986), p. 133-52.
This article stresses the importance of cultural decolonization in nation building and
theorizes that the disorientation and alienation of youth in the anglophone Caribbean
(including Grenada) is 'rooted in the institutional flimsiness and superficial planning in
the area of cultural development'.

512 **A successful maroon project.**
Bob Lindsey. *Caribbean Contact*, vol. 17, no. 10 (March 1990), p. 7.
A report on a self-help programme in the poorest region of Grenada (St. Andrew's Parish on the island's east coast), initiated by the Caribbean Conference of Churches (CCC) and the Grenada Save the Children Development Agency. Housing projects, leadership training, nutrition courses, periodic group evaluations on the work, family life workshops, fund raising endeavours and social get-togethers are all part of this maroon project.

513 **Inlaw terms and affinal relations in a Grenadian fishing community.**
Judy Smith McDonald. *Caribbean Studies*, vol. 12, no. 4 (Jan. 1973), p. 44-51.
A study of kinship in the fishing sector of Gouyave, a small town on Grenada's west coast.

514 **Social stratification and the free coloured in the slave society of the British Windward Islands.**
Bernard Marshall. *Social and Economic Studies*, vol. 31, no. 1 (March 1982), p. 1-39.
An investigation of the relationship between whites, free persons of colour and slaves on Grenada, Trinidad and Tobago, Dominica, and St. Vincent during the early 1820s. The author, a professor of history at the University of the West Indies, Mona, Jamaica, observes that these relationships are determined by colour, class and legal status.

515 **Father-absence and delay of gratification: cross-cultural comparison.**
Walter Mischel. *Journal of Abnormal and Social Psychology*, vol. 63, no. 1 (July 1961), p. 116-24. bibliog.
A comparison of the personality differences between black groups on Grenada and Trinidad as well as a study of children's preferences for delayed gratification to the variable of the absence or presence of a father in the child's home on these two island nations.

516 **With a Carib eye.**
Edgar Mittelholzer. London: Secker & Warburg, 1958. 192p.
The Guyanese author describes Grenadian society as divided between an upper class (whites and mulattos) and peasants (blacks) with no middle class to speak of.

517 **Kinship and community in Carriacou.**
M. G. Smith. New Haven, Connecticut: Yale University Press, 1962. 347p. maps.
An excellent study of the culture and society of Carriacou which should be of interest to anybody concerned with kinship study of folk societies.

518 **Kinship and household in Carriacou.**
M. G. Smith. *Social and Economic Studies*, vol. 10, no. 4 (1961),
p. 455-72.
An analysis based on surveys conducted at various locations in Carriacou of the kinship
system, the organization of mating and household management.

519 **Stratification in Grenada.**
M. G. Smith. Berkeley, California: University of California, 1965.
271p. bibliog.
Smith identifies four strata within the Grenadian élite: at the top, the white plantocracy
educated in Great Britain and Barbados. Secondly, the light brown stratum which
imitates the white élite. Next, the medium brown and mulatto stratum consisting of
professionals and medium level executives. Fourthly, at the bottom of the grouping:
the dark pigmented group.

Women

520 **Women and the law in the Commonwealth Caribbean.**
Norma M. Forde. Cave Hill, Barbados: University of the West
Indies, 1982. 125p. (Women in the Caribbean Project, vol. 1).
Grenadian laws dealing with marriage, dissolution of marriage, maintenance,
matrimonial property, domicile, abortion, bigamy, prostitution and marital coercion
are discussed in this fine monograph.

521 **Blaze of fire.**
Nesha Z. Haniff. Toronto, Ontario: Sister Vision, 1988. 220p.
This book deals with significant contributions made by Caribbean women. The
Grenadian woman mentioned in this volume is Louise Rowley who served in the civil
service of Grenada for almost forty years (1930-69) and became Grenada's first woman
permanent secretary. The author teaches at the Center for Afro-American Studies at
the University of Michigan.

522 **What revolution brought Grenadian women.**
Margaret Jayko. *Militant*, vol. 47, no. 44 (2 Dec. 1983), p. 4.
A member of the editorial staff of the *Militant* lists the PRG's many programmes and
laws which, according to her, meant that Grenada's women were making great
progress in their battle for equal rights.

523 **The significance of the Grenada Revolution to women in Grenada.**
Rita B. Joseph. *Bulletin of Eastern Caribbean Affairs*, vol. 7, no. 1
(March-April 1981), p. 16-19.
The head of the Women's Desk at the PRG's Ministry of Education and Social Affairs
lists what in her opinion, are the many accomplishments of the Grenadian Revolution

regarding the advancement of women's rights. The régime of former Prime Minister Eric Gairy is accused of practising sexual exploitation and preventing women's participation in governmental affairs.

524 **Women on the march.**
Pat Kane. *Intercontinental Press*, vol. 20, no. 2(25 Jan. 1982), p. 32-3.
Leaders of the National Women's Organization (NWO) in Grenada hail the PRG's measures to help women (such as outlawing discrimination, introducing paid maternity leave and equal pay) as great accomplishments in the fight for Grenadian women's rights.

525 **Women's growing role in revolutionary Grenada.**
Colleen Levis. *Intercontinental Press*, vol. 18, no. 43 (17 Nov. 1980), p. 1192-93.
An interview about Grenadian women's advances under the PRG with the secretary of women's affairs in the Ministry of Education, Youth, and Social Affairs, Phyllis Coard.

526 **Women and the state: women's movements in Grenada and their role in the Grenadian Revolution, 1979-1983.**
Rosemary A. Porter.   PhD dissertation, Temple University, Philadelphia, Pennsylvania, 1986. 588p. (Available from University Microfilms, Ann Arbor, Michigan, order no. 86-27500).
An analysis of the relationship of women and women's organizations to the Grenadian state before and after the 13 March 1979 revolution.

527 **Women in the new Grenada.**
Patsy Romain. *Intercontinental Press*, vol. 19, no. 12 (6 April 1981), p. 336-37.
A member of the National Executive of the National Women's Organization (NWO) discusses the day-to-day activities, day-care projects, participation in the militia, and health improvement plans of her organization.

528 **Alimenta Bishop – a profile in courage.**
Rickey Singh. *Caribbean Contact*, vol. 12, no. 11 (April 1985), p. 4.
A columnist and former editor of *Caribbean Contact* uses the occasion of International Women's Day (8 March) to draw a sympathetic portrait of seventy-year-old Alimenta Bishop whose fifty-seven-year-old husband, Rupert, was killed by Eric Gairy's thugs on 21 January 1974, and whose son, Maurice, was executed by members of the PRA on 'Bloody Wednesday', 19 October 1983.

529 **Reproductive rights of women.**
Baxter Smith. *Intercontinental Press*, vol. 20, no. 24 (28 June 1982), p. 576.
Claudette Pitt, a leader of the National Women's Organization (NWO) explains the difficulties of convincing Grenadian women of the benefits of birth control, given the opposition of the predominant Catholic Church.

530 **Women chart revolutionary course.**
Baxter Smith. *Intercontinental Press*, vol. 21, no. 1 (17 Jan. 1983), p. 32.

A report on the 6-7 December 1982 Congress of Grenada's National Women's Organization NWO which lists some of the changes in the status of women brought about by the Grenadian Revolution.

531 **Grenada's women – four years after March 1979.**
Annette Walker. *Caribbean Contact*, vol. 10, no. 10 (Feb. 1983), p. 12.

Among the accomplishments which women achieved since the Grenadian Revolution, the article lists a law providing equal pay for equal work and a maternity leave law which gives female employees in all occupations the right to two months' maternity leave for each childbirth.

532 **Grenada's women move forward with the revolution.**
Annette Walker. *Freedomways*, vol. 23, no. 1 (1983), p. 23-28.

An interesting account of the role that women played in developing the Grenadian Revolution by the director of international affairs programming at WBAI–FM radio station in New York City.

533 **Grenadian women under the New Jewel Movement.**
Dessima Williams. *Transafrica Forum*, vol. 4, no. 3 (Spring 1987), p. 53-67.

The PRG's ambassador to the OAS discusses the advances in the fields of employment, health, and education which Grenadian women, according to her, made from 1979 until 1983.

Social Services, Health and Welfare

534 **Grenada's importance: its geographic location and its symbolism.**
Marvin Alisky. *Vital Speeches*, vol. 50, no. 5 (15 Dec. 1983),
p. 159-60.
A professor of political science at Arizona State University delivered this address
before the Valley of the Sun Kiwanis Club on 9 November 1983. In the course of his
speech, he made the unfounded claim that the US medical students on Grenada 'had
been threatened with death' and had been told 'they would be shot on sight if they left
their dormitories'.

535 **Changing perspectives on health care development in Grenada since the
revolution.**
Candia Alleyne. *Bulletin of Eastern Caribbean Affairs*, vol. 7, no. 1
(March-April 1981), p. 12-16.
A positive evaluation of the health care programme of the PRG which is described as
'preventative' rather than 'curative' by the author, a nutritionist with the Ministry of
Health at St. George's.

536 **Community involvement and participation in Grenada.**
Candia Alleyne. *CAJANUS*, vol. 15, no. 1 (June 1982), p. 5-12.
The head of the nutrition unit of the Grenadian Ministry of Health discusses the
organizational structures (Parish Coordinating Councils, Zonal Coordinating Councils,
National Organization of Women, etc.) through which the PRG was able to involve
communities in primary health care and nutrition.

537 **Health in Grenada.**
David F. Clyde. London: Vade-Mecum, 1985. 415p. map. bibliog.
A comprehensive historical and sociological study of the medical service in Grenada
from 1700 to 1984 by a medical officer and malariologist. The book contains accounts

of the outbreak of Boulam Fever (1793) and cholera (1854) which destroyed up to a tenth of Grenada's population.

538 **Day care in Grenada.**
Monica Clyne. *CAJANUS*, vol. 3, no. 6 (Dec. 1970), p. 323-29.
Statistics on the variety of day care on Grenada during the Gairy régime, provided by the Chief Nursing Officer of Grenada at a workshop dealing with food, nutrition and development for St. Lucia, St. Vincent and Grenada held in Grenada on 13-15 October 1970.

539 **Epidemiology of mongoose rabies in Grenada.**
C. O. R. Everard, George M. Baer, Andrew James. *Journal of Wildlife Diseases*, vol. 10, no. 3 (July 1974), p. 190-96.
An examination of the outbreak of rabies which was found in 0.5-3.7% of mongooses trapped on Grenada between 1968 and 1972. The behaviour of rabid mongooses is described, and the virus titers in organs of some of the animals are recorded. The article is accompanied by a map of Grenada showing the localities of capture for 124 mongooses with rabies SN antibodies.

540 **High prevalence of anaemia established in Grenada's population.**
CAJANUS, vol. 19, no. 4 (1986), p. 179-84.
A report on the pioneering efforts of the Government of Grenada in collaboration with the Caribbean Food and Nutrition Institute (CFNI) to deal effectively with the problem of anaemia by quantifying the national prevalence rate, identifying the vulnerable groups, clarifying the major causes and guiding decisions relating to intervention programmes.

541 **The St. George's medical school issue.**
Michael Hoyos. *Bulletin of Eastern Caribbean Affairs*, vol. 10, no. 1 (March-April 1984), p. 25-27.
The president of the Barbados Association of Medical Practitioners firmly opposes the relocation of the St. George's Medical School from Grenada to Barbados, calling that medical school 'a privately-owned foreign business' with no social commitment to the host country.

542 **Mongoose rabies in Grenada.**
A. H. Jonkers, F. Alexis, R. Loregnard. *West Indian Medical Journal*, vol. 18, no. 3 (Sept. 1969), p. 167-70.
An account of the attempts by Grenada's health department to reduce the incidence of rabies on the island by trapping mongooses.

543 **An American pathologist's view of medicine on the island of Grenada.**
Eugene J. Mark. *Journal of the American Medical Association*, vol. 26, no. 17 (5 May 1989), p. 2554-54.
A North American pathologist from the Massachusetts General Hospital at Boston, describes the activities of Project HOPE on Grenada. Since 1983, this organization has arranged for United States physicians to provide medical care for Grenada in the areas

of general surgery, pediatrics, radiology and pathology. The author himself, served for Project HOPE at the 150-year-old General Hospital at St. George's for one month as physician and pathologist. He draws a grim picture of the primitive state of medicine on the island, claiming that 'practicing medicine in Grenada is like practicing medicine on another planet'.

544 Faith healing and medical practice in the southern Caribbean.
Frances Mischel. *Southwestern Journal of Anthropology*, vol. 15, no. 4 (Winter 1959), p. 407-17.

An initial study of the Afro-American religious cult of Shango on Grenada and Trinidad, led the author to compare the problem of bush or faith healing to legitimate medical practice on those two island nations. Mischel found the greatest difference between Grenada and Trinidad in the attitude of medical doctors towards problems of mental health. In Trinidad, doctors will not send mental patients to bush doctors because 'such practices smack of pagan Africa'. On Grenada, where medical facilities in the rural areas are much more primitive, doctors will often refer psychosomatic patients to bush doctors.

545 St. George's University medical issue in Barbados.
E. R. Walrond. *Bulletin of Eastern Caribbean Affairs*, vol. 10, no. 2 (May-June 1984), p. 13-17.

The vice dean of the faculty of medicine at the University of the West Indies, Cave Hill, Barbados, describes the fierce controversy which exploded over the relocation of the St. George's University Medical School to Barbados. According to the vice dean, Prime Minister Tom Adams and the Ministry of Health defend the stationing of this school on Barbados, whereas the medical profession, the University of the West Indies and the political opposition vigorously oppose the presence of this medical school on Barbadian soil.

Politics and Government

546 **Political change and public opinion in Grenada 1979-1984.**
Patrick Emmanuel, Farley Brathwaite, Eudine Barriteau. Cave Hill,
Barbados: University of the West Indies, 1986. 168p. bibliog.

Occasional Paper No. 19 of the Institute of Social and Economic Research (Eastern
Caribbean) of the University of the West Indies at Cave Hill, Barbados, renders an
excellent analysis of the multi-faceted political development which transpired on
Grenada in the wake of the collapse of the Grenadian Revolution in October 1984.
The book also documents the results of the Institute's polls on Grenada which revealed
that the Grenadian people still held Maurice Bishop in high esteem and felt that the
Grenadian Revolution had produced many positive results. The PRG's measures
against freedom of the press and free elections were, however, overwhelmingly
criticized.

547 **Democracy and crisis in the Eastern Caribbean.**
Paget Henry. San German, Puerto Rico: Universidad Interamericana
de Puerto Rico, 1986. 28p. (CISCLA Documento de Trabajo, no. 27).

This essay by a Caribbeanist at the University of Virginia, analyses the impact of the
economic and political crisis tendencies of two Eastern Caribbean societies – Grenada
and Antigua – on patterns of democratic growth and contraction.

548 **Politics Caribbean style: lessons from Grenada.**
Anthony P. Maingot. *Caribbean Review*, vol. 14, no. 2 (Spring 1985),
p. 4-6, 36-67.

A vivid, perceptive account of the first elections held on Grenada after the October
events of 1983. The author teaches sociology and directs the graduate programme in
International Studies at Florida International University at Miami, Florida.

Constitution and Legal System

Constitution

549 **Changing Caribbean constitutions.**
Francis Alexis.   Bridgetown: Carib Research & Publications, 274p.
bibliog.
A prominent Grenadian politician and legal scholar has written this survey of
constitutional changes adopted by the independent Commonwealth Caribbean
countries. Specific references to Grenada may be found on pages 50-61 and 109-16.

550 **Three cases of constitutionalism and cuckoo politics: Ceylon, British
Guiana and Grenada.**
Archie Singham.   *New World Quarterly*, vol. 2, no. 1 (1959), p. 23-33.
Just as cuckoos in cuckoo clocks serve only an ornamental purpose, so does the 1959
constitution in Grenada represent a mere showpiece under the quasi-dictatorship of
Eric Gairy, according to the author.

Legal system

551 **Opening address to the American Association of Jurists Conference.**
Maurice Bishop.   St. George's: Government Information Service,
1982. 19p.
Maurice Bishop, who used to be a practising lawyer himself, delivered this speech to
the American Association of Jurists Conference which met at The Dome at Grand
Anse, Grenada on 10 March 1982. In his speech, the Grenadian prime minister gave a
short history of the development of the world's legal system before launching into a

bitter attack on the Reagan Administration. Towards the end of his speech, Bishop asserted 'that there can be no equality before the law if real and concrete social and economic rights are the preserve of only a privileged minority'.

552 **Law and the 'revolution': a review of post-revolution laws in Grenada.**
Andrew Burgess. *Bulletin of Eastern Caribbean Affairs*, vol. 7, no. 1 (March-April 1981), p. 20-25.

A lecturer at the faculty of law of the University of the West Indies asserts that the laws issued by the PRG were based on pragmatism and not revolutionary theory.

553 **Grenada and current law of the sea problems.**
Anselm Clouden. Halifax, Nova Scotia: Dalhousie University, 1980. 238p.

A member of the Grenada delegation to the Third United Nations Conference on the Law of the Sea analyses the effects of geography, navigation, pollution, marine scientific research, fishing and delimitation of maritime boundaries upon Grenada in light of extended coastal research.

554 **Grenada consolidated index of statutes and subsidiary legislation to 1st January, 1978.**
Cave Hill, Barbados: University of the West Indies, 1978. 45p.

The laws covered by this index are the Statutes and Subsidiary Legislation in force on 31st December 1958 contained in volumes 1 to 6 of the 1958 Revised Edition of the Laws of Grenada and Ordinances and Acts enacted and Statutory Rules and Orders made between 1 January 1959 and 31 December 1977 and some of the United Kingdom legislation in force in Grenada.

555 **Grenada Laws 1988.**
St. George's: Government Printing Office, 1989. 354p.

This book contains the Principal Legislation (Ordinances) act, the Subsidiary Legislation (Orders, Proclamations, Rules, Regulations) and Imperial Legislation (applicable to the state passed during the year). The volume includes the controversial Value Added Tax Provisional Order which created a storm of protest.

556 **An appraisal of the prison system in Grenada.**
Carlton D. Hosten. Cave Hill, Barbados: University of West Indies, 1974. 41p.

This thesis draws a horrifying picture of Grenada's Richmond Hill Prison which was originally built by the French during the 18th century as a military hospital but in 1880 was converted into Grenada's only prison.

557 **The laws of Grenada.**
London: Waterlow & Sons, 1897. 983p.

This volume contains Acts and Ordinances, Order of the Queen in Council creating the Court of Appeal for the Windward Islands, Supreme Court Rules, Acts of Parliament relating specially to the West Indies, Royal Proclamations of 1764 and 1784 and list of Acts of Parliament relating to the Colonies.

558 **How revolution changed legal system.**
Baxter Smith. *Intercontinental Press*, vol. 20, no. 18 (17 May 1982),
p. 428-29.
In an interview with Baxter Smith, the legal counsel in Grenada's Ministry of Justice,
Miles Fitzpatrick, remarks that Grenada's labour legislation before the revolution was
100 years out of date, thereby necessitating the PRG's emphasis on workers' and
women's rights.

559 **The revised laws of Grenada.**
Daniel Thomas Tudor. London: Waterlow & Sons, 1911. 2 vols.
Volume 1 contains laws pertaining to legislation, general revenue, religion and
education, registration, naval and military affairs, protection of agricultural and other
natural products, commerce and trades, and civil and criminal jurisdiction. Volume 2
includes laws dealing with land and civil and criminal jurisdiction.

Foreign Relations

General

560   **Grenada urges peaceful settlement of Malvinas islands dispute.**
Intercontinental Press, vol. 20, no. 17 (10 May 1982), p. 394.

A press statement released by the Permanent Mission of Grenada to the United
Nations in New York on 22 April 1982, which illustrates Grenada's support for
Argentina during the Falklands crisis, the only anglophone country in the Caribbean to
do so.

561   **Statement delivered by H. E. Unison Whiteman, Minister of Foreign
Affairs of the People's Revolutionary Government of Grenada to the
Second Special Session on Disarmament at the United Nations on
Wednesday 23rd June, 1982.**
Unison Whiteman.   St. George's: Government Information Service,
1982. 13p.

In his speech, the Grenadian Minister of Foreign Affairs of the PRG deplores the fact
that the armaments race is speeding up year after year, while poverty in the Third
World becomes more catastrophic all the time. The address contains vitriolic attacks
upon the governments of Israel, the Union of South Africa and the United States.

562   **'US shows determination to police the world by military might'.**
Unison Whiteman.   *Militant*, vol. 47, no. 41 (11 Nov. 1983), p. 9-11.

A speech delivered by the Grenadian foreign minister to the United Nations General
Assembly on 13 October 1983, six days before he was murdered on Grenada alongside
Maurice Bishop. The speech is a good summary of the foreign policy which the PRG
pursued during its four-and-a-half years in power.

563 **From revolutionary solidarity to military defeat: the foreign policy of Grenada, 1979-1983.**
David E. Lewis. In: *The Caribbean after Grenada.* Edited by Scott B. MacDonald, Harald M. Sandstrom, Paul B. Goodwin, Jr. New York: Praeger, 1988. p. 55-67. bibliog.
Although sympathetic to the Grenadian Revolution, the author criticizes the PRG for ignoring the near omnipotence of the United States in the Caribbean.

With Canada

564 **Bishop's last stand.**
Jared Mitchell. *Maclean's*, vol. 96, no. 44 (31 Oct. 1983), p. 17-18.
The final crisis of the Grenadian Revolution (19 October 1983) from a Canadian perspective. Even after Maurice Bishop's execution, Prime Minister Pierre Trudeau vowed to continue Canadian aid to Grenada.

With other Caribbean countries

565 **Regional comments: Barbados – Grenada relations.**
Eudine Barriteau. *Bulletin of Eastern Caribbean Affairs*, vol. 6, no. 5 (Nov.-Dec. 1980), p. 22-30.
This article reviews the bitter personal feud which had erupted between Barbadian Prime Minister Tom Adams and Grenadian Prime Minister Maurice Bishop by November 1980.

566 **Trinidad keeps its health minister and football team from Grenada.**
Merle Hodge. *Caribbean Contact*, vol. 8, no. 4 (Aug. 1980), p. 18.
Trinidadian writer Merle Hodge denounces the continual hostility of the Trinidadian government towards the PRG which, according to her, was illustrated by the Trinidadian government's refusal to send its minister of health to a CARICOM Health Ministers' Conference which met at St. George's, Grenada on 15 July 1980.

567 **Barbados regime attacks Grenada revolution.**
Sam Manuel. *Intercontinental Press*, vol. 18, no. 44 (24 Nov. 1980), p. 1222.
An account of the harassment of a Grenadian cabinet member, Minister of Agriculture Unison Whiteman, at the Grantley Adams Airport on Barbados.

568 **Belize and revolutionary Grenada: a partnership in the Caribbean, 1979-1983.**

Kai Schoenhals. In: *Central America: Historical Perspectives on the contemporary crises.* Edited by Ralph Lee Woodward, Jr. Westport, Connecticut: Greenwood, 1988, p. 193-218.

An examination of the strange partnership between Grenada under the revolutionary Prime Minister, Maurice Bishop, and Belize under the conservative Prime Minister, George Price. The essay is based on research in the captured Grenadian Document Collection at the US National Archives in Washington, DC.

569 **Message to Grenada: an interview with Edward Brathwaite.**

Chris Searle. *Race and Class*, vol. 22, no. 4 (Spring 1981), p. 387-94.

In the course of an interview with Chris Searle, the prominent Barbadian poet Brathwaite makes some illuminating comparisons between the very different societies of Barbados and Grenada.

570 **Summit 'a success for Grenada'.**

Baxter Smith. *Intercontinental Press*, vol. 20, no. 36 (13 Dec. 1982), p. 859.

A description of the CARICOM Conference held on 16-18 November 1982 at Ocho Rios, Jamaica during which Barbados and Jamaica attempted to expel Grenada and Guyana and failed.

571 **The Jamaica reaction: Grenada and the political stalemate.**

Carl Stone. *Caribbean Review*, vol. 12, no. 4 (Autumn 1983), p. 31-32, 60-63.

Jamaica's leading pollster and newspaper columnist states that the October 1983 events on Grenada lent a new element of uncertainty to political trends in Jamaica where both major political parties (PNP and JLP) must now move closer towards the centre, the PNP to overcome its leftist image and the JLP to minimize its lack of populism.

572 **Trinidad's displeasure with Grenada.**

Jeremy Taylor. *Caribbean Contact*, vol. 8, no. 2 (June 1980), p. 7.

In an interview with Jeremy Taylor, Trinidad and Tobago's Minister for Caribbean Community Affairs, Mervyn de Souza, expresses his government's grave reservations towards the PRG.

573 **Towards one Caribbean – 'The Declaration of St. George's'.**

Bulletin of Eastern Caribbean Affairs, vol. 5, no. 3 (July-Aug. 1979), p. 13-16.

A set of agreements entered upon during a summit meeting between representatives of the governments of Dominica, Grenada and St. Lucia on 16 July 1979, which called for greater unity between the anglophone, francophone, Dutch and Spanish-speaking Caribbean.

With Cuba

574 **A Pyrrhic military victory and a profound moral defeat.**
Fidel Castro.   Havana: Editora Politica, 1983. 19p.
The funeral speech for the Cubans who died on Grenada, rendered by Fidel Castro on Revolution Square at Havana on 14 November 1983.

575 **Cuba's renewed support for violence in Latin America.**
In: *American Foreign Policy Current Documents 1981.* Washington: Department of State, 1984, Document 663, p. 1207-23.
In a report submitted to the Subcommittee on Western Hemisphere Affairs of the Senate Foreign Relations Committee on 14 December 1981, the Department of State lists the penetration of Grenada by Cuba.

576 **Bishop's Cuba, Castro's Grenada: notes toward an inner history.**
Mark Falcoff.   In: *The Communist challenge in the Caribbean and Central America.* Howard J. Wiarda, Mark Falcoff, Ernest Evans, Jiri Valenta, Virginia Valenta. Washington: American Enterprise Institute for Public Policy Research, 1987, p. 187-97. bibliog.
An exploration of the relationship between the People's Revolutionary Government of Grenada with Cuba and the Soviet Union.

577 **The Cuban and Soviet challenge in the Caribbean basin.**
Edward Gonzalez.   *Orbis*, vol. 29, no. 1 (Spring 1985), p. 73-94.
A professor of political science at UCLA and resident consultant to the Rand Corporation, makes much of the alleged policy differences between Cuba and Grenada which have yet to be proven.

578 **The Cuban yoke.**
Maxwell Harrow.   *National Review*, vol. 33, no. 11 (12 June 1981), p. 666.
A West Indian businessman describes Grenada under Bishop as 'a lovely island sold down the river to Cuba by a bunch of London School of Economics dropouts' and claims that Grenadian troops have been dispatched to El Salvador.

579 **Hearings and markup before the Committee on Foreign Affairs House of Representatives Ninety-Eighth Congress Second Session on S. Con. Res. 80; H. R. 4504; H. Res. 383; H. R. 4835; H. Res. 437. February 17, 29; March 14, 1984.**
Washington: US Government Printing Office, 1984. 129p.
This government document contains treaties between the PRG, the Soviet Union and Cuba concerning the delivery of arms and ammunition to Grenada.

580 **How Cubans aid revolution.**
Pat Kane. *Intercontinental Press*, vol. 20, no. 16 (3 May 1982),
p. 380-81.
Cuban aid to Grenada in the fields of health care, culture, housing sports facilities, agro-industries, transportation, and the maintenance and development of the island's electricity system are discussed in this artcle.

581 **Soviet activities in Latin America and the Caribbean.**
James H. Michel. In: *American Foreign Policy Current Documents 1985*. Washington: Department of State, 1986, Document 527,
p. 929-34.
In a prepared statement before a subcommittee of the House Foreign Affairs Committee, 28 February 1985, the Principal Deputy Assistant Secretary of State for Inter-American affairs, Michel, asserts that Grenada 'became the focal point of anti-democratic activities throughout the Caribbean. In doing this, Grenada surrendered a large part of its sovereignty to the Cubans and Soviets'.

582 **Truth about Cuba's internationalist role.**
Geoff Mirelowitz. *Intercontinental Press*, vol. 21, no. 22 (14 Nov. 1983), p. 651-52.
A summary of Cuban-Grenadian relations (1979-83) and a refutation of the claim that Cuba was using Grenada as a stepping stone to export revolution and terrorism to the rest of the region.

583 **This 'rubbish' of a Cuban naval base in Grenada.**
Rod Prince. *Caribbean Contact*, vol. 9, no. 12 (April 1982), p. 5.
A British journalist, after visiting Grenada, declared that all reports that the Cubans are building a naval base at Calivigny on Grenada are pure inventions.

584 **What 'Newsweek' didn't print: full text of interview with Fidel Castro.**
Patricia Sethi. *Intercontinental Press*, vol. 22, no. 8 (30 April 1984), p. 246-50.
The complete text of an interview with Cuban President Fidel Castro which was conducted in December 1983 by *Newsweek* correspondent Patricia Sethi. In its 9 January 1984 edition, *Newsweek* left out more than half the interview. Much of the interview revolves around Grenada and contains fascinating glimpses into the Cuban relationship with Maurice Bishop and Castro's hostility towards the Coard faction and the RMS.

With Britain

585 **Our man in Grenada.**
Patrick Cosgrave. *Encounter*, vol. 63, no. 2 (July-Aug. 1984),
p. 40-43.
The former political editor of *The Spectator*, believes that Great Britain should have
participated in the invasion of Grenada and criticizes Prime Minister Margaret
Thatcher and Foreign Secretary Geoffrey Howe for not joining Reagan's 'rescue
mission'.

586 **Grenadian lessons: the protracted conflict.**
Brian Crozier. *National Review*, vol. 35, no. 24 (9 Dec. 1983),
p. 1534.
A criticism of Prime Minister Margaret Thatcher's failure to approve of the US
intervention in Grenada.

With France

587 **French aid and politics in this region: Bishop's Paris visit a plus.**
Greg Chamberlain. *Caribbean Contact*, vol. 10, no. 7 (Nov. 1982),
p. 11.
A report on a visit by Maurice Bishop to France and his meeting with French President
François Mitterand during September 1982. Bishop, who was the first Anglo-
Caribbean leader ever officially to visit France, was able to obtain French aid for
Grenada and the East Caribbean in general.

588 **New boost for agriculture.**
Fred Murphy. *Intercontinental Press*, vol. 20, no. 34 (15 Nov. 1982),
p. 810.
An account of Maurice Bishop's three-day visit to France in mid-September 1982,
during which he received French President François Mitterand's promise that Grenada
will receive French assistance in the development of agriculture, agro-industries, food
distribution, education and public health.

With the Soviet Union

589 **The bear in the back yard: Moscow's Caribbean strategy.**
Timothy Ashby.   Lexington, Massachusetts; Toronto: Lexington
Books, 1987. 240p. map.

Chapter four (p. 81-101) of this book by a policy analyst for Latin American affairs
with the Heritage Foundation in Washington, DC is devoted to Grenada. The author
views the Grenadian Revolution as a Soviet plot to seize control of the Caribbean.

590 **Cold war in a hot country.**
Richard Buel.   *National Review*, vol. 32, no. 23 (14 Nov. 1980),
p. 1392, 1414-15.

According to this article, the Grenadian Revolution was hatched in the Kremlin with
the intention of seizing the oil fields of Trinidad and Venezuela and disrupting the vital
US shipping lanes during any future war.

With the United States

591 **The mote in Reagan's eye.**
George Alagiah.   *South*, no. 32 (June 1983), p. 20.

The author questions the frequent assertion by the Reagan Administration that
Grenada represents a threat to the security of the United States.

592 **US relations with Grenada.**
Stephen W. Bosworth.   In: *American Foreign Policy Current
Documents 1982*. Washington: Department of State, 1985, Document
687, p. 1441-44.

In a statement before a subcommittee of the House Foreign Affairs Committee on 15
June 1982, the Principal Deputy Assistant Secretary of State for Inter-American
Affairs, Bosworth, outlines the steps which the PRG would have to take in order to
establish normal relations with the United States.

593 **'We will always have a special interest in Grenada'.**
George Bush. In: *American Foreign Policy Current Documents 1985*.
Washington: Department of State, 1986, Document 544, p. 980-81.

A speech delivered by Vice President George Bush on 14 March 1985, at Tanteen
Field, Grenada, during which he congratulated the Grenadian people for their return
to democracy and vowed to come to the aid of Grenada again if 'the unprincipled,
antidemocratic forces and their foreign allies in the Communist bloc will once again
work to subvert the freedoms Grenada now enjoys'.

594   **Securing independence: Grenada faces 'massive resistance' from the United States.**
Charlie Cobb.   *Transafrica Forum*, vol. 1, no. 2 (Autumn 1982), p. 89-94.

A contributing editor for *Africa News* traces the hostility of the US government towards revolutionary Grenada.

595   **Country reports on human rights practices for 1981. Report submitted to the Committee on Foreign Affairs US House of Representatives and the Committee on Foreign Relations US Senate by the Department of State.**
Washington: US Government Printing Office, 1982. p. 435-44.

This report accuses the PRG of many human rights' violations such as holding political prisoners without warrant, restricting freedom of the press and refusing to hold free elections.

596   **US policy in Latin America.**
Kenneth W. Dam.   In: *American Foreign Policy Current Documents 1983*. Washington: Department of State, 1985, Document 608, p. 1267-72.

In an address before the General Assembly of the Organization of American States on 14 November 1983, US Deputy Secretary of State, Kenneth W. Dam, claims that the US intervention on Grenada conformed to articles 22 and 28 of the OAS charter and article 52 of the UN charter.

597   **Grenadian tours California, answers US lies.**
Raúl González, Sam Manuel.   *Militant*, vol. 47, no. 29 (5 Aug. 1983), p. 7.

A report on the California tour of the Grenadian consul general to the United States, Joseph Burke, during which the Grenadian diplomat refuted President Reagan's claim that the new airport under construction on Grenada represents a threat to the security of the United States.

598   **Four years of US aggression.**
Ernest Harsch.   *Intercontinental Press*, vol. 21, no. 21 (7 Nov. 1983), p. 633.

A survey of the unremitting hostility of the United States towards the Grenadian Revolution.

599   **US government monitoring of outbreak of violence in Grenada.**
John Hughes.   In: *American Foreign Policy Current Documents 1983*. Washington: Department of State, 1985, Document 655, p. 1394-97.

During a press briefing on 20 October 1983, Department of State spokesperson, John Hughes, expresses concern for the safety of the 1,000 US citizens on Grenada but, otherwise, gives no hint what the attitude of the US government will be towards the newly established Revolutionary Military Council under General Hudson Austin.

600 **The role of Cuba in international terrorism and subversion.**
Fred C. Iklé. In: *American Foreign Policy Current Documents 1982.*
Washington: Department of State 1985, Document 677, p. 1406-18.
In the course of addressing the question of Cuban penetration of the Eastern
Caribbean before a subcommittee of the Senate Judiciary Committee on 11 March
1982, the Under Secretary of Defence for Policy, Iklé, makes the often-repeated, but
never proven, assertion that PRG Minister of National Mobilization, Selwyn Strachan,
boasted that Cuba would eventually use the new airport on Grenada to supply troops
in Angola and 'that because of its strategic location, the airport may also be used by
the Soviet Union'.

601 **The United States confronts change in Latin America.**
David T. Jervis. PhD dissertation, Temple University, Philadelphia,
Pennsylvania, 1985. 444p. (Available from University Microfilms,
Ann Arbor, Michigan. order no. 85-21094).
An examination of US hostility towards six revolutionary governments in Latin
America and the Caribbean: Cuba (1958-61), the Dominican Republic (1965), Chile
(1969-73), Nicaragua (1979-85), El Salvador (1979-85) and Grenada (1979-83).

602 **Oh, what a lovely war!**
Jonathan Kwitny. *Mother Jones*, vol. 9, no. 5 (June 1984),
p. 27-33, 46.
An interesting account of the Revolutionary Military Council's desperate attempts to
be obliging to the United States and the North American medical students on
Grenada. According to the author, a reporter of the *Wall Street Journal*, all of the
RMC's efforts were ignored by the Reagan Administration which was determined to
put an end to Marxism on Grenada.

603 **The real virus: Prime Minister Maurice Bishop responds to Reagan's
initiative.**
Samori Walker. *Caribbean Perspective*, vol. 1, no. 5 (Summer 1982),
p. 12-16.
An editor and contributing editor interview Maurice Bishop about Ronald Reagan's
Caribbean Basin Initiative (CBI) and early 1982 visit to Barbados during which Reagan
remarked that Grenada was attempting to spread the 'Communist virus' throughout
the region. Bishop asserts that the real virus is Reagan's attempt to revert life in the
United States to the epoch of unrestrained capitalism of the previous century.

604 **Grenada's prime minister reports US trip a success.**
Malik Miah. *Militant*, vol. 47, no. 23 (24 June 1983), p. 5.
A description of a press conference held on 9 June 1983, during which Maurice Bishop
declared that the three main objectives of his visit to the United States had been met.
He defined his objectives as furthering the close relations between Grenadians and
North American blacks, promoting a better understanding of the Grenadian
Revolution and initiating a dialogue with the Reagan Administration with a view of
normalizing relations between the United States and Grenada.

605 **Caribbean conflict: cold war in the sun.**
Janet Henshall Momsen. *Political Geography Quarterly*, vol. 3, no. 2
(April 1984), p. 145-51.
A member of the department of geography at the University of Newcastle upon Tyne,
England, analyses the powerful outside forces which have dominated the Caribbean.
The author describes the challenge of the Grenadian Revolution to United States
hegemony in the region.

606 **The impact of Grenada on the Caribbean: ripples from a revolution.**
Robert A. Pastor. In: *Latin America and Caribbean contemporary
record, 1983-1984.* Edited by Jack W. Hopkins. New York; London:
Holmes & Meier, 1985, vol. 3, p. 11-33. bibliog.
A former senior staff member (1977-81), responsible for Latin American and
Caribbean Affairs on the National Security Council in the White House, concludes that
the impact of Grenada 'will be something more than a ripple and something less than a
revolution'.

607 **Peacekeeping agreement between the United States of America and
Grenada effected by exchange of notes signed at St. George's March 12
and 13, 1984. (Treaties and other International acts Series 10963.)**
Washington: US Government Printing Office, 1984. 6p.
An exchange of notes between the Grenadian Governor-General, Paul Scoon and US
Ambassador Charles A. Gillespie, which formalized the status of US peacekeeping
forces on Grenada.

608 **'It isn't nutmeg that's at stake in the Caribbean and Central America. It
is the US national security'.**
Ronald Reagan. In: *American Foreign Policy Current Documents
1983.* Washington: Department of State, 1985, Document 614,
p. 1285-90.
The Reagan speech which alarmed the PRG more than any of his other addresses
because the US president claimed that the USSR and Cuba were not only building an
air force base, but also a naval base on Grenada which was threatening the national
security of the US. Reagan delivered this speech to the annual meeting of the National
Association of Manufacturers on 10 March 1983.

609 **Lebanon and Grenada: the use of US armed forces.**
Ronald Reagan. *Vital Speeches*, vol. 50, no. 3 (15 Nov. 1983),
p. 66-69.
In this famous speech, President Reagan asserts that the United States was forced to
intervene militarily on Grenada because that country 'was a Soviet-Cuban colony being
readied as a major military bastion to export terror and undermine democracy. We got
there just in time'.

Foreign Relations. With the United States

610 **Peace and national security.**
Ronald Reagan. In: *American Foreign Policy Current Documents 1983*. Washington: Department of State, 1985, Document 13, p. 56-62.

An address delivered on 28 March 1983, over nation-wide radio and television by President Reagan who drew an alarming picture of the militarization of Grenada which he denounced as a Cuban-Soviet 'power projection in the area'. The speech greatly perturbed the PRG.

611 **President Reagan's visit to Grenada.**
Ronald Reagan. In: *American Foreign Policy Current Documents 1986*. Washington: Department of State 1987, Document 477, p. 809-12.

The text of the speech delivered by President Reagan at Queen's Park on the occasion of his state visit to Grenada on 20 February 1986.

612 **President's remarks, Bridgetown, April 8, 1982.**
Ronald Reagan. *Department of State Bulletin*, vol. 82, no. 2063 (June 1982), p. 38.

During a visit to Barbados, President Reagan expressed his concern with the overturn of Westminster parliamentary democracy in Grenada and warned 'that country [Grenada] now bears the Soviet and Cuban trademark which means that it will attempt to spread the virus among its neighbors'.

613 **US commitment to preserving democracy in Grenada.**
Ronald Reagan. In: *American Foreign Policy Current Documents 1986*. Washington: Department of State, 1987, Document 476, p. 808.

Responding to questions submitted to him by Caribbean journalists on 18 February 1986, President Reagan declares that 'the United States is fully aware of its commitment to preserving democracy in Grenada and will stand by it in times of need'.

614 **'US marines and US army rangers have now been withdrawn from Grenada'.**
Ronald Reagan. In: *American Foreign Policy Current Documents 1983*. Washington: Department of State, 1985, Document 667, p. 1425-26.

In this letter of 8 December 1983, President Reagan informed the Speaker of the House of Representatives, Thomas P. O'Neill, Jr., that US marines and US army rangers were withdrawn from Grenada and less than 2,700 US armed forces personnel remain on the island.

615 **Grenada as looking glass: playing the 'Russian game' in the Americas.**
Andrew Reding. *Christianity and Crisis*, vol. 44, no. 7 (30 April 1984), p. 159-60.

A searing denunciation of US policy towards Grenada which is compared to President McKinley's policy towards the Philippines. The author claims that President Reagan has adopted a North American version of the 'Brezhnev Doctrine' for the Caribbean.

616   **Grenada: the struggle against destabilization.**
Chris Searle.   London: Writers & Readers Publishing Cooperative,
1983. 164p. bibliog.
Written by an uncritical British admirer of the Grenadian Revolution who played a
major role in developing the educational reforms of the PRG, this work blames all of
the problems of Revolutionary Grenada as well as the events of 19 October 1983 on
destabilization efforts on the part of the US government. The appendix contains
interesting interviews with Maurice Bishop and Cheddi Jagan.

617   **Testimony of Sally A. Shelton before the Sub-Committee on Inter-**
American Affairs, US House of Representatives. 15 June 1982.
Sally A. Shelton.   *Bulletin of Eastern Caribbean Affairs*, vol. 8, No. 5
(Nov.-Dec. 1982), p. 12-17.
The former United States ambassador to Grenada (1979-81) blames the Grenadian
Revolution of 13 March 1979 upon the corrupt and tyrannical rule of Eric Gairy and
warns Washington not to isolate the Bishop régime and to threaten it militarily.

618   **Telecommunications: radio communications between amateur stations**
on behalf of third parties. Treaties and other international acts series
10855.
Washington: US Government Printing Office, 1986. 4p.
An arrangement between the USA and Grenada concerning radio communications
which was effected by an exchange of notes signed at St. George's on 5 and 8
December 1983.

619   **United States policy toward Grenada. Hearing before the Subcommittee**
on Inter-American Affairs of the Committee on Foreign Affairs House of
Representatives Ninety-Seventh Congress Second Session June 15, 1982.
Washington: US Government Printing Office, 1982. 100p.
Testimonies by Stephen M. Bosworth, Principal Deputy Assistant Secretary of State
for Inter-American Affairs, Sally A. Shelton-Colby, former U.S. Ambassador to the
Eastern Caribbean, Randall Robinson, executive director of Transafrica, and
congressmen Mervyn M. Dymally (California) and George W. Crockett (Michigan)
before a hearing on US policy towards Grenada.

620   **Government warns of invasion.**
Steve Wattenmaker.   *Intercontinental Press*, vol. 21, no. 7 (18 April,
1983), p. 190.
An account of a press conference held by the PRG's foreign minister at the United
Nations on 28 March 1983, during which Whiteman warned that the Reagan
Administration was getting ready to invade Grenada.

621   **An open letter to the Congress and to the people of the United States.**
Dessima Williams.   *Congressional Record*, vol. 130, no. 58 (8 May
1984), p. 3,558-59.

After observing that both Grenada and the United States had been victims of British
imperialism, the former Grenadian ambassador to the Organization of American
States states that her country did not really become independent until the New Jewel
Revolution of March 1979. Denouncing the intervention on Grenada in October 1983
she writes, 'In real terms, the invasion of Grenada and the continuing occupation
remains a fundamental negation of Grenada's sovereignty. In defence of your nation's
proud history, you cannot allow this unjustified and illegal invasion of a nation of
110,000 people and 133 square miles to pass as "a victory for democracy."' This open
letter was placed in the *Congressional Record* by Congressman George W. Crockett,
Jr. of Michigan.

Economics

622 **Economic memorandum on Grenada. Report no. 3825 – GRD.
Document of the World Bank.**
Washington: Latin America and the Caribbean Regional Office, The
World Bank, 1982. 133p. map.
A World Bank document published on 4 August 1982 which gives a generally
favourable appraisal of the economic undertakings of the Bishop régime. Valuable
information on the agriculture, agro-industry, forestry, fisheries, tourism, manufacturing
and construction industries of Grenada.

623 **Foreign economic trends and their implications for the United States –
October 1988 Grenada.**
Washington: US Department of Commerce, International Trade
Administration, 1988. 10p.
A positive report on Grenada's economy prepared by the American Embassy at St.
George's. This 1988 report gives helpful advice to potential US investors.

624 **Grenada: economic report The International Bank for
Reconstruction/The World Bank.**
Washington: 1985. 90p. (A World Bank Country Study).
This economic report suggests for Grenada 'a comprehensive fiscal reform to improve
incentives for productive activities, a strengthening of public sector finances through
the reorganization and reduced role of the public sector and reform of the public
enterprises, promotion of private investment through an improved incentive system
and upgraded economic infrastructure, reduction of the high level of unemployment
and continuation of the liberalization of the economy, particularly in the areas of trade
and price control'.

Economics

625 **Group dynamics and the development of a fish-marketing co-operative: the La Baye fishermen – townsmen of Grenada, West Indies.**
George M. Epple. PhD dissertation, Brandeis University, Waltham, Massachusetts, 1973. 565p. (Available from University Microfilms, Ann Arbor, Michigan, order no. 73-32377).

A study of the social and economic factors affecting the development and acceptance of a fishermen's marketing cooperative in the vicinity of Grenville, Grenada.

626 **Incalculability as a feature of sugar production during the eighteenth century.**
Douglas Hall. *Social and Economic Studies*, vol. 10, no. 3 (Sept. 1961), p. 340-52.

Basing his conclusions upon a minute examination of the late 18th century accounts of the Westerhall Estate on Grenada, a lecturer in economic history at the University College of the West Indies observes that the owners of West Indian sugar plantations 'seldom had any realistic idea of how their enterprise stood financially, or what its prospects were'.

627 **Masses take part in economic planning.**
Pat Kane. *Intercontinental Press*, vol. 20, no. 6 (22 Feb. 1982), p. 127-28.

A report on the First National Conference of Delegates of Mass Organizations on the Economy on 29 January 1982, which was attended by close to 1,000 Grenadians who were called upon by the PRG to participate in the planning of the Grenadian budget.

628 **Grenada and the IMF: the PRG's extended Fund Facility Program, 1983.**
Claremont D. Kirwan. *Latin American Perspectives*, vol. 16, no. 3 (Summer 1989), p. 121-44.

A former consultant (1980-83) on economic planning to the PRG, who now teaches economics at UWI argues that the People's Revolutionary Government believed that once an IMF 'seal of approval' was granted to Grenada via an Extended Financial Fund agreement, increased levels of participation of both domestic and foreign capital in Grenada's development efforts would occur

629 **Spaceport Grenada.**
Jack D. Kirwan. *Space World*, vol. U-10-250 (Oct. 1984), p. 3.

An assistant editor of *Energy Journal*, published at the University of Arizona, suggests that 'Grenada could be for private spaceship launching what Switzerland is for banking because of its nearness to the equator and lack of bureaucracy'.

630   **Grenada, the Caribbean Basin, and the European Economic Community.**
Scott B. MacDonald, Albert L. Gastmann.   In: *The Caribbean after Grenada.* Edited by Scott B. MacDonald, Harald M. Sandstrom, Paul B. Goodwin, Jr. New York: Praeger, 1988. p. 229-50.
The authors conclude that 'though US hegemony remains a factor, the Caribbean is no longer an American lake, especially as the EEC countries have extended a greater influence in the region since the Grenadian and Nicaraguan Revolutions in 1979'.

631   **The development of underdevelopment in Grenada.**
Naraine Persaud.   PhD dissertation, Florida State University, Tallahassee, Florida, 1985. 317p. (Available from University Microfilms, Ann Arbor, Michigan, order no. 85-28709).
Studying the microstate of Grenada, the author concludes that 'primacy cannot be attributed to economic factors as major determinants of underdevelopment'.

632   **Revolutionary Grenada: a study in political economy.**
Frederic L. Pryor.   New York: Praeger, 1986. 359p. bibliog.
The only satisfactory account of the People's Revolutionary Government's economic policies. Written by a noted professor of economics at Swarthmore College in Pennsylvania, this book is based on painstaking research in the captured Grenadian Document Collection located at the US National Archives, Modern Military Headquarters Branch in Washington, DC. The author also conducted extensive interviews with representatives of all segments of Grenadian society.

633   **Report on the national economy for 1981 and the prospects for 1982.**
St. George's: Government Printing Office, 1981. 77p.
An optimistic report delivered by the then Deputy Prime Minister and Minister of Planning, Finance and Trade, Bernard Coard, to the Grenadian people on Friday, 29 January 1981 at The Dome, Grant Anse, St. George's, Grenada.

634   **Report on the national economy for 1982 and the budget plan for 1983 and beyond.**
St. George's: Government Printing Office, 1983. 172p.
A report on the Grenadian economy and its future prospects presented by Bernard Coard, the PRG's Deputy Prime Minister and Minister of Planning, Finance and Trade to the National Conference of Delegates of Mass Organisations on 24 February 1983, at The Dome, Grand Anse, St. George's.

635   **The value added tax in Grenada: the lessons not learnt.**
Wendell A. Samuel.   *Bulletin of Eastern Caribbean Affairs*, vol. 13, no. 2 (May-June 1987), p. 10-20.
A lecturer at the department of economics at the University of the West Indies weighs the advantages and disadvantages of the Value Added Tax which was introduced in Grenada during 1987 in order to shift the tax base from income to consumption without taking into account the peculiarities of the Grenadian economy.

Economics

636 **The second invasion of Grenada.**
Fortune, vol. 109, no. 3 (6 Feb. 1984), p. 36.

A report on the trip of a group of North American business people (among them representatives of Control Data, MacGregor Sporting Goods) who travelled to Grenada 'to help make the tiny Caribbean island a bastion of free enterprise'.

637 **'The consumer comes first.'**
Baxter Smith. *Intercontinental Press*, vol. 20, no. 19 (24 May 1982), p. 456.

An explanation of how the PRG keeps a lid on prices through the Marketing and National Importing Board (MNIB), a state enterprise which imports all cement, rice, raw sugar and some fertilizers.

638 **The economic and social development of Grenada.**
Clive Y. Thomas, L. Coke, S. DeCastro, A. Norton, H. McKenzie, B. Persaud, N. Miller, E. St. Cyr. Mona, Jamaica: University of the West Indies, 1968. 237p.

A detailed report on the economic and social conditions on Grenada by the University of the West Indies Development Mission which consisted of experts in the fields of botany, economics, sociology, geography and the social sciences from the three campuses of the UWI. The report includes the background of resource endowments, economic structure and projections, sectoral analysis: problems and recommendations as well as problems of social structure and the organization of social services.

639 **Grenada: honeymoon island on honeymoon.**
Myfanwy van de Velde. *The Courier*, no. 96 (March-April 1986), p. 23-33.

A positive survey of Grenada's economic development which includes an interview with Prime Minister Herbert Blaize.

Finance and Banking

640 **A Grenadian budget.**
Devonson LaMothe. *Caribbean Contact*, vol. 13, no. 11 (April 1986), p. 2.
A discussion of Herbert Blaize's controversial proposal in February 1986 to abolish the income tax and replace it by VAT which was to tax Grenadians on how much they spend rather than on how much they earn.

641 **Grenada's budget fears.**
Devonson LaMothe. *Caribbean Contact*, vol. 15, no. 11 (April 1988), p. 2.
A criticism of the Blaize Government's 1988 Grenadian budget proposal which, according to this article, heralds continued social and economic grim times for the majority of Grenadians.

642 **Let them eat sardines.**
Devonson LaMothe. *Caribbean Contact*, vol. 17, no. 1 (June 1989), p. 6.
A critical analysis of George Blaize's 1989 budget proposal which, according to this article, comes down hard on Grenada's urban and rural poor.

643 **The saga of an airline.**
Devonson LaMothe. *Caribbean Contact*, vol. 17, no. 7 (Dec. 1989), p. 7.
The tale of Grenada's national airline, Grenada Airways, which was founded in June 1985 and dissolved in November 1986, leaving behind debts of almost East Caribbean $3 million, which became the responsibility of Grenadian taxpayers.

Finance and Banking

644 **Big revolution small country: the rise and fall of the Grenada Revolution.**
Jay R. Mandle. Lanham, Maryland: North-South, 1985. 103p.
The second chapter of this volume constitutes a useful probe into the financial undergirdings of the Grenadian Revolution.

645 **Clean bill of health for the outcast of the islands.**
Rod Prince. *South*, no. 28 (Feb. 1983), p. 70-71.
An analysis of Grenada's economy under the PRG which claims that it was the glowing World Bank Report on Grenada which prevented Jamaica and Barbados from succeeding in their efforts to expel Grenada from CARICOM.

646 **The Grenada Development Bank.**
Francis Robertson, Alistair Keens-Douglas. *The Grenadian Farmer*, vol. 4, no. 4 (Nov./Dec. 1989), p. 8-10.
Advice to Grenadian farmers on how to go about obtaining credits from the Grenada Development Bank for crops like cocoa, nutmegs, bananas and vegetables as well as for farm buildings, anti-erosion land terracing, livestock rearing and processing, packaging, storage and marketing of agricultural products.

647 **'To construct from morning': making the people's budget in Grenada.**
Chris Searle, Don Rojas. St. George's: Fedon Publishers, 1982. 168p.
A booklet by the PRG which explains how ordinary Grenadians participated in the development of the national budget.

648 **The national income and the national accounts of Barbados; Antigua; St. Christopher, Nevis and Anguilla; Dominica; St. Lucia; St. Vincent and Grenada.**
Nora M. Siffleet. *Social and Economic Studies*, vol. 1, no. 3 (July 1953), p. 5-139.
Grenada's production account, consumption account, public authorities accounts (central and local government), capital account and balance of payments may be located on pages 104-16. The author observes that 'the estimation of incomes in Grenada is complicated by the multiplicity of occupations which may be followed by any one individual'.

649 **Fiscal reform: an analytical review of the Grenada experience.**
Karl Theodore. *Bulletin of Eastern Caribbean Affairs*, vol. 13 no. 2 (May-June 1987), p. 28-36.
An appraisal of fiscal reforms in Grenada under the New National Party administration by a lecturer in the Department of Economics, University of the West Indies at St. Augustine, Trinidad. The author concludes that in order to make the newly installed VAT more efficient, the Grenadian government will have no choice but to reintroduce some sort of income tax.

External Trade

650 **The foundations for future production and export of West Indian citrus.**
Dennis McFarlane. *Social and Economic Studies*, vol. 13, no. 1
(March 1964), p. 118-56.

Page 153 of this article contains a table which projects the production, export, and consumption of citrus on Jamaica, Dominica and Grenada (including Carriacou) for the years 1961-76.

651 **EEC – Grenada cooperation.**
Bob Visser. *The Courier*, no. 96 (March-April 1986), p. 36-37.

An outline of the economic cooperation between Grenada and the European Economic Community by the EEC's Resident Adviser in Grenada, Bob Visser.

Industry

652　**A relic of the past; standard for the future.**
　　Alister Hughes.　*The Greeting Tourist Guide*, vol. 1, no. 2 (Oct. 1988),
　　p. 12-18.

A prominent Grenadian editor and journalist renders a detailed history of the production of rum on Grenada which takes place at the four rum distilleries of Woodlands, Westerhall, River Antoine and Dunfermline. Alister Hughes gives a lucid account of the complicated process of manufacturing rum the old fashioned way.

653　**Marquis: Grenada's straw capital.**
　　Alister Hughes.　*Discover Grenada, Carriacou, Petit Martinique*, (Jan.
　　1990), p. 44-47.

Grenada's most prominent journalist explores the village of Marquis, outside of Grenada's second town of Grenville, where most of the island's straw articles are made out of tropical wild pine.

654　**The nutmeg industry of Grenada.**
　　J. M. Mayers.　Kingston: Institute of Social and Economic Research
　　of the University of the West Indies, 1974. 50p. (Working Paper no. 3).

This brochure discusses the production and marketing of Grenada's nutmegs and mace, the background to the Grenada Cooperative Nutmeg Association, the finances of that association, the Nutmeg Industry (Amendment) Act of 1971, and the future prospects of Grenada's nutmeg industry. Valuable statistical tables accompany this paper.

655 **Cacao industry of Grenada.**
Harley Porter Milstead. *Economic Geography*, vol. 16, no. 2 (April 1940), p. 195-203.

This article deals with the physical environment, disease and insect pests, wind protection, harvest and curing as well as exports and trends of production of the cocoa crop on Grenada.

656 **Launching a schooner in Carriacou.**
Bruce Procope. *Caribbean Quarterly*, vol. 4, no. 2 (Dec. 1955), p. 122-31.

A blow-by-blow account, accompanied by interesting drawings, of the building and launching of a schooner on Carriacou, where boat building is an ancient and honoured craft.

Agriculture and Rural Conditions

657 **Yields of maize (Zea mays L.) in four Caribbean islands as influenced by variety and plant density.**
R. A. Baynes. *Tropical Agriculture*, vol. 49, no. 1 (Jan. 1972), p. 37-49.

A comparison of tropical hybrid maize cultivars with local island selections which was carried out over a three year period on Barbados, Grenada, St. Vincent and St. Lucia by a professor at the University of the West Indies. The author discovered that in Grenada and St. Vincent, 71.6 thousand plants per hectare were associated with the highest yields, whereas in Barbados and St. Lucia, a plant density of 35.1 thousand plants per hectare appeared to be adequate to achieve high yields.

658 **To Grenville on market day.**
Jenny Bingham. *The Greeting Tourist Guide*, vol. 2, no. 2 (Oct. 1989), p. 18-21.

The produce market of Grenada's second largest town is vividly described by the director of Stylus Communication, UK, public relations consultants to the Grenada Department of Tourism.

659 **Fragmentation of holdings: a study of small farms in Grenada.**
John S. Brierley. *Tropical Agriculture*, vol. 55, no. 2 (April 1978), p. 135-40.

A professor of geography at the University of Manitoba at Winnipeg, Manitoba, Canada, examines the nature of farm fragmentation and its impact upon land use patterns on Grenada. The author concludes that much of Grenada's idle land could be effectively used and farming practices made more intensive if time and energy were not consumed in accommodating fragmentation. He suggests programmes of land consolidation as a means of improving land use patterns and practices.

660 **Harvesting history in the hills of Bacolet.**
Jan Carew. *Journal of Caribbean Studies*, vol. 3, no. 1-2
(Spring/Autumn 1982), p. 49-62.

A Guyanese novelist and professor at Northwestern University, Evanston, Illinois, relates his experiences in the Grenadian countryside where he and his wife helped with improved agricultural methods during the Grenadian Revolution.

661 **Note on the identification and distribution of Moko disease in Grenada.**
D. K. Cronshaw, J. E. Edmunds. *Tropical Agriculture*, vol. 57, no. 2
(April 1980), p. 171-72.

An investigation into the outbreak of bacterial wilt (Moko disease) of banana and bluggoe on Grenada, caused by a SFR strain of Race 2 *Psudomonas solanacearum*. The authors, who visited the island during February 1978, found the outbreak largely confined to Grenada's northern parish of St. Patrick.

662 **The Caribbean basin to the year 2000.**
Norman A. Graham, Keith L. Edwards.   Boulder, Colorado:
Westview, 1984. 166p.

A comparative analysis of demographic, economic and resource use trends in seventeen Caribbean basin countries. Grenada is discussed on pages 56-62. The authors state that Grenada's economy is quite different from most agricultural economies of the Caribbean basin because there exists on Grenada a lack of dominance of any single crop which means that if the price of one Grenadian commodity becomes depressed on the world market, the economy still functions reasonably well with the revenue obtained from other crops.

663 **Part-time farming in Grenada: factors affecting off-farm work by small-farm operators.**
Henry G. Hitz. PhD dissertation, University of Maryland, College
Park, Maryland, 1984. 208p. (Available from University Microfilms,
Ann Arbor, Michigan, order no. 85-14535).

The review of an empirical model which explains participation and hours of off-farm work among a cross section of farmers in three rural areas of Grenada.

664 **Grenada's farming gains under fire.**
Mohammed Oliver. *Militant*, vol. 48, no. 7 (2 March 1984), p. 9, 16.

A report on the dismantling of state-owned farms on Grenada and their return to their previous private owners, a process which, according to the author, will result in great unemployment among Grenada's agricultural workers.

665 **Grenada mobilizes for agricultural development.**
Mimi Pichey. *Intercontinental Press*, vol. 19, no. 13 (13 April 1981),
p. 360-61.

A valuable discussion of such PRG agricultural programmes as the 'idle lands for idle hands' (1980) scheme and the National Cooperative Development Agency (NACDA) which assisted in the formation of farming, bakery, plumbing, furniture-making, and fishing cooperatives.

Agriculture and Rural Conditions

666 Cacao cultivation in Grenada.
F. J. Pound. *Tropical Agriculture*, vol. 15, no. 1 (Jan. 1938), p. 18-19.

An agronomist with the Department of Agriculture on Trinidad concludes that the intensive cultivation of Grenada's cocoa fields serves to diminish the extremes of fluctuations in water content of the soil by supplying a well aerated soil mulch through which excess water will drain away, and by forcing the feeding roots below the surface where they are less liable to dry out.

667 Results of the Grenada Agricultural Survey 1982.
St. George's: Ministry of Planning, 1984. 87p.

The results of the 1981 Agricultural Census which provide massive statistics on such agricultural topics as the total production of mangoes, avocadoes, soursops, golden apples, cloves, nutmegs as well as the number of pickaxes, hoes, spades, shovels and rakes owned by Grenadian farmers.

668 How revolution affects rural areas.
Baxter Smith. *Intercontinental Press*, vol. 20, no. 33 (1 Nov. 1982), p. 787-88.

A discussion of the PRG's efforts to involve young Grenadians in agriculture, which still plays a central role in the island's life.

669 Projection of cocoa output in Grenada, Trinidad and Jamaica, 1960-75.
Clive Y. Thomas. *Social and Economic Studies*, vol. 13, no. 1 (March 1964), p. 97-117.

This article evaluates the long-term supply position of cocoa in the major Caribbean producing countries. The section on Grenada (p. 95-101) deals with the organisation of production, processing and marketing and projections for future output.

670 The nutmeg: a spice story.
Myfanwy van de Velde. *The Courier*, no. 96 (March-April 1986), p. 34-35.

A short essay dealing with the importance of nutmeg production to Grenada. According to the article, it provides income and employment to 7,450 Grenadians.

671 Carriacou – an island with a sustainable agricultural system.
Cecil Winsborrow. *The Grenadian Farmer*, vol. 4, no. 4 (Nov./Dec. 1989), p. 14-15.

A description of the transformation of the formerly practised, export-orientated monoculture on Carriacou into the present subsistence farming carried out by part-time farmers.

Transportation

672 **Report on traffic surveys conducted in St. George's, Grenada.**
H. T. Dyer, G. Nimmerfjord.   St. Ann's Court, Barbados: UN
Physical Planning Office, 1968. 56p. maps.

A transportation study of St. George's carried out by the United Nations Physical
Planning Office for the purpose of providing a scientific and rational basis for the
planning of the future road system, car parking and other transport facilities in and
around the Grenadian capital.

Employment and Manpower

673 **Grenada – fight unemployment with production!**
Maurice Bishop.   Stoneleigh, England: Britain-Grenada Friendship
Society, 1982. 20p.

A speech given by Maurice Bishop at the conference on unemployment held at The
Dome at Grand Anse, Grenada, on 28 June 1982. The prime minister discussed his
government's efforts to reduce unemployment by encouraging people to return to
agricultural life instead of moving to towns or emigrating to the United States or
Canada.

674 **Employment in Grenada in 1960.**
Jack Harewood.   *Social and Economic Studies*, vol. 15, no. 3 (Sept
1966), p. 203-38.

A description of changes in the employment situation on Grenada during the inter-
censal period 1946-60 and the attempt to link those changes with demographic
developments on the island. Comparisons are drawn with other West Indian islands,
particularly Trinidad and Tobago.

675 **Help yourself: a career guidance booklet.**
Jacinta C. Johnson.   St. George's: NP, 1984. 125p. bibliog.

A brochure written for the purpose of advising young Grenadians in choosing a career,
applying for jobs and becoming familiar with the higher institutions of learning in the
Caribbean, United Kingdom, Canada and the United States. Good information on
post-secondary institutions in Grenada (p. 15-34), areas of study for careers in
Grenada (p. 35-70) and scholarships available to Grenadians (p. 115-20).

676 **The revolution vs. joblessness.**
Baxter Smith. *Intercontinental Press*, vol. 20, no. 32 (18 Oct. 1982), p. 772-73.

A discussion of the PRG's plan to create 6,000 new jobs over a period of three years (3,000 in agriculture, 2,000 in construction, 500 in tourism, 100 in agro-industries, and the rest in teaching and other sectors) in order to wipe out unemployment on Grenada.

Labour Movement and Trade Unions

677 **In the spirit of Butler: trade unionism in Free Grenada.**
St. George's: Fedon, 1982. 104p.

This PRG booklet contains autobiographical material by such Grenadian labour leaders as Cacademo Grant, Vincent Noel and Fitzroy Bain as well as some of the PRG's laws that were designed to protect trade unionism.

678 **Butler versus the king: riots and sedition in 1937.**
Edited by W. Richard Jacobs. Port of Spain: Key Caribbean, 1976.
254p. bibliog.

Letters, speeches and court records of Tubal Uriah Buzz Butler, a Grenadian who organized the oil field workers on Trinidad and led them in a violent strike during 1937 which became known as the 'Butler Riots'. Accused of sedition by the British Colonial Government, Butler was sent to prison for six years on Nelson Island.

679 **How revolution transformed a union.**
Pat Kane. *Intercontinental Press*, vol. 20, no. 11 (29 March 1982), p. 256-57.

The transformation of the Technical and Allied Workers Union (TAWU), consisting of 1,000 Grenadian telephone and electricity workers, truck drivers, transport workers, mechanics and postal workers, by the Grenadian Revolution.

680 **Revolution and the dockworkers.**
Pat Kane. *Intercontinental Press*, vol. 20, no. 15 (26 April 1982), p. 354-55.

An account of the hostility towards the Grenadian Revolution by the leadership of the Seamen's and Waterfront Workers Union (SWWU) under Eric Pierre.

681 **Winning farm workers to the revolution.**
Pat Kane, Nancy Walker, Ned Dmytryshyn. *Intercontinental Press*, vol. 20, no. 8 (8 March 1982), p. 176-77.
An interview with the president of the Agricultural and General Workers Union Fitzroy Bain, who was executed alongside Maurice Bishop on 19 October 1983.

682 **Gairy begins disruptive tactics in Grenada.**
Devonson LaMothe. *Caribbean Contact*, vol. 13, no. 7 (Dec. 1985), p. 10.
A description of an effective strike by Eric Gairy's Grenada Manual Maritime and Intellectual Workers' Union (GMMIWU) which illustrates that the former Grenadian prime minister still has substantial support among Grenada's agricultural population.

683 **Grenada's public servants protest.**
Devonson LaMothe. *Caribbean Contact*, vol. 17, no. 8 (Jan. 1990), p. 6.
The description of a week-long strike of the Grenada Union of Teachers (GUT), the Technical and Allied Workers Union (TAWU) and the Public Workers Union (PWU) against the Blaize government during December 1989. The strike, according to the author, constituted the *coup de grace* against the five-year reign of Prime Minister Herbert Blaize.

684 **'Our objective is workers power.'**
Errol McLeod, Gerry Kangalee. *Intercontinental Press*, vol. 22, no. 10 (128 May 1984), p. 322-25.
In an interview, the first vice-president and the assistant education officer of Trinidad and Tobago's Oilfields Workers Trade Union (OWTU), point out the profound differences between the economy, class structure and trade union movement between Grenada and Trinidad and Tobago.

685 **US targets Grenada's unions.**
Fred Murphy. *Intercontinental Press*, vol. 22, no. 2 (6 Feb. 1984), p. 34-35.
The author claims that the Reagan Administration through the American Institute for Free Labor Development (AIFLD) is attempting to destroy the trade unions which backed the Grenadian Revolution.

686 **Public workers fight to transform their union.**
Baxter Smith. *Intercontinental Press*, vol. 20, no. 31 (4 Oct. 1982), p. 744-45.
A description of the efforts of Wayne Sandiford and his November 12 Committee to revolutionize the Public Workers Union (PWU) which is one of the largest trade unions of Grenada with a membership of 1,200.

Labour Movement and Trade Unions

687 **Compulsory recognition of trade unions in Grenada.**
Lindel Smith. *Bulletin of Eastern Caribbean Affairs*, vol. 5, no. 3 (July-August 1979), p. 39-41.

A criticism of the Trade Union (Recognition) Act which was passed by the PRG on 18 May 1979.

688 **Educating for class-struggle unionism in Grenada.**
Diane Wang. *Intercontinental Press*, vol. 18, no. 29 (28 July 1980), p. 782-84.

The speeches of several Grenadian trade union leaders (Anselm De Bourg, John Ventour, Danny Roberts and Vincent Noel) who supported the PRG.

689 **How unions helped to make a free Grenada.**
Diane Wang. *Militant*, vol. 44, no. 30 (8 Aug. 1980), p. 8-9.

A discussion of the massive unionization of Grenada's labour force and the passage of pro-labour laws under the PRG.

Statistics

690 **Grenada abstract of statistics 1979.**
St. George's: Central Statistics Office, 1979. 146p.
Invaluable statistics on the area and climate, population, housing, agriculture, trade, tourism, travel, transport and communication, industrial statistics, government revenue, prices, financial statistics, national accounts, and social statistics on Grenada.

Environment

691 **Proceedings of the conference on environmental management and economic growth in the smaller Caribbean islands.**
Edited by William S. Beller. Washington: Department of State, 1979. 187p. (Publication 8996).

The transactions at the Conference on Environmental Management and Economic Growth in the Smaller Caribbean Islands which was held at the Caribbean Development Bank Conference Center at Wildey, St. Michael, Barbados on 17-21 September 1979. Three Grenadian officials participated: Anthony Boatswain, an economist, and Ron Smith and John Paul Fletcher, both engineers. Their comments are listed on pages 123-25.

692 **The overdevelopment of Carriacou.**
Bonham C. Richardson. *Geographical Review*, vol. 65, no. 3 (July 1975), p. 390-99.

The author points out that 18th-century plantation clearings disrupted Carriacou's ecosystem and caused great ecological damage. Further ecological harm was wrought by subsequent cropping and overgrazing. Labour migration and remittances have sustained life on the island which would become endangered by a shut-off of emigration since Carriacou is not self-sustaining.

Education

693 Address by comrade Maurice Bishop Prime Minister People's Revolutionary Government of Grenada to executive board of UNESCO.

Maurice Bishop. St. George's: Government Printing Office, 1982. 15p.

A speech delivered by Maurice Bishop on 18 September 1982 at UNESCO headquarters at Paris during which the Grenadian prime minister explained the changes which had occurred under his rule in Grenada, particularly in the field of education.

694 Education is production too!

Maurice Bishop. St. George's: Ministry of Education, 1981.

A speech by Maurice Bishop at the re-opening of the second year of the National-In-Service Teacher Education Programme (NISTEP) delivered on 15 October 1981.

695 'Emulation is the seed that brings the fruit of excellence'.

Maurice Bishop. St. George's: Ministry of Education, 1981. 19p.

An address given by Maurice Bishop at The Dome, Grand Anse on 29 October 1981 on the occasion of national emulation night for outstanding students and educators. The Grenadian prime minister expounds on the principle of emulation in the educational policy of the PRG and singles out for special recognition, F. F. Mahon, an ex-principal at River Sallee Government School who for forty-two years (1888-1930) devoted his life to his students instead of emigrating in order to earn more money. Bishop also praises the role which the Christian churches have played in the development of the Grenadian Educational system.

696 The education reform process in Grenada 1979-81.

George J. Brizan. St. George's: Institute for Further Education, 1981. 162p. map. bibliog.

A study of the educational reforms undertaken by the PRG after its accession to power in 1970. The areas of education selected for examination were teacher education, curriculum development and adult education. The author is an educator and historian who has served as Grenada's minister of agriculture and is presently (1990) minister of finance.

697 **New York reception celebrates 'year of education' in Grenada.**
Steve Clark. *Militant*, vol. 47, no. 2 (28 Jan. 1983), p. 3.

During a reception for supporters of the Grenadian Revolution held on 16 January 1983, at Brooklyn, New York, NJM central committee member, Kamau McBarnette, explains the importance assigned to education by the PRG.

698 **Education for true liberation and economic independence.**
St. George's: 1982. 37p.

A handbook of norms and guidelines for the primary adult education programme prepared by the National Technical Commission of the Centre for Popular Education.

699 **Reaching beyond the grasp: a revolutionary approach to education.**
Carlyle A. Glean. *Bulletin of Eastern Caribbean Affairs*, vol. 7, no. 1 (March-April 1981), p. 5-11.

A critical exploration of the PRG's National In-Service Teacher Education Programme (NISTEP) and the Community School Day Programme (CSDP).

700 **Government of Grenada Request for External Capital Assistance in the Field of Technical/Vocational Education.**
St. George's: Ministry of Education, 1983. 412p. map.

A project preparation document which was drawn up by a Grenadian government working party for the purpose of securing external capital assistance in order to improve the quality of technical and vocational education and training in the country. Essential reading for anyone interested in the problems of the Grenadian educational system.

701 **Social and educational change in a revolutionary society: Grenada 1930-1981.**
Wycherley V. Gumbs. PhD dissertation, University of Pittsburgh, Pittsburgh, Pensylvania, 1982. 270p. (Available from University Microfilms, Ann Arbor, Michigan, order no. 82-19926).

This dissertation compares the educational systems of Grenada, Cuba and the People's Republic of China before and after the revolutionary process in each country.

702 **Grenada launches literacy drive.**
Ernest Harsch. *Intercontinental Press*, vol. 18, no. 40 (27 Oct. 1980), p. 1105-08.

A report on the drive to wipe out illiteracy in Grenada.

703 **Each one teach one, we learn together.**
Didacus Jules. *Caribbean Contact*, vol. 8, no. 10 (Feb. 1981), p. 15.

A St. Lucian, who temporarily halted his studies at the University of the West Indies, in order to aid the PRG's literacy campaign, relates the efforts of the Centre for Popular Education (CPE) in which he played a leading role.

704 **Strategies and mechanisms for planning and implementing functional literacy programmes in the Caribbean.**
Didacus Jules. *Bulletin of Eastern Caribbean Affairs*, vol. 13, no. 1 (March-April 1987), p. 79-83.

The resident consultant of the National Research and Development Foundation, St. Lucia and former permanent secretary of the ministry of education of the PRG in Grenada, states that the eradication of illiteracy must be a political act. The literacy programmes of Jamaica and Grenada (1979-83) are discussed.

705 **Grenadian volunteers in Nicaragua.**
Pat Kane. *Intercontinental Press*, vol. 20, no. 7 (1 March 1982), p. 150.

The story of twenty Grenadians who volunteered to go to the anglophone part of Nicaragua (Bluefields) to help in the battle against illiteracy there.

706 **Whole country a school.**
Pat Kane. *Intercontinental Press*, vol. 20, no. 7 (1 March 1982), p. 150-1.

A discussion of the educational reforms under the PRG, including the Centre for Popular Education and the National In-Service Teacher Education Program.

707 **We work and play together.**
Edited by Catalina Lajud. St. George's: Centre for Popular Education, 1982. 51p.

This reader (Marryshow Reader Infant 1c) is the result of the cooperative efforts between the CPE of the Ministry of Education, Grenada, and the publishing house Pueblo y Education of the Ministry of Culture in Cuba. Before the Grenadian Revolution, Grenadian children were taught how to read from discarded United States textbooks which showed white children in an environment unfamiliar to Grenadian children. This Marryshow Reader displays black children and adults, involved in activities typical of Grenadian daily life. After the liquidation of the Grenadian Revolution, this reader was eliminated from the Grenadian school system.

708 **Let us learn together.**
St. George's: Centre for Popular Education, Ministry of Education, 1980. 104p.

A primer designed by the PRG's Centre for Popular Education's campaign to stamp out illiteracy. The text extols Grenadian and Caribbean unity and lauds various measures undertaken by the PRG to improve agriculture, medical services and education.

Literature

General

709 **Words unchained: language and revolution in Grenada.**
Chris Searle. London: Zed, 1984. 260p. map.

An English writer, teacher and poet illustrates how language changed during the Grenadian Revolution (1979-83) through the poems, essays, calypsos of Grenadians from all walks of life. The book contains interesting interviews with such Caribbean authors as George Lamming, Andrew Salkey, Earl Loveland, C. L. R. James, Martin Carter and Edward Kamau Brathwaite.

Children's books

710 **Tim tim tales from Grenada.**
Edited by Beverley A. Steele, Bruce St. John. St. George's: UWI Extra Mural Department, [n.d.]. 88p.

A collection of thirty-four Grenadian children's tales and six children's songs which were published in honour of the tenth anniversary of the founding of the Cave Hill Campus of the University of the West Indies.

Poets

711   A flag on the island.
Rolstan Adams.   *Caribbean Quarterly*, vol. 20, no. 1 (March 1974),
p. 44.

A poem by a Grenadian writer and literary critic who wrote the words to the Grenadian national anthem.

712   Calaloo.
Merle Collins.   *Freedomways*, vol. 24, no. 3 (1984), p. 195-6.

The most famous poem by Grenada's poet Merle Collins.

713   Poems of life.
Leonard Merrydale Comisiong.   Barrie, Ontario: Earth Printing,
1985. 103p.

Poetry by a Grenadian physician and chief medical officer in Grenada until his death in 1980. Many of his poems deal with his love for his country, e.g. 'Ode to Grenada' and 'Ode to Carriacou'.

714   Tongues of the new dawn: an anthology of poems.
Edited by Didaçus Jules, Valerie Cornwall.   Bridgetown: 1981. 65p.

Poems, some of them for the PRG's literacy campaign, recited during the festival of the revolution, 10-13 March 1981. Several of the poems were written by Chris De Riggs, a noted poet and the PRG's minister of health.

715   Freedom has no price: an anthology of poems.
Bridgetown: 1980. 88p.

This anthology includes poetry in praise of the Grenadian Revolution, by people of all ages and all strata of Grenadian society, which was recited during the festival of the revolution, 1-13 March 1980.

716   Grenada: the poets respond.
The Black Scholar, vol. 15, no. 3 (May-June 1984), p. 15-21.

A collection of poetry from the United States and the Caribbean, responding to the tragic events on Grenada during October 1983.

717   Grenada: tongues of the new dawn.
Race and Class, vol. 25, no. 3 (Winter 1984), p. 27-36.

Poems by Grenadian poets (Garvin Nantambu, Stuart Jacob Ross, Michael 'Senator' Mitchell, Merle Collins, Kojo de Riggs, Helena Joseph and Allan Lowe) who supported the revolution.

Literature. Poets

718 **'Essentially, my poetry is all about the revolution' says Merle.**
Chris Searle. *Free West Indian*, vol. 3, no. 70 (20 Nov. 1982), p. 12.
An English teacher and writer interviews Merle Collins, a Grenadian poetess, who during the Grenadian Revolution worked in the Ministry of Foreign Affairs.

719 **'My main form of expression is poetry' says Valdon Boldeau.**
Chris Searle. *Free West Indian*, vol. 3, no. 72 (27 Nov. 1982), p. 8.
A Grenadian poet relates to the English teacher, Chris Searle, how he is increasingly setting his poems to music now that he has learned how to play the guitar.

Architecture

720 **A brief assessment of the chief military monuments of Grenada, Saint Vincent, Saint Lucia, Antigua.**
David Buisseret. *Caribbean Quarterly*, vol. 16, no. 1 (March 1970), p. 58-67.
A useful account of the construction and present condition of the many fortifications that dot the hills overlooking the harbour of St. George's.

721 **The elusive deodand: a study of the fortified refuges of the Lesser Antilles.**
David Buisseret. *Journal of Caribbean History*, vol. 6 (May 1973), p. 43-80.
St. George's forts are more numerous and more interesting than those located on the Lesser Antilles according to this article which also states that 'West Indian fortifications had developed not to command a strategic point, as was most commonly the case in Europe, but to serve as a refuge for non-combatants (and final citadel for combatants) in time of war'.

722 **Sedan-chair porches: a detail of Georgian architecture in St. George's.**
J. R. Groome. *Caribbean Quarterly*, vol. 10, no. 3 (Sept. 1964), p. 31-33.
A teacher at Grenada Boys Secondary School discovered at least three sedan-chair porches on Georgian homes in the Grenadian capital. According to the author, these types of porches have become all but extinct in England.

Architecture

723 **Two tales of a city.**
Alister Hughes. *The Greeting Tourist Guide*, vol. 2, no. 2 (Oct. 1989), p. 22-26.

The first tale involves a building in St. George's known as 'La Chapelle'. It was in this edifice that the Roman Catholic priest Anthony O'Hannon preached to a large congregation of slaves and the less fortunate in the 1820s. The priest's radical views created a temporary schism within Grenada's Catholic Church. The other tale revolves around the statue of 'Christ of the Deep' which is located on St. George's Carenage and commemorates the help which the Grenadian people extended to the passengers of the Italian cruise liner, *Bianca C.*, when it caught fire off Grenada's coast on 22 October 1961.

The Arts

General

724 **Of culture and sovereignty.**
George A. V. Belle. *Caribbean Contact*, vol. 10, no. 10 (Feb. 1983), p. 13.
An extensive report by a lecturer in political science, UWI, about the Conference of Intellectual and Cultural Workers held at St. George's, Grenada during November 1982 and attended by many prominent journalists, artists, poets and actors of the Caribbean region.

725 **Address by Cde. Maurice Bishop, Prime Minister of the People's Revolutionary Government, at the opening of the Caribbean Conference of Intellectual Workers.**
Maurice Bishop. St. George's: National Convention Centre, 1982. 31p.
In his speech to the First Caribbean Conference of Intellectual Workers on 20 November 1982, Maurice Bishop called for the unity of the entire Caribbean and the elimination of alien cultural influences emanating from the world of the former colonial lords.

Visual arts

726   Grenada sketches in black and white.
W. Dieterle.   St. George's: NP, 1986. 54p.
Pleasant sketches of many facets of Grenadian life by an artist who visited Grenada during 1985 and 1986.

727   Women, art, and culture in the new Grenada.
Betty La Duke.   *Latin American Perspectives*, vol. 11, no. 3 (Summer 1984), p. 37-52.
A description of the development of art during the Grenadian Revolution by an art teacher at Southern Oregon State College. The article contains photographs of sculptures by Grenadian artists Kerrain Nedd and Sylvester Augustis Holder.

Music and dance

728   Lyrics by The Flying Turkey.
Cecil Belfon.   *Race and Class*, vol. 25, no. 1 (Summer 1983), p. 77-81.
The lyrics to two calypsos written by a Grenadian calypsonian who was a strong supporter of the Grenadian Revolution whose message he incorporated into his music.

729   The history and tradition of Carriacou's Big Drum Dance.
Christine David.   *The Greeting Tourist Guide*, vol. 2, no. 2 (Oct. 1989), p. 8-12.
A detailed account of the renowned African Nation Dance (popularly known as the Big Drum Dance) by which some of Carriacou's inhabitants maintain their African heritage to this day. Reproductions of painting by Grenadian artists Canute Caliste and Frankie Francis illustrate this article.

730   The future in the present.
C. L. R. James.   Westport, Connecticut: Lawrence Hill, 1977. 268p.
These selected writings of the late Trinidadian historian, poet, playwright and politician contain a chapter on the Mighty Sparrow (Francisco Slinger), the most famous calypsonian of the West Indies who was born on Grenada. The author calls him 'in every way a genuinely West Indian artist' and 'a living proof that there is a West Indian nation'. The chapter contains the words of some of the Mighty Sparrow's calypsos.

731 **The Big Drum Dance of Carriacou.**
Annette C. MacDonald. *Revista/Review Interamericana*, vol. 8, no. 4
(Winter 1978/79), p. 570-76.
The associate professor of theatre arts at San Jose State University in San Jose,
California, describes the religious and social aspects of the Big Drum Dance on
Carriacou.

732 **Memory songs: community, flight and conflict in the Big Drum**
Ceremony of Carriacou, Grenada.
Lorna A. McDaniel. PhD dissertation, University of Maryland,
College Park, Maryland, 1986. 311p. (Available from University
Microfilms, Ann Arbor, Michigan, order no. 86-25687).
The author, calling her method 'historical ethnomusicology', uses the Big Drum
Ceremony as the major source from which to examine religious thought, social
attitudes and family patterns of the slave and post-emancipation populations on
Carriacou.

733 **The people's commentator: calypso and the Grenada revolution.**
Chris Searle. *Race and Class*, vol. 25, no. 1 (Summer 1983), p. 45-58.
An interview with the Grenadian calypsonian Cecil Belfon ('The Flying Turkey') by
the British educator and poet Chris Searle. The interview sheds a great deal of light
upon the development of calypso in Grenada and the Caribbean in general.

Photography

734 **Grenada Carriacou and Petit Martinique: islands of treasure.**
Kristina Lagerkvist-Doyle. St. George's: Gail Smith, 1980. 38p.
Magnificent photographs of the three islands that constitute the nation of Grenada.

735 **Grenada portfolio.**
Arbon Jack Lowe. *Américas*, vol. 29, no. 9 (Sept. 1977), p. 33-40.
Stunning photographs of various parts of Grenada.

Folklore

736 **Folklore of Carriacou.**
Christine David. Wildey, Barbados: Coles Printery, 1985. 54p. maps
A Carriacouan educator and school principal writes about the folk culture of her native
island. The contents of this booklet include such typical Carriacouan traditions as the

The Arts. Folklore

Big Drum Dance, maroons, boat building and beliefs dealing with life after death. Information on local medicines as well as a glossary of dialect and slang may be found towards the end of the book.

Festivals

737 **Carnival fever.**
Norma Sinclair. *The Greeting Tourist Guide*, vol. 1, no. 2 (Oct. 1988), p. 20-21.
A detailed account of the different phases of the Grenadian carnival that is divided into the Kiddies Carnival, the Queen Show and Panorama (the steel band competition). Colourful photographs of Grenada's carnivals illustrate this article.

Customs

738 **More on truth, fact, and tradition in Carriacou.**
Donald R. Hill.' *Caribbean Quarterly*, vol. 20, no. 1 (March 1974), p. 45-59.
A distinguished anthropologist enters into a controversy between two other students of Carriacouan culture (W. A. Redhead and M. G. Smith) and, after siding mostly with Smith, makes his own contribution by an analysis of customs and religion on that Grenadian island.

Food and Drink

739 **Trade winds: a Caribbean cookery book.**
Christine Mackie.   Bath, England: Absolute Press, 1986. 174p.
bibliog.

A musician and piano teacher who has travelled to the Caribbean for over fifteen years, collected over 100 recipes of Caribbean cookery. The volume is accompanied by a short history of the region as well as a glossary of Caribbean fruits, vegetables, spices and dishes. Grenadian dishes which are listed include: Grand Anse black pudding (p. 36), crawfish in butter and garlic, Grenadian style (p. 44), calaloo soup (p. 81-82), pigeon pea soup (p. 87), and Grenada cucumber salad (p. 114).

Sports and Recreation

740 **Grenada, Carriacou and Petit Martinique: the sailing mecca.**
Peter Evans, Chris Doyle. *The Greeting Tourist Guide*, vol. 1, no. 1
(May 1988), p. 38-41.
Two yachtsmen explore the reason for Grenada's great popularity among the world's
yachtspersons. The reason, according to them, is Grenada's great abundance of
anchorages which are all within a few miles of each other. Carriacou's anchorages are
also highly praised.

741 **Easter regatta marks upswing in Grenada yachting.**
Barbara Lloyd. *Sail*, vol. 15, no. 7 (July 1984), p. 108-09.
An account of the Grenada Yacht Club Easter Regatta, 18-22 April 1984, for which
forty yachts showed up, a fact which, according to the author, indicates that Grenada is
rapidly recovering from the crisis year of 1983.

742 **Carib cruises the West Indies.**
Carleton Mitchell. *National Geographic Magazine*, vol. 93, no. 1
(January 1943), p. 1-56.
The author, who was to undertake another sailing trip to Grenada two decades later
and again report about it in *National Geographic Magazine*, describes his first sailing
adventure to Grenada in this article which gives a vivid account of the Grenadian
carnival.

743 **Finisterre sails the Windward Islands.**
Carleton Mitchell. *National Geographic Magazine*, vol. 128, no. 6
(Dec. 1965), p. 755-801.
Anybody interested in sailing the Caribbean ought to read this exciting account of the
voyage of a thirty-eight-foot ocean-cruiser racer called *Finisterre* from Grenada to
Dominica. The author, who began sailing at the age of ten on Lake Pontchartrain,
Louisiana, describes Grenada as the most beautiful island of the Caribbean. On

Carriacou, Wilfred A. Redhead, then district officer there, gave a reception for the crew.

744 **On the sporting scene.**
Norma Sinclair. *The Greeting Tourist Guide*, vol. 2, no. 1 (March 1989), p. 13-14.

An informative article about sport events on Grenada which involve swimmers, scuba divers, cyclists, fishermen, golfers and yachtspersons. Among yacht contests listed, there are the Carl Schuster round-the-island race, the race for the Girl Pat trophy and the Southern Caribbean Ocean Racing Circuit (SCORC).

Art Galleries and Museums

745 Carriacou: small island – big museum.
Ann Katzenbach. *Liat Islander*, vol. 21 (Jan. 1990), p. 43-45.

The story of the Carriacou Museum which started out in a tiny building behind a rum shop, was transferred to a former coffin shop, but since 1986 is located in a two-storey building which was constructed with the aid of the governments of the United States, Canada and Great Britain as well as donations from private firms and individuals. The articles in the museum consist of Amerindian and African artifacts as well as the written records and furnishings of English and French settlers from the 17th to the 19th century.

746 The Grenada National Museum.
Wilfred Redhead. *The Greeting Tourist Guide*, vol. 1, no. 2 (Oct. 1988), p. 45.

A retired Grenadian civil servant takes the reader through the Grenada National Museum's collection which ranges from articles used by the Caribs and Arawaks to Empress Josephine's bath tub as well as harpoons used in whaling around the Grenadines.

Mass Media

General

747 **Talking with whom?**
Aggrey Brown, Roderick Sanatan. Mona, Jamaica: University
Printery and School of Printing, 1987. 272p.

A report on the state of the media in the Caribbean by Aggrey Brown, the Jamaican
director of CARIMAC (The Caribbean Institute of Mass Communication) and
Roderick Sanatan, the Trinidadian head of the Communications Unit of the
CARICOM Secretariat. Information on the media organizations of Grenada can be
found on p. 111-26.

748 **Grave charges, so Torchlight goes out.**
Alister Hughes. *Caribbean Life and Times*, vol. 1, no. 2 (Dec. 1979),
p. 53-54.

An account of the closing of the opposition paper *Torchlight* by the PRG which
claimed that this newspaper was trying to stir up the Rastafarians against the
government.

749 **Caribbean media and the Grenada affair.**
Rickey Singh. *Caribbean Contact*, vol. 12, no. 1 (Jan.-Feb. 1984),
p. 14.

The address which the editor of *Caribbean Contact* delivered on 2 December 1983 to a
seminar at Kingston, Jamaica, on the occasion of the fortieth anniversary of the Press
Association of Jamaica (PAJ). Singh denounces most of the Caribbean media for
slavishly supporting Reagan's 'rescue mission'.

Mass Media. Newspapers and magazines

750   **Extreme bias alleged.**
      Ian St. Bernard.   *Caribbean Contact*, vol. 16, no. 2 (July 1988), p. 14.
A former member of the Revolutionary Military Council (RMC) complains in a letter
to *Caribbean Contact* that the Caribbean media has taken a biased position towards the
seventeen Grenadians accused of murdering Maurice Bishop and many of his
followers.

751   **The press and the military: some thoughts after Grenada.**
      Donald Atwell Zoll.   *Parameters*, vol. 14, no. 1 (Spring 1984),
      p. 26-34.
A writer and lecturer explores the historical relationship between the military and the
press and comes to the conclusion that in the case of the Grenada intervention both the
press and the Pentagon must share the responsibility for the crisis of confidence which
occurred between them in 1983. The author calls for the restoration of a
complementary working relationship between the media and the military.

Newspapers and magazines

752   **The Beacon.**
      St. George's: Y., Marryshow, 1990- . weekly.
This weekly has more foreign news than any other Grenadian newspaper. Its local and
regional coverage is also extensive. The editor is a son of T. A. Marryshow.

753   **Business Watch.**
      Port-of-Spain: 1989- . weekly.
Although printed in Trinidad, this paper reports exclusively on Grenadian business
news as well as political developments. It is paid for by advertisements and is
distributed free of charge.

754   **Grenada Guardian.**
      Bridgetown: Coles Printery, 1984- . weekly.
Founded in August 1984, this political paper is the official organ of former Grenadian
Prime Minister Eric Gairy's Grenada United Labour Party (GULP).

755   **The Grenadian Tribune.**
      St. George's: West Indian Publishing Company, 1989- . fortnightly.
Published under the slogan 'the pen is mightier than the sword', this political paper is
the official voice of the National Democratic Congress (NDC). The editor is Leslie
McQueen.

756 **Informer.**
St. George's: C. Briggs, 1985- . weekly.
Calling itself 'a non-partisan, non-political weekly that tells it as it is', this paper has been called 'a scurrilous rag', by a leading Grenadian journalist. Dwelling on sensational news and printing the many rumours that constantly arise in a minuscule island such as Grenada, this paper has the highest circulation (6,500) of any weekly in Grenada. The managing director and sole owner of the *Informer* is business executive, Errol Maitland.

757 **The National.**
Bridgetown: Coles Printery, 1984- . weekly.
Founded in November 1984, this political newspaper is the official voice of Grenada's New National Party (NNP) whose leader Herbert Blaize was Grenada's prime minister (1984-89).

758 **The Grenadian Voice.**
St. George's: L. Pierre, 1984- . weekly.
The *Grenadian Voice*'s first issue actually came out in 1981 when a group of prominent Grenadians (including the journalist Alister Hughes and the present editor Leslie Pierre) decided to come out with an opposition newspaper to the PRG's *Free West Indian*. The Bishop régime quickly closed down this paper (its second issue was never distributed) and confined its editor, Leslie Pierre, to Richmond Hill Prison from which he was not to emerge until October 1983. The current *Grenadian Voice*, which is non-political, contains sections devoted to local news, commentary, news from Carriacou and Petit Martinique, agricultural developments, religion, arts, culture and entertainment as well as sports.

Professional periodicals

759 **Bulletin of Eastern Caribbean Affairs.**
Cave Hill, Barbados: Institute of Economic and Social Research,
University of the West Indies, 1975- . bimonthly.
Required reading for any serious student of the Eastern Caribbean. Almost every issue contains information on Grenada. This journal consists of articles, summaries of current events, bibliographies, book reviews and documents.

760 **CAJANUS.**
Kingston: Caribbean Food and Nutrition Institute, 1967- . quarterly.
The official journal of the Caribbean Food and Nutrition Institute which strives to better the food and nutrition situation in the anglophone Caribbean. Since Grenada is a member of CFNI, the quarterly contains occasional articles on that nation's health and nutrition condition.

Mass Media. Professional periodicals

761 **Caribbean Contact.**
Bridgetown: Caribbean Conference of Churches, 1971/72- . monthly.
The only regional monthly of the Caribbean which brings news about the entire Caribbean basin, although it is largely directed at the anglophone Caribbean. Practically every issue has articles on Grenada. One of the few newspapers of the Caribbean which were sympathetic towards the Grenadian Revolution, which earned it the dislike of Barbadian Prime Minister Tom Adams and the US embassy at Bridgetown. Edited by Colin Hope, this paper shows great independence. Its circulation stands at 22,000.

762 **Caribbean Quarterly.**
Mona, Jamaica: Department of Extra-Mural Studies, University of the West Indies, 1951- . quarterly.
An interdisciplinary journal devoted primarily to the anglophone Caribbean which frequently contains contributions dealing with Grenada. On the occasion of Grenada's attainment of independence in 1974, this periodical dedicated an entire issue (March 1974) to Grenada.

763 **Caribbean Review.**
Miami, Florida: Florida International University, 1972- . quarterly.
A nicely illustrated magazine, edited by Barry Levine, that appeals to both the general public and scholars who are concerned with the Caribbean. This journal makes it a point to present diverse views on controversial topics. The review contains frequent articles on Grenada. Excellent bibliographical lists on recent publications on the Caribbean in each issue.

764 **Caribbean Studies.**
Rio Piedras, Puerto Rico: Institute of Caribbean Studies, University of Puerto Rico, 1961-62- . quarterly.
A scholarly interdisciplinary journal which frequently contains articles on Grenada.

765 **The Greeting Tourist Guide.**
St. George's: D. Gideon, 1988- . biannual.
Besides containing information on hotels, restaurants, taxis, and church services, this glossy tourist magazine contains articles about all aspects of Grenada by some of that country's leading writers.

766 **The Grenadian farmer.**
St. George's, Grenada: Botanic Gardens, Ministry of Agriculture, 1985- .
Founded in December 1985, this irregularly published journal of the Ministry of Agriculture advises the farmers of Grenada, Carriacou and Petit Martinique on such topics as irrigation, food processing, poultry raising, bee keeping, farm loan applications and other agricultural pursuits. In order to stimulate interest and pride in agriculture, the journal selects a Farmer of the Month as well as a Farmer of the Year. The editor is Alastair Keens-Douglas.

767 **Grenada Newsletter.**
St. George's: A. Hughes, 1973- . monthly.

Factual reporting about economic and political developments in Grenada by that country's most prominent journalist who opposed dictatorial tendencies in both the Gairy and Bishop régimes (he was jailed by the Revolutionary Military Council in October 1983). The *Grenada Newsletter* will not accept any advertisement which, according to the editor, would subject the paper to possible pressure from powerful interest groups. The *Grenada Newsletter*'s printing press is located in Alister Hughes' own house.

Encyclopaedias and Directories

768 **Biographical dictionary of Latin American and Caribbean political leaders.**
Edited by Robert J. Alexander. New York; Westport, Connecticut; London: Greenwood, 1988. 509p.

This biographical dictionary contains biographies of Maurice Bishop, Herbert Blaize, Eric Gairy and Theophilus Albert Marryshow.

769 **Caribbean Business Directory 1988/89.**
Antigua; Barbados; Cayman Islands; Jamaica; St. Lucia; Trinidad; Miami, Florida: Caribbean Publishing, 1989. 230p.

Besides some general information on the government, economy, business, political trends and airline access to Grenada, this guide contains the names and telephone numbers of most businesses on Grenada on pages 134-37.

770 **Caribbean and Central American data book.**
Washington: Caribbean/Central American Action, 1987. 383p.

Information on the geography, population, history, government, political parties, trade unions, education, transportation and communications, newspapers, airlines and US business firms in Grenada may be found on pages 153-59.

771 **The Cambridge encyclopedia of Latin America and the Caribbean.**
Edited by Simon Collier, Harold Blakemore, Thomas Skidmore. Cambridge, England: Cambridge University Press, 1985. 465p. maps. bibliog.

A one-volume encyclopedia of the physical environment, economy, population, history, politics and society as well as culture of Latin America and the Caribbean. References to Grenada may be found on pages 290-94.

772   **The Grenada year book.**
Bridgetown: Advocate, 1964. 85p. map.

A small volume which contains information on Grenadian history, tourist attractions, fishing, livestock, transportation, electoral system, industries and air services. This year book compares poorly with the *Grenada handbook and directory 1946* (q.v.).

773   **Research guide to Central America and the Caribbean.**
Kenneth J. Grieb, editor-in-chief, Ralph Lee Woodward, Jr., Graeme S. Mount, Thomas Mathews, associate editors.   Madison, Wisconsin; London: University of Wisconsin, 1985. 431p.

Scattered references to Grenada can be found throughout this invaluable guide. A good summary of the archive and resource depositories on Grenada may be located on pages 375-82.

774   **Caribbean writers: a bio-bibliographical-critical encyclopedia.**
Edited by Donald Herdeck.   Washington: Three Continents, 1979. 943p. map. bibliog.

An immensely useful bibliography of the authors of the anglophone, francophone, Dutch and Spanish-speaking Caribbean. The lives and works of four Grenadian authors are cited: Delana de Coteau (Abdul Malik), Syl Lowhar, Theophilus Albert Marryshow and Wilfred A. Redhead. Unfortunately this encyclopedia appeared just prior to the Grenadian Revolution (1979-83) which produced an outburst of new Grenadian authors.

775   **Caribbean investment handbook.**
Claude M. Jonnard.   Park Ridge, New Jersey; London: Noyes Data Corporation, 1974. 285p.

Grenadian history, vital and social statistics, taxes, investment opportunities, tourism, real estate, economic and financial conditions as well as foreign trade regulations, are covered on pages 118-25 of this book.

776   **The Grenada handbook and directory 1946.**
Compiled by E. Gittens Knight.   Bridgetown: Advocate, 1946. 392p. map.

The most complete handbook on Grenada that was ever published. It contains information on the history, geology, churches, tax system, meteorology, judicial system, education, and flora and fauna of Grenada.

777   **Historical dictionary of the British Caribbean.**
William Lux.   Metuchen, New Jersey: Scarecrow, 1975. 266p. (Latin American Historical Dictionaries no. 12).

Information on Grenada may be found under the rubric: Windward Islands (p. 225-47).

Encyclopaedias and Directories

778 **Caribbean patterns.**
Harold Mitchell. New York; Toronto: John Wiley, 1972. 2nd ed. 505p. bibliog.

A political and economic study of the Caribbean area which contains references to Grenada throughout the volume. The author is a research professor of Latin American studies at Rollins College, Florida.

779 **South America, Central America and the Caribbean, 1988.**
London: Europa, 1988. 683p.

An annual survey of the political and economic life of the region in general and the forty-seven countries and territories which constitute it in particular. Information on the climate, public holidays, currency, external trade, principal crops, government, banking, trade and industry as well as tourism of Grenada, may be found on page 377.

780 **Theses on the Commonwealth Caribbean 1891-1973.**
London, Ontario: The Commonwealth Caribbean Resource Centre, Office of International Education, University of Western Ontario, 1974. 136p.

This list of theses on the Commonwealth Caribbean contains works on Grenada on pages 1 and 16.

Bibliographies

781 **Bibliography of geological literature of possible relevance to work of regional beach erosion control programme.**
Caribbean Industrial Research Institute (CARIRI). St. Augustine, Trinidad: CARIRI, 1972. 10p.
This pamphlet describes source material contained at the library of the UWI at St. Augustine, the Seismic Research Unit, UWI, St. Augustine, the Technical Information Service, CARIRI, and computer-based GEO-RFF (Geological Reference File) maintained by the American Geological Institute. Four items pertain to Grenada.

782 **Bibliography of the English-speaking Caribbean.**
Parkersburg, Iowa: Caribbean Booksellers, 1979- .
A bibliography of the anglophone Caribbean, published on an irregular basis, which lists works in English from North America, Europe and the Caribbean that relate to the arts, humanities and social sciences. It lists many articles and books which deal with Grenada.

783 **Bibliography on Grenada – works of sociological interest.**
Caribbean Quarterly, vol. 20, no. 1 (March 1974), p. 69-70.
The special issue of *Caribbean Quarterly* which was issued on the occasion of Grenada's attainment of independence on 7 February 1974, contains this short but useful bibliography.

784 **Bibliography on the Caribbean.**
Castries: Morne Educational Complex Library, 1962. 30p.
Pages 11 and 12 of this bibliography deal with articles and books on Grenada.

Bibliographies

785 **Our ancestral heritage: a bibliography of the roots of culture in the English-speaking Caribbean.**
Compiled by Edward Kamau Brathwaite. Kingston: Savacou Publications, 1977. 194p.

This bibliography contains the following subject areas: bibliographical references and studies, Caribbean background, the Amerindians, Europe, European settlers and settlements, histories and accounts, modern plantations and planters, slave, slavery and slave society, the European alter-Renaissance in the Caribbean, the European church and mission in the Caribbean, Africa and Africans in the New World, Africa in the Caribbean. A number of the partially annotated entries deal with Grenada.

786 **The CARICOM Bibliography.**
Georgetown: Caribbean Community Secretariat Information and Documentation Section, 1977- . annual.

This bibliography includes materials which are published by the member states of the Caribbean Community and Common Market of which Grenada is a part. The bibliography is divided into a classified subject section and an alphabetical section.

787 **The complete Caribbeana 1900-1975: a bibliographic guide to the scholarly literature.**
Lambros Comitas. Millwood, New York: KTO Press, a US division of Kraus-Thomson Organization, 1977. 4 vols. maps.

The most complete and useful bibliography of the non-Hispanic, non-Haitian Caribbean which contains 17,000 references, including 115 pertaining to Grenada.

788 **Latin America and the Caribbean: a dissertation bibliography.**
Edited by Carl W. Deal. Ann Arbor, Michigan: University Microfilms International, 1978. 164p.

This bibliography, compiled by the Latin American librarian at the University of Illinois, contains five dissertations which deal with Grenada: three in anthropology (p. 8) and two in earth sciences (p. 28).

789 **Sources for West Indian studies: a supplementary listing, with particular reference to manuscript sources.**
Kenneth E. Ingram. Zug, Switzerland: Inter Documentation, 1983. 412p.

The author, a retired librarian at the University of the West Indies at Mona, Jamaica, has listed 1,169 annotated items of materials located in 135 Australian, European and West Indian repositories. Forty-eight of these entries pertain to Grenada.

790 **The English-speaking Caribbean: a bibliography of bibliographies.**
Alma Jordan, Barbara Comissiong. Boston, Massachusetts: G. K. Hall, 1984. 411p.

An annotated bibliography of 1,406 items by the chief and deputy librarians of the University of the West Indies at St. Augustine, Trinidad. The entries are organized by subject matter. Many references to Grenada may be found in the index of this volume.

791　**Bibliography of Grenada.**
Compiled by Beverley A. Steele.　St. George's: University of the West
Indies, Department of Extra Mural Studies, 1983. 119p.

The best existing bibliography on Grenada by a sociologist and resident tutor of the
UWI in Grenada. The bibliography covers general works, religion, social science,
statistics, demography, sociology, women, politics and government, economics,
tourism, laws, education, linguistics, science, medicine, agriculture, cookery, arts and
recreation, and literature.

792　**Grenada: a select bibliography.**
Audine C. Wilkinson.　Cave Hill, Barbados: University of the West
Indies, 1988. 99p. (Occasional Bibliography No. 11).

An excellent bibliography of material on Grenada which is available at the Cave Hill
campus of the University of the West Indies at Barbados. These sources on Grenada
are located at three sites: the Institute of Social and Economic Research (ISER), the
main library, and the law library. The compiler of this guide is administrative assistant
at the ISER (EC) library at Cave Hill.

793　**Grenada: a select bibliography.**
Audine C. Wilkinson.　*Bulletin of Eastern Caribbean Affairs*, vol. 7,
no. 1 (March-April 1981), p. 41-48.

An excellent select bibliography consisting of books, articles, documents, pamphlets,
papers and theses compiled by the librarian of ISER at UWI, Cave Hill, Barbados.

Index

The index is a single alphabetical sequence of authors (personal and corporate), titles of publications and subjects. Index entries refer both to the main items and to other works mentioned in the notes to each item. Title entries are in italics. Numeration refers to the items as numbered.

177

Map of Grenada

This map shows the more important towns and other features.

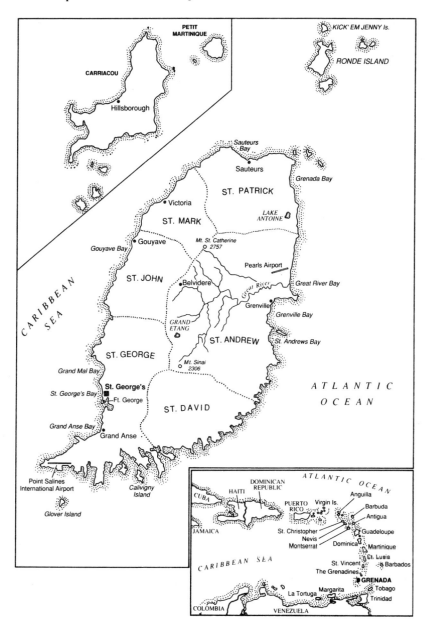